Confronting Crime

Cambridge Criminal Justice Series

Published in association with the Institute of Criminology, University of Cambridge

Published titles

Community Penalties: change and challenges, edited by Anthony Bottoms, Loraine Gelsthorpe and Sue Rex

Ideology, Crime and Criminal Justice: a symposium in honour of Sir Leon Radzinowicz, edited by Anthony Bottoms and Michael Tonry

Reform and Punishment: the future of sentencing, edited by Sue Rex and Michael Tonry

Confronting Crime: crime control policy under New Labour, edited by Michael Tonry

Sex Offenders in the Community: managing and reducing the risks, edited by Amanda Matravers

Confronting Crime

Crime control policy under New Labour

Edited by

Michael Tonry

WILLAN
PUBLISHING

Published in association with the Institute of Criminology, University of Cambridge by

Willan Publishing
Culmcott House
Mill Street, Uffculme
Cullompton, Devon
EX15 3AT, UK
Tel: +44(0)1884 840337
Fax: +44(0)1884 840251
e-mail: info@willanpublishing.co.uk
website: www.willanpublishing.co.uk

Published simultaneously in the USA and Canada by

Willan Publishing
c/o ISBS, 920 NE 58th Ave, Suite 300
Portland, Oregon 97213-3786, USA
Tel: +001(0)503 287 3093
Fax: +001(0)503 280 8832
website: www.isbs.com

First published 2003

ISBN 1-84392-022-0

British Library Cataloguing-in-Publication Data
A catalogue record for this book is available from the British Library

Project management by Deer Park Productions
Typeset by GCS, Leighton Buzzard, Beds
Printed and bound by T.J. International, Padstow, Cornwall

Contents

Notes on contributors

Larry Bill is Detective Chief Inspector, Bath, Avon and Somerset Constabulary.

Richard Crowley is the Chief Crown Prosecutor for Cambridgeshire.

David A. Green has an MPhil from the Institute of Criminology, Cambridge and is now studying for a PhD.

Rod Hansen is Chief Superintendent and Commander in Charge in the Bath district, Avon and Somerset Constabulary.

Mike Hough is Director of the Institute for Criminal Policy Research, School of Law, King's College, London.

Gareth V. Hughes is a consultant clinical and forensic psychologist at Kneesworth House Hospital and a Research Fellow of the Institute of Criminology, Cambridge.

Neil Hutton is Professor of Criminal Justice and co-director of the Centre for Sentencing Research in the Law School at the University of Strathclyde.

Amanda Matravers is Lecturer in Criminology and Director of the MSt course in Applied Criminology and Police Studies at the Institute of Criminology, Cambridge.

Neil McKittrick is a Circuit Judge based in the Peterborough Crown Court.

Darian Mitchell is Head of Service Delivery for Substance Misuse, London Probation Area, National Probation Service.

Nicola Padfield is Senior Lecturer at the Institute of Criminology and a fellow of Fitzwilliam College, Cambridge.

Ken Pease is Professor of Criminology at Huddersfield University.

Sue Rex is Senior Research Associate at the Institute of Criminology, Cambridge.

Jenny Roberts was formerly Chief Probation Officer, Hereford and Worcestershire.

Michael E. Smith is Professor of Law at the University of Wisconsin.

Michael Tonry is Professor of Law and Public Policy and Director of the Institute of Criminology, Cambridge, and Sonosky Professor of Law and Public Policy at the University of Minnesota.

Preface

Michael Tonry

Punishment politics, policies and practices in England and Wales have undergone nearly continuous change since the late 1980s and even a temporary halt is nowhere in sight. The milestones seen through contemporary eyes are the Criminal Justice Act 1991 and the government's omnibus Criminal Justice Bill of 2002. The former attempted fundamental changes based on premises the latter repudiates.

The 1991 Act is premised on normative ideas about proportionality, just deserts and fairness to offenders, and a belief that government can do little to affect crime rates through changes in punishment. The 2002 Bill is premised on instrumental ideas about deterrence, incapacitation and fairness to victims, and a belief that changes in punishment can significantly affect crime rates.

The 1991 Act took shape in a time of widespread agreement in government that crime policies should be substantive, moderate and as humane as the practical realities of Her Majesty's Prison and Probation Services allowed. The 2002 Bill took shape at a time when makers of crime policy were at least as concerned by tabloid front pages and focus group summaries as they were about the content of the policies they promoted.

This book takes a hard-headed, practical-minded look at punishment policies and proposals of the past five years, and considers whether and how they might work. The texts mostly examined are John Halliday's 2001 Review of the Sentencing Framework, the 2002 government White Paper *Justice for All* and the 2002 Criminal Justice Bill. The focus is on the substance of the problems the proposals address.

The essays originate from two sources: a Cambridge Crime Policy Conference convened in November 2002 to examine the proposals set out in the White Paper, and the Cambridge Sentencing Policy Study Group which met regularly between October 2000 and April 2002 and which examined a wide range of sentencing and corrections policy issues, giving particular attention to the Halliday report's then-new proposals. Both are unusual among academic meetings in that they were composed primarily of experienced practitioners and policy-makers with only a leavening of academics. The rationale for this is that practitioners are so much closer to the ground that they see things academics miss. A mix of practitioners and academics brings to bear the best features of the overlapping intellectual worlds they separately inhabit.

Among the essays, therefore, some are written by practitioner-academic teams, some by practitioners, some by academics. All have been substantially expanded and updated since they were first written. Although the essays have named authors who put fingers to keyboards, all are informed by the diverse perspectives and experiences of the participants in the conferences for which they were first prepared.

It was an effort to establish in England and Wales a programme of ongoing policy seminars attended by senior practitioners and officials from diverse professional backgrounds, together with a small number of researchers and policy analysts, which would explore cutting-edge problems that transcend organisational and bureaucratic boundaries. Such programmes, typically called 'Executive Sessions', have been convened on criminal justice subjects since the late 1970s at the Kennedy School of Government at Harvard and elsewhere. Many, especially on policing subjects, have proven influential and contributed to the formulation of important policy changes. The immediate predecessor to the Cambridge Sentencing Policy Study Group was a series of Executive Sessions on Sentencing and Corrections convened at the University of Minnesota from 1997 to 2000. Several members of the Cambridge Group have contributed to this volume. We are grateful to those writers – Richard Crowley, Neil McKittrick, Sue Rex, Jenny Roberts and Michael E. Smith – and almost as grateful to the other attendees, without whose presence and insight these papers and this volume would be lesser things: Niall Campbell, Neil Clarke, Cressida Dick, David Faulkner, Richard Gebelein, John Halliday, Jim Gomersall, Peter Jones, Collette Kershaw, Alison Liebling, Amanda Matravers, Mary Anne McFarlane, Christopher Pitchers and Graham Towl.

Whereas the Study Group met five times, the Crime Policy

Conference met but once, for three days. The aim was more focused – to examine closely and assess critically the proposals set out in the 2002 White Paper. Here too the idea was taken seriously that practitioners and academics working together will see more than will either group working alone. As a result, almost all the papers prepared for that conference were co-authored. We are grateful to those authors, many of whom were surprised to receive matchmaking letters inviting them to write a paper with someone with whom the idea had neither been discussed nor even considered. Most of those approached accepted and we are all the beneficiaries: Larry Bill, Richard Crowley, Rod Hansen, Mike Hough, Gareth V. Hughes, Neil Hutton, Amanda Matravers, Darian Mitchell, Nicky Padfield and Ken Pease. Here again the other attendees made the papers better and we much appreciate their willingness to give three days of their lives to the enterprise: Andrew Ashworth, Simon Clements, Withiel Cole, Frances Flaxington, Loraine Gelsthorpe, David Green, Christine Lawrie, Darian Mitchell, Colin Roberts, John Spencer, John Stafford, Bryan Turner, Andrew von Hirsch and Alan Wilkie.

We hope this book and these essays will contribute usefully and insightfully to policy debates that have been going on for a decade, and will continue for at least as long. Readers will decide for themselves whether that hope is justified.

Michael Tonry
Cambridge
September 2003

Chapter 1

Evidence, elections and ideology in the making of criminal justice policy

Michael Tonry

The Labour government has undertaken a root-and-branch remaking of the criminal justice system of England and Wales. This includes reorganising the criminal justice agencies, setting performance targets and goals, looking for ways to increase cost-effectiveness and efficiency, and altering the statutory framework in numerous ways.

Processes have been underway since 1999 that look toward fundamental changes in the ways criminal courts are organised and operate and in the ways convicted offenders are dealt with. Five major government documents serve as milestones. The first, *The Way Forward* (Home Office 2001a), is a Labour government policy document published just before the 2001 national elections. The second is the final report of the Home Office Review of the Sentencing Framework, *Making Punishments Work* (Home Office 2001b), commonly known as the Halliday Report after its director, John Halliday. The third is the report of the Review of the Criminal Courts, commonly called the Auld Report after its director, Sir Robin Auld (Auld 2001). The fourth is a government White Paper, *Justice for All* (Home Office 2002a), which set out policy proposals partly based on the Auld and Halliday reports. The fifth is the Criminal Justice Bill introduced into Parliament in November 2002. Because the emphasis in this book is mostly on policy proposals relating to the punishment of offenders, I devote greatest attention to the Halliday Report, the White Paper and the Criminal Justice Bill.

Part of the backdrop is the government's expressed but schizophrenic commitment to 'evidence-based policymaking'. The schizophrenia can be seen in sometimes startling contrasts between the government's rationalistic claims to engage in evidence-based policy-making, and its determination always and on all issues to be seen as tough on crime. Many millions of pounds have been devoted to piloting and evaluating new criminal justice programmes in the name of evidence-based policy. Preoccupation with media imagery, however, has led to support for policies for which there is no significant evidence base – including mandatory minimum sentences, Neighbourhood Watch, ubiquitous CCTV, preventive detention and weakening of procedural protections against wrongful convictions – to knee-jerk responses to shocking incidents like the New Year's Eve 2002 gun killings in Manchester and to rhetoric like this from the 2002 White Paper: 'The people are sick and tired of a sentencing system that does not make sense' (Home Office 2002a: 86).

Looking to see whether proposals are based on evidence is not the same thing as looking to see whether they are based on rigorously vetted findings from social science research or whether they accord with the policy preferences of academics. Academics have no special standing in these matters and systematic evidence can come from many places (Tonry and Green 2003). Not all systematic evidence comes from empirical research. Some comes from thoughtful analysis of official statistics. Much comes from professional experience and simple observation. The important question, however, is whether policy-making gives good-faith consideration to the credible systematic evidence that is available, or whether it disregards it entirely for reasons of ideology or political self-interest.

In section II below, I take the idea of 'evidence-based policy' seriously and ask what the evidence is and whether the major clusters of proposals in the White Paper and the Criminal Justice Bill take it into account. A number of proposals take the idea of evidence seriously. More do not. To lay a stage for that discussion, I canvass in section I reasons that have been offered for why criminal justice policies have become more repressive under the Labour government even than they were during the 'Prison Works' period of the last Conservative government of John Major.

I. Why?

The answer is that Parliament enacted tougher sentencing laws, Home Secretaries put those tougher laws into effect, magistrates and judges sent more people to prison and for longer times, the Parole Board became more risk averse and rates of recall and revocation increased, and the probation service shifted away from its traditional supervision and social service ethos to a surveillant and risk-management ethos. In other words, every component of the English criminal justice system became tougher.

In a sense, then, there is a simple explanation for the current prison population – things got tougher all along the line – but that begs, or merely rephrases, the question. Why did things get tougher all along the line?

England's record and rising prison population is a remarkable phenomenon because it occurred during a period of generally declining crime rates and, except at the margins as yet, without the aid of mandatory minimum sentence laws, three-strikes laws, and truth in sentencing. Unlike in the United States, no plausible case can be made that a long-term increase in the imprisonment rate or enactment of tougher sentencing laws led to the decline in crime rates, and that continued increases or at least current levels are required to maintain momentum.

For a variety of reasons, the claim that US imprisonment increases caused crime rates to fall as much as they did is difficult to make (Harcourt 2001; Zimring *et al* 2001). The common-sense correlation is there though. It comports with most people's intuitions about deterrence and incapacitation, and so it is not surprising that many people believed prison works. In England, however, the deterrence-and-incapacitation logic is harder to argue when crime rates began to fall before imprisonment rates began to rise. It's also harder to countenance in England in 2002, when we know that crime rates have been falling in every Western country since the mid-1990s, irrespective of whether imprisonment rates have risen (England, the Netherlands, the US), fallen (Finland, Canada, Denmark) or held steady (Germany, Scotland, Sweden) (Tonry and Frase 2001; Tonry 2001). When crime rates in the US began to decline, by contrast, no one knew that crime rates would soon be falling almost everywhere, which made it possible to believe the declines were a uniquely US phenomenon that could be explained by reference to uniquely American developments.

Nor, conversely, can it plausibly be claimed that rising crime rates in England led to more convictions, which led to more prison sentences, which led to rising prison populations. Crime rates have been falling, which makes the English prison population trend even harder to explain. At least after a brief transition period, less crime should produce fewer convictions, fewer prison sentences and fewer prisoners. Other developments are more than offsetting the tendency of falling crime rates to lead to falling imprisonment rates.

Many explanations have been offered for why penal policies became

3

increasingly severe in England and America. I'll review the five major ones. The first, associated in England with Sir Anthony Bottoms and in America with David Garland, is postmodernist angst. The material and existential uncertainties of late modernity, Bottoms observed, have produced a public sensibility he famously labelled 'populist punitiveness' (1995). Garland, in his *Culture of Control* (2001), developed a similar argument though in more detail. Rising crime rates in the 1970s and 1980s combined with economic transformation, globalisation, personal insecurity, loss of confidence in the state and rapid social change to weaken support for welfare institutions, reduce sympathy for the disadvantaged and strengthen receptivity to easy answers. The major, and fatal, flaw of this argument is that essentially the same developments occurred in every Western country but harsh crime policies were adopted and prison populations leapt only in a few. Somehow, Scotland, Canada, Germany and all of Scandinavia escaped the penal policy influence of postmodernist angst.

A second explanation is racial. American penal policy trends are said by some to be the result of cynical and deliberate efforts (Edsall and Edsall 1991) or functional processes (Wacquant 2001) in which crime is a proxy for race and penal policy is a way to keep criminals (blacks) in their subordinate place. Whatever the power of those arguments in the United States, they can't explain English developments. The Civil Rights Movement has not had a galvanising influence in England, none of the major parties is strongly dependent on Afro-Caribbean support as the US Democrats are on black voters, and even today Afro-Caribbeans make up less than 3 per cent of the English population. Race relations in England may be highly charged but over the long term, at least in relation to Afro-Caribbeans, they have not been a central or dispositive issue in partisan politics. And, in any event, most Western countries are as much or more troubled by ethnic tension as England is, and in every country some visible minority group is heavily over-represented in the crime, victimisation and imprisonment statistics (Tonry 1997). The racial hues of the crime problem can't be the English answer.

A third, associated with David Garland (2001) and the American sociologist Jonathan Simon (e.g. Caplow and Simon 1999), relates to the weakness of the state. The arguments are somewhat different. Garland refers to the 'crisis of the state' and argues that the state can no longer meet many basic needs, including crime control, but must nonetheless be seen to be doing so. Policies aren't really meant to work but to express solidarity with public anxiety and good values. Simon's 'Governing through Crime' argument is that loss of confidence in the state's power to do good, coupled with the influence in the United States of single-issue political groups, has required politicians to seek out symbolic issues which offend no one powerful on which to campaign. Issues like crime, welfare, immigration, and recently terrorism satisfy those criteria, and accordingly are the focus of political campaigns. Politicians cannot govern unless they are elected, and symbolic crime issues are what get people elected. Simon's argument is too idiosyncratically American to have broad explanatory force but Garland's, if right, should explain developments in all Western countries. It doesn't, and there is no reason why it should uniquely do so in England.

A fourth is that public opinion willed current policies and politicians and public officials responded. This has some validity but not much. Certainly it is true that political figures, from Lord Bingham famously observing that the courts must respond to what he saw as public demands for harsher punishments to Michael Howard invoking public opinion to explain his Bulger case decisions and Jack Straw promoting ASBOs (anti-social behaviour orders), claim to be moved by the public will. There are two major problems with this. First, for as long as people have been surveying public opinion about crime and punishment, the same findings have recurred: crime rates are believed to be higher than they really are and sentences and judges to be too lenient; typical crimes are imagined to be the exceptional cases featured in the media rather than the mundane cases that clog the courts; the public does not understand how the system works (Walker and Hough 1988). There is nothing special about public opinion findings in the 1990s to explain why penal severity ratcheted upward then rather than earlier. The second problem, as shown in the US by sociologist Katherine Beckett (1997), is that close analyses of media content and public opinion survey results show that media and political preoccupation with crime generally precede rather than follow up ticks in public concern. Public opinion by itself can't be the answer.

The fifth is political. Politicians for reasons of self-interest have cynically raised public concern about crime in order to offer proposals to assuage it and to win public favour by doing so. There is much evidence that conservative American politicians did this from the 1960s onwards, believing that most Democrats would oppose harsher policies and in a political shouting match would lose credibility with the electorate (Edsall and Edsall 1991). Public duels between emotional 30-second soundbites and lengthy assertions that things are more complicated than they appear are always won by the soundbiter. This is the standard account in England (Downes and Morgan 2002). From the late 1970s onwards, Tories were more inclined than Labour politicians to promote toughness, believing Labour would lose the soundbite duels. In the waning days of the Major government, the Tories are said in desperation to have tried to win public favour with a tough-on-crime platform. Labour, like Bill Clinton opposing Bob Dole in 1992, is said to have decided never to let the Right get to their right on crime issues. It worked politically in the sense that it checked the Tories but it failed substantively because it locked both parties into unreflective toughness. Jack Straw was as single-mindedly tough and worried about focus groups, the *Daily Mail* and political symbols as Michael Howard was, and David Blunkett, after waffling for a while, adopted the same posture.

That serial recital of arguments is no doubt oversimplified. All the things I described, and others, have influenced opinion and policy. Nonetheless, the bottom line is that current policies, political rhetoric and punishment patterns are as they are because politicians, however motivated, wished it so.

Looking on the bright side, that conclusion means that directions can change if politicians wish it so. Looking on the dark side, however, as the proposals in the White Paper and the Criminal Justice Bill testify, the Labour government shows no signs of wishing to return to policies that are more moderate, substantive, humane and effective than those it has promoted since taking office.

II. What?

In this section, I discuss seven bundles of proposals in the White Paper and the Criminal Justice Bill. They run a gamut from sensible and substantive through muddled and bound-to-fail to cynical and disingenuous. Proposals to strengthen the Crown Prosecution Service and rationalise the filing of criminal charges and to replace a congeries of inflexible community penalty statutes with a single community punishment order are in the first category. Proposals concerning sentencing guidelines and 'custody-minus' sentences cannot be reconciled with the idea of evidence-based policy-making. They are hopelessly muddled and bound to fail. Retention of mandatory minimum sentences and the fundamental weakening of procedural protections against wrongful convictions are cynical and disingenuous. Proposals for extended sentences for dangerous offenders are over-broad and over-inclusive and take insufficient cautionary account of the relevant evidence.

Charging

England and Wales came very late to the establishment of independent professional prosecutors and the Crown Prosecution Service is conspicuously weak as a result. It is often outgunned by private counsel in individual cases. Politically, its low credibility and lack of institutional authority mean that it is not an effective political counterweight to the views and preferences of the judiciary and that it has little voice in sentencing of individual cases.

Prosecutors in most other Western countries are forces to be reckoned with. In most European civil law countries, public prosecution has long been the task of high-status cadres of professionally trained, career civil servants who move back and forth between the judiciary and prosecution. A strong constitutional commitment in the United States to separation of powers gives prosecutors independent bases of political power and complete independence from the judicial branch of government.

In England and Wales, by contrast, there was no independent prosecution service until 1985. Charges were filed by the police and cases were prosecuted, depending on their complexity and political sensitivity, by police solicitors or publicly engaged private counsel. When the Crown Prosecution Service ('CPS') was established, Andrew Sanders and Richard Young report, '[t]he government ... built the CPS around the pre-existing system' (2002: 1057). The police retained substantial power to charge, caution and summons, but prosecutors were given authority to discontinue cases. This meant that the prosecutor remained entirely dependent on information provided by the police and, as a result, 'that the CPS is primarily a police prosecution agency is hardly surprising' (p. 1058).

This may all have been sensible as a matter of cautious, incremental institutional change, but the result has been that the CPS is not a powerful agency. To become one it will need greater authority, greater resources and stronger leadership. The charging proposals are a step in that direction. The White Paper and the Bill propose various ways in which police and prosecutors might work together more efficiently and in particular that for most significant crimes the power to charge suspects be shifted from the police to the prosecutor (Home Office 2002a: chapter 3). These are sensible, experienced-based increments in the long-term transition from police solicitors to independent prosecutors.

The changes are desirable from an efficiency perspective: prosecutorial screening before charges will reduce the frequency of dismissals and discontinuances for evidentiary insufficiency, will enhance prospects for consistency in charging and will facilitate the development of prosecutorial diversion programmes. No doubt police and prosecutors will always complain about the other but it is hard to doubt that allocating authority over charges to the agency that prosecutes them will be more effective and consistent than splitting authority over prosecutions. The changes are also desirable as steps toward the gradual empowerment of the CPS. The evidence on which these proposals are based is mostly experiential, but they count as sensible evidence-based policy-making.

Community punishment orders

So does this. Halliday proposed the creation of a simple penal system of four broad kinds of sanctions: confinement, community/confinement hybrids, community punishment orders and financial penalties. He did this to tidy up confused and complicated prior arrangements and to allow sentencers more accurately to tailor sentences to offenders' circumstances.

When Halliday wrote in 2001, English sentencers chose from a menu that included, besides confinement, curfew orders, probation orders, community service orders, combination orders, drug treatment and testing orders, attendance centre orders, exclusion orders and drug abstinence orders. Each had its own governing statutory language. The proliferation, said Halliday, was 'not helpful to understanding sentencing. The present law … is complex and should be simplified and made more understandable' (Home Office 2002b: 38). His solution was the creation of a single community punishment order that could encompass any from among a wide range of supervision, treatment, training, work, reparation, residential and other conditions.

Halliday, however, had another main reason for his proposal: the growing and increasingly credible body of evidence on 'what works'. The research literature shows, Halliday said, 'Some things can work for some people, provided the right programmes are selected and implemented properly' (Home Office 2001b: 7). Further, 'if the programmes are developed and applied as intended, and to the maximum extent possible, reconviction rates might be reduced by 5–15 percentage points (i.e., from the present level of 56 percent to [perhaps] 40 percent)' (*ibid*.). Halliday also took note of the work of the Joint Accreditation Panel which is weighing evidence of crime-reductive effectiveness and classifying programmes on the basis of the evidence.

To ensure that sentences were informed by relevant information about programmes appropriate for different types of offenders at the outset and over time, Halliday proposed a much larger role for judges than now exists, including the proposal that they serve as 'sentence managers' throughout the implementation and evolution of a sentence. Part of the rationale was that circumstances alter over time – offenders do especially well or poorly, commit minor or major breaches – and that conditions might often profitably be changed toward greater or lesser intrusiveness or intensity. Halliday argued that having a single judge involved in all those decisions would make for better-informed decisions and achieve various efficiencies.

Reasonable people can differ about the community punishment order proposal. A system of smorgasbord sentencing, in which judges can impose any conditions they like, might result in the piling-on of conditions that taken in aggregate are sometimes too burdensome relative to the seriousness of the offence (Halliday tried to address this by creating three tiers of offences punishable by community penalties, with limitations on available conditions). The proposal might also be accused of making heroic assumptions about governmental capacity for delivering effective programmes. Rigorously evaluated programmes shown to be effective are difficult to replicate. When they have been successfully replicated, the next step of going 'up to scale' by implementing across an entire bureaucratic setting has proven almost impossible (US Surgeon General 2001: chapter 5).

The critiques raise important issues which can be addressed in various ways. The key points are that Halliday offered a proposal based on an informed understanding of existing practice and of the evaluative literature on correctional treatment programmes, and that the government adopted it and carried it forward in the White Paper (renamed a 'customised community sentence'; Home Office 2002a: 91) and the Criminal Justice Bill. Chalk one up for evidence-based policy.

The examples of the Crown Prosecution Service as the charging authority and community punishment orders are not very exciting (except to prosecutors, judges and probation officers who must live with them), but they are evidence-based. The next two examples are of proposals that were evidence-based as offered by Halliday but have been altered by government for political reasons in ways that make them sure to fail.

Custody plus and minus

Recognising that the seriousness of some minor crimes, or the cultural sensibilities of some magistrates, would inevitably result in some short confinement sentences, Halliday proposed a hybrid 'custody plus' sentence which would combine confinement with, in effect, a community punishment order overseen by a judicial 'sentence manager'. Typically known as 'split sentences', such punishments are common in the United States. Halliday also proposed that custody plus sentences include no more than three months real time in custody, thereby in conjunction with other proposals eliminating confinement sentences between three and six months real time.

The government rejected the recommendation that judges be given responsibility as sentence managers (McKittrick and Rex, in this volume), but did in the White Paper (Home Office 2002a: 92–3) and the Bill propose custody plus sentences. So far, so good. The evidence supporting the concept of custody plus sentences is the same as that for the community punishment order discussed in the preceding subsection.

But the White Paper also proposed the creation of 'custody minus' sentences, and here the evidence base falls apart. Custody minus sentences would be a form of suspended prison sentence, and the full range of conditions possible in any other community sentence would be available. The possibility would exist that conditions could be changed if the offender were doing especially well or poorly, but 'any breach will lead to immediate imprisonment' (Home Office 2002a: 93; lest anyone miss the point, it is repeated on pp. 91 and 94).

There are serious problems here (Roberts and Smith, in this volume). Many offenders breach conditions. In 1999, official breach rates for probation, community service orders and combination orders were 18, 30 and 29 per cent respectively (Home Office 2002b: appendix 6), and those were only the breaches that were noticed and acted on. However, people who receive such sentences are usually minor offenders. Even they, though, as a combined group experience 56 per cent reconviction rates within two years from beginning their community penalties. Among released prisoners, those serving short sentences have the highest reconviction rates (60 per cent within two years for those serving a year or less).

A very large percentage of people sentenced to custody minus, certainly a majority, will commit the kinds of breach that should trigger 'immediate imprisonment'. The NEW-ADAM programme has shown that 65 per cent of arrestees in 1999–2000 tested positive for drugs and 29 per cent for heroine and cocaine (Bennett, Holloway and Williams 2001). Drug dependence is a chronic, relapsing condition, and most offenders receiving a no-drug-use condition will fail at least once, and many will fail more than once (Hough and Mitchell, in this volume). And a large percentage of offenders will fail to appear for community service, work or training, violate electronic tagging rules or commit other non-criminal technical breaches. If the 'immediate imprisonment' approach to breaches is adopted and followed, most custody minus offenders will wind up in prison.

There are other problems. First, everything we know about creation of 'new' community-based penalties meant to serve as prison alternatives, which custody-minus is, tells us that net-widening judges as often as not use the new penalty for offenders who would otherwise have received something lesser (Petersilia and Turner 1993). This is especially likely under the White Paper's recommendations since custody-plus sentences will eliminate real-time sentences of between three and six months; judges inclined to impose something longer than three months can impose a custody minus sentence with twelve months suspended, knowing that the breached offender will serve longer than three months.

Second, programmes involving closer supervision than heretofore, and intensive supervision programmes generally, which custody minus is, seldom result in higher rates of breach for new crimes but typically result in higher rates of breach for technical violations (*ibid*.). When these two robust findings are combined, the creation of a new prison alternative often results in higher overall rates of imprisonment (basically through the ratcheting-up effects of net-widening combined with higher breach rates; those genuinely diverted from prison will have their normal failure rate).

Custody-minus including immediate imprisonment for every breach fails to satisfy the evidence-based policy criterion on three grounds: it takes no account of predictably high rates of failure to comply with conditions, of foreseeable net-widening and of higher rates of technical breaches associated with intensive supervision. Custody-minus will fail to achieve its purpose, in the aggregate, of reducing use of imprisonment. Equally predictably, it will result in some wilful circumvention of the breach rules by probation officers and magistrates who do not believe particular breaches are so serious that imprisonment is an appropriate response.

The sensible way to avoid these predictable but undesirable effects would have been to resist the 'immediate imprisonment on failure' temptation and allow case-by-case consideration of what responses particular failures warrant.

The only reasons I can imagine for the odd combination of a prison-diversion programme with an automatic-imprisonment-on-failure rule are ignorance, which isn't credible, or a wish to appear tough before the media and the public. The better alternative would have been to explain that prisons are too full of people who don't need to be there, that short prison sentences are destructive, that prisons are overcrowded and over-expensive, and accordingly that Her Majesty's government will create a new, more constructive and less expensive community sanction for non-dangerous offenders.

Sentencing guidelines

Halliday urged, as an essential component of his comprehensive proposals, 'that new guidelines for the use of discretion will be an essential part of the new framework' (Home Office 2001b: viii). Because his proposals would radically change English punishment policies, processes and practices, Halliday insisted that *comprehensive* guidelines would be necessary to assure consistent application of the new system and avoid gross disparities in treatment. I stress the word 'comprehensive' to emphasise the scope of the proposed guidelines:

> The statute would require guidelines to be drawn up so they would include:
>
> descriptions of graded seriousness levels, covering all the main offences;
>
> presumptive 'entry points' of sentence severity in relation to each level (including circumstances justifying a community sentence);
>
> how credit for absence of previous convictions and escalating sentence severity for increasing numbers and types of previous convictions should operate, and subject to what limits ...;
>
> how multiple offences of the same type should be dealt with;
>
> other grounds for aggravation and mitigation.
>
> (Home Office 2002b: 54)

The proposed guidelines would cover all offences in magistrates' and higher courts, and be very detailed, including criteria for community penalties and for taking account of prior convictions. The proposed guidelines are orders of magnitude more comprehensive and detailed than existing guideline judgments issued by the Court of Appeal or existing guidelines for magistrates' courts (Ashworth 2000). The guidelines are to be developed by an 'independent body', which in the White Paper is called the Sentencing Guidelines Council. Halliday proposed three models for the council: the Court of Appeal wearing another hat; a body chaired by the Lord Chief Justice composed entirely of judges and magistrates and appointed by the Lord Chancellor; or an independent body composed of people from a wide range of back-grounds (Home Office 2002b: 55–7).

Existing evidence provides three reasons to predict that the sentencing guidelines envisaged by the White Paper will fail. First, guidelines commissions/councils composed solely of judges invariably fail to develop guidelines that significantly constrain sentencing judges' discretion. Second, the scheme proposed in the Criminal Justice Bill, which involves roles for the Sentencing Guidelines Council, the existing Sentencing Advisory Council and the Court of Appeal, is much too complex to work. Third, the White Paper abandons Halliday's call for comprehensive guidelines and envisages incremental changes to the existing guideline judgments issued by the Court of Appeal.

Judge-dominated commissions

In another essay (Tonry 2002), I've explained why Halliday's first and second models are doomed to failure. The White Paper and the Criminal Justice Bill propose the second model. The ample American experience with sentencing councils (called commissions in the States) demonstrates that councils composed solely of judges never manage to develop meaningful guidelines. Partly this is because judges are not policy-makers and are unaccustomed to participating in administrative rule-making (which is what guideline drafting is). Partly it is because judges typically oppose meaningful guidelines in principle, believing strongly that judges should be given wide discretion in setting sentences. Partly it is, as a consequence, because judges are less likely than others to believe that current sentences are arbitrary, inconsistent, inappropriate or otherwise in need of alteration. In a considerable number of American states, including Maryland, Florida, Michigan and New Jersey, sentencing commissions composed solely of judges were constituted for the (seldom publicly admitted) express purpose of pre-empting the creation of commissions or enactment of laws that might adopt sentencing policies judges disliked (Tonry 1987).

Judges are typically happy with the status quo. Recent but telling evidence for this can be found in a summary of comments sought out by Hilary Benn MP as part of an ongoing Review of Correctional Services. One generally held view Benn reported was that 'short sentences are particularly ineffective' (Benn 2003: 7). Halliday and the White Paper both said similar things. They are too short to serve rehabilitative or incapacitative ends, but long enough to damage offenders and their families.

One might reasonably expect another widely held view that Benn reports: 'Almost all respondents felt there is currently an overemphasis on the use of custody' (p. 7). However, Benn qualifies this by noting, 'Some sentencers argued that the current balance is right'.

The section of Benn's report on the use of imprisonment ends thus: 'It is striking that while most of those observing the sentencers feel that too much use is being made of custody, the sentencers themselves support the current balance between custodial and non-custodial penalties' (p. 8). Ian Dunbar and Andrew Langdon, sometime Directors of Inmate Administration and Operational Policy in the Prison Service, describe this as a pervasive problem:

> [F]or 40 years or more, it has not been possible to align sentencing policy with the capacity of the penal system in any way that the judiciary will accept. In crude terms, the courts have usually overfilled whatever prison capacity has been available, and whenever new types of non-custodial penalties have been provided to relieve pressure on the prisons, they have largely been used to punish people who would previously have received a more lenient disposal.
>
> (1998: 59)

Commissions/councils composed solely or mostly of judges have always failed in the US, which raises a general reason to doubt the wisdom of the White Paper's proposals. The not-unrepresentative judicial attitudes Benn summarises help explain why.

Complexity
The White Paper indicates that the Sentencing Guidelines Council will develop guidelines that will apply in all courts and in every individual case. The existing Sentencing Advisory Panel will 'offer advice' to the Council. No mention is made of the existing and future guideline judgments issued by the Court of Appeal, but other White Paper comments suggest they will continue to exist and that the Sentencing Advisory Panel will continue to offer advice concerning them. Setting aside Parliament and various interested constituencies, the White Paper and Bill envision three major bodies, two composed solely of judges, involved in the policy process. That wasn't necessary. The Sentencing Advisory Panel could have been folded into the new Council, and Court of Appeals judges could, with others, have been made members. The key point, though, is that drafting comprehensive guidelines is an enormously complicated job and a majority of commissions elsewhere (including of those not composed solely of judges) have failed. Giving the job to a new Council which must share power and authority with

two other already existing bodies reduces the odds of success to near zero.

Comprehensiveness

Halliday made it clear that the guidelines must be comprehensive and apply to all courts if the rest of the proposed radical overhaul were to work. The White Paper plays lip service to this, proposing '… a consistent set of guidelines that cover all offences and should be applied whenever a sentence is passed' (Home Office 2002a: 89). However, a later passage makes it clear that the process envisaged is one of incremental additions to the body of existing guideline judgments, with 'individual guidelines being issued to judges and magistrates … as and when they are completed' (Home Office 2002a: 90).

Unfortunately, it doesn't and can't possibly work that way. Comprehensive guidelines cannot be drafted from the bottom up, taking existing guidelines and building around them. One reason this doesn't work is that gross anomalies inevitably arise. It will be sheer coincidence, for example, if the existing guidelines for burglary involving a theft and possession of a gun call for the same sentence as existing guidelines for robbery involving the same amount of property and possession of a gun. Another, much more important reason it can't work is that drafting comprehensive guidelines necessarily entails policy trade-offs. If longer sentences for sex crimes are wanted, then sentences for something else must be shortened. Looking at the sentencing system, and sentences, as a whole is an inherent part of drafting comprehensive guidelines. It can't be done piecemeal (Hutton, in this volume).

The government in section 153 of the Criminal Justice Bill avoided these problems by eviscerating Halliday's proposals and backing away from its own less ambitious proposals in the White Paper. First, no mention is made in section 153 of entry points, sentences for concurrent offences or aggravating and mitigating circumstances, and only the vaguest mentions are made of offence seriousness and criminal histories. Second, comprehensive guidelines were abandoned as a goal. What the Council will do is entirely up to itself. The Bill merely provides that 'The Council may from time to time consider whether to frame sentencing guidelines,' which are elsewhere defined as 'guidelines relating to the sentencing of offenders, which may be general in nature or limited to a particular category of offence or offender' (sections 153(1) and (4)).

The government effectively abandoned the goal of comprehensive sentencing guidelines in favour of new institutional arrangements that provide the appearance of doing something while in all likelihood doing nothing that would not have happened under the existing arrangement between the Sentencing Advisory Panel and the Court of Appeal.

Mandatory minimum sentences

Mandatory minimum sentences do not achieve their aims and always produce unwanted side-effects of arbitrariness, unjust sentences in individual cases, hypocritical efforts at circumvention, and substantial unwarranted sentencing disparities (between like-situated cases in which the mandatory penalty is imposed and cases in which it is circumvented) (Tonry 1996: chapter 4). This is well-known and common ground among experienced public officials and scholars who specialise in sentencing.

Halliday defined mandatory minimums as outside his remit, and did not examine the evidence for and against their use. He did point out, however, that 'many contributors to the review have argued against these sentences, on the grounds that they are inherently likely to result in some disproportionately severe sentences' (Home Office 2001b: 15). He also suggested, without expressing his own view, that at some later time, if the guidelines were in place and working, Parliament might want to reconsider the wisdom of existing mandatory minimums.

Though Halliday proposed no changes, the government felt obliged, gratuitously, to emphasise its support for mandatories. In an auxiliary document to the White Paper, the government summarised its reactions to Halliday's and Auld's recommendations. Accurately noting that Halliday suggested no more than a review someday of whether mandatories would still be needed, the document reports 'We believe that the current provisions are satisfactory' (Home Office 2002b: 10).

This is a particularly clear instance of the evidence pointing one way and the government marching decisively in the other. The story is well-known of the passage of mandatory minimum legislation for drug crimes, violent crimes and burglary in the final days of the last Conservative government (e.g. Downes and Morgan 2002). Michael Howard's proposals for such laws were widely seen as bows to law-and-order symbolism, as frantic and cynical efforts to appeal to what Tony Bottoms (1995) labelled populist punitiveness in the electorate, and it was widely expected that the new Labour government would allow them to languish, unimplemented. Instead, in its own bow to the same audience, Jack Straw put them into force. Evidence notwithstanding, the current government appears committed to mandatory minimums. This is a clear evidence of a victory of cynicism and political symbolism over substance.

Extended sentences for dangerous offenders

Policy-makers in every country worry about pathologically violent and sexual offenders. The profoundly difficult problem, however, is that serious violent and sexual offences are very difficult to predict. The danger is great that people who would not commit such offences in future will be confined unnecessarily.

Halliday proposed the creation of a new kind of determinate sentence for especially dangerous offenders in which release would not be automatic when half was served but would require an individualised decision by the parole board. Halliday cautioned that the indeterminate sentence should be used 'only when there were *high* risks of re-offending and *serious* harm' (emphasis added). Serious harm he defined as death or serious personal injury. He worried that it might be misused or over-used: 'It will be important to set a threshold for this sentence to assure that it is used for dangerous offenders, and not used inappropriately' (Home Office 2001b: 32–3). And at the end of the sentence, the offender would have to be released. Mental health commitments might be appropriate at that point for some, but the rest would have to be allowed to get on with their lives. Some might someday commit a new serious crime, but the need to balance risk and liberty requires that risks be taken.

The White Paper's proposals for violent and sexual offenders are profoundly anti-civil-libertarian and reject all of Halliday's limits and cautions. Instead, some offenders would be sentenced to indeterminate sentences and be held 'until their risks are considered manageable in the community'. They would remain in custody 'until the Parole Board was *completely satisfied* that the risk had sufficiently diminished' and the prisoner could then remain on licence for the rest of his or her life (Home Office 2002a: 95, emphasis added). 'Completely satisfied' is a test that can never be met. Others would receive sentences up to nine years longer than their current crime justifies and be subject to confinement up to the full length of the sentence rather than, like other prisoners, being entitled to release after serving half.

Nowhere in the discussion of sentences for violent and sexual offences is there a trace of nuance or subtlety, a suggestion that the proposals involve fundamental trade-offs, or that prospective predictions of dangerousness are devilishly difficult and much more often than not inaccurate (Matravers and Hughes, in this volume). Roger Hood and Stephen Shute (2002) have shown, for example, that the English Parole Board is highly inaccurate when predicting which parole applicants will later commit serious crimes.

The Criminal Justice Bill sets out two pairs of extended sentence provisions (one member of each pair is for offenders under age 18 and one for those over) for offenders deemed to present especially serious risks to public safety. First, for persons convicted of a 'serious' offence punishable by life imprisonment or a determinate term of ten years or more, and concerning whom 'the court is of the opinion that there is a significant risk to members of the public of serious harm occasioned by the commission by him of further [serious] offences', the court 'must' impose either a life sentence or a prison sentence for an indeterminate period (sections 205, 206). Second, for persons convicted of sexual or violent offences that are not 'serious' offences, but about whom 'the court is of the opinion [etc.]', the court must impose an additional increment of punishment beyond that deserved for the current offence up to an additional five years for violent offences and nine years for sexual offences (sections 207, 208).

There are three major problems with the scheme. First, it sets no actuarial or scientific criteria for judicial determinations of dangerousness, even though uncontroversial research has for more than 30 years shown that predictions of future serious violence are much more often wrong than right (e.g. Monahan 1981; Hood, Shute and Wilcox 2000) and that clinical predictions (as by judges or social workers or mental health specialists) are less reliable than actuarial predictions (Meehl 1954; Monahan forthcoming). The Bill, with no more guidance than the vague language quoted in the preceding paragraph, leaves the decision to the individual judge.

Second, with apologies for the intricacy of what follows, the proposal is broadly over-inclusive. The life and indeterminate sentence provisions (sections 205, 206) apply to 'serious offences' which are defined as 'specified offences' punishable by imprisonment for life or ten or more years. The up-to-nine-year extended term provisions also apply to specified offences. 'Specified' offences, which may be sexual or violent, are listed in Schedule 14 to the Bill. Some of the 98 offences listed there are incontrovertibly serious – manslaughter, kidnapping, rape – but others are not. Specified offences include, for example, assault with intent to resist arrest, carrying a firearm, destroying property, causing death by dangerous driving, incest, soliciting by men and permitting a girl under 16 to use premises for intercourse. One need not imply that these are necessarily trivial forms of misconduct to observe that they are seldom likely to justify extended terms on grounds of dangerousness. The gravamen of this tortured exegesis is that current or past convictions for quite trivial crimes could lead to lengthy or indeterminate deprivations of liberty.

Third, for anyone previously convicted of a specified offence, the judge must assume that the offender presents a serious risk of harm. An extended sentence must be imposed unless the judge 'considers that it would be unreasonable to conclude there is such a risk' (section 209).

The extended sentence provisions, no matter what else they may be, are not evidence-based.

Trial and procedural matters

The White Paper and the Criminal Justice Bill propose a wide range of changes in how trials are conducted and in related procedures and rules (Padfield and Crowley, in this volume). These include abrogation of the many-centuries-old double jeopardy rule, elimination of rules forbidding admission of hearsay evidence, allowing admission into evidence of information about offenders' prior offences and narrowing of jury trial rights. The reasons for the traditional rules are straight-forward. The imbalance of power and resources between the state and any individual is so great, and the stress, anxiety and expense of defending oneself in a trial so burdensome, that the double jeopardy rule forbids putting any individual through that twice. The hearsay rules exist as a protection against inaccurate information and through that against wrongful convictions. The rules against admitting information about prior crimes into evidence are intended to increase the likelihood that convictions occur because the evidence justifies it rather than, prejudicially, because the prior convictions show the defendant to be an unattractive person. Jury trial rights are meant to protect the liberty of citizens and ensure that ordinary people agree with the state functionaries who file criminal charges. All of these proposals are made in the names of 'rebalancing the system in favour of the victim' and reducing the frequency of wrongful acquittals. No credible evidence is provided on either the frequencies of wrongful acquittals or estimates of the increased numbers of wrongful convictions that will occur if the proposed changes are adopted.

These would all be radical diminutions in procedural protections of people accused of crimes in England and Wales. No empirical evidence is given in the White Paper that the problems any of the proposed changes are meant to address are quantitatively important. That is, no evidence is given to show that large numbers of guilty people are avoiding convictions because of the existing rules. No doubt some are, but equally there is no doubt that some innocent people are convicted under the current rules and that more would be if they were abrogated or weakened. At least since the time of Blackstone, wise consensus has existed that wrongful acquittals are a far less worrisome problem than are wrongful convictions. Most of the proposals described in this subsection, if adopted, will increase the number of wrongful convictions. The double jeopardy rule change will expose acquitted people to retrial because politicians decide it is in their political interest to do so. These also are not proposals for evidence-based policy-making.

III. Evidence-based policy-making?

It may simply have been unrealistic to imagine that the Labour government would take its evidence-based policy rhetoric seriously in relation to crime. Rightly or not, like it or not, Labour in the early 1990s saw its weak anti-crime credentials as an electoral handicap and resolved to adopt Bill Clinton's approach to crime policy: never let the conservatives get to your right (Downes and Morgan 2002). For Clinton this meant signing 1994 legislation that extended the death penalty to 60 additional federal crimes. For Labour it meant endorsing the anti-liberal provisions of the Criminal Justice Act 1993 and the repressive provisions of the Criminal Justice and Public Order Act 1994.

Policy-making does not always take account of the best available evidence or sometimes of any systematic evidence at all. Risk aversion should not be surprising concerning a subject considered politically sensitive by the government of the day, even though the two Labour governments have had such large majorities that a little risk-taking might seem safe. The question considered in this final section is: what are the risks that led the government, after so many years of such extensive consideration of criminal justice reform, and so much money spent on research in the name of evidence-based policy, to submit so flawed a set of proposals to Parliament? There appear to be three.

Placating the judiciary

First, most peculiarly, is the risk that the judiciary would oppose proposed changes to the sentencing system. This is the only plausible explanation for the gradual abandonment of Halliday's primary proposals. All of the main proposals for changes to the sentencing framework that have been widely discussed in recent years derive from the Halliday report. The Labour government policy document published just before the 2001 national elections, *The Way Forward* (Home Office 2001a), explicitly held its fire on this subject in anticipation of the release of Halliday's report a few months later. For Halliday, sentencing guidelines were a central and essential component of his proposals, without which many of the other specific proposals would not be workable. The guidelines were to be comprehensive and detailed and cover all offences. In the nature of things they would have had to be built from the ground up. The White Paper waffled a bit, referring both to comprehensive guidelines and the possibility that they would be developed piecemeal. The Criminal Justice Bill abandons the idea of comprehensive guidelines in favour of such piecemeal and evolutionary augmentation of existing appellate judgments as a Sentencing Council composed solely of judges chooses to undertake.

There were other major retreats from Halliday. He, for example, examined the research evidence on the deterrent effects of changes in penalties and concluded that there 'seems to be no link between marginal changes in punishment levels and changes in crime rates' (Home Office 2001b: 8). Accordingly he concluded that 'any new sentencing framework should make no assumptions about deterrence. To change the framework in order to achieve a deterrent effect would not be justified. Nor, contrary to widespread belief, is there evidence to support making deterrence a specific purpose of sentencing in individual cases' (Home Office 2001b). Judges, however, famously believe in deterrence, as evidenced by the Court of Appeal's evisceration in *Cunningham* (1993) 14 Cr App R (S) 444, of the Criminal Justice Act 1991's just-deserts approach by interpreting the statutory phrase 'commensurate with the seriousness of the offence' to mean 'commensurate with the punishment and deterrence that the seriousness of the offence requires' (Ashworth 2001: 78). The first clause of the sentencing chapter of the Criminal Justice Bill begins: 'Any court dealing with an offender in respect of his offence must have regard for the following purposes of sentencing – (a) the punishment of offenders, (b) the reduction of crime (including its reduction by deterrence …' (section 126(1)). This language expressly authorises judges to take deterrence into account in imposing sentences on particular offenders. The judges won again.

Finally, more generally, the organisation of the Sentencing Council is the least threatening to the judiciary imaginable. The Council will be chaired by the Lord Chief Justice, appointed by the Lord Chancellor, and composed solely of judges and magistrates. The existing Sentencing Advisory Panel will be retained, even though its work will become completely redundant. The rationale for all this, as indicated in the Explanatory Notes accompanying the Bill, is 'to ensure proper judicial independence'. This notion that respect for judicial independence requires that judges be given authority over formulation of sentencing policies or standards is, as Andrew Ashworth (2000) repeatedly has demonstrated, a nonsense. Parliament has that authority and can delegate it as it wishes. The principle of judicial independence protects individual litigants by forbidding executive or political influence in the resolution of individual cases.

I have no idea why the judiciary has been so placated, and why it is to be given complete authority over the development of guidelines far less substantial than those Halliday proposed. My best guess is that the Labour government at day's end does not much care what form sentencing guidelines take, does not much care how the proposed reform of sentencing works out and therefore sees no reason to expend any political energy or capital on the subject.

Stalemating the Tories

The second risk is that the Conservatives may try to regain the laurels as toughest-on-crime. Many of the provisions of the Criminal Justice Bill can be understood on the rationale that the best defence is a good offence. They will play well in soundbites. Mandatory minimum sentences may have no discernible deterrent effects and demonstrably do injustice in individual cases, but they sound tough. The proposal for extended terms for dangerous offenders may be loosely defined and over-broad, and thereby present sizeable risks that people will wrongly receive greatly extended sentences, but they also sound tough. For the reasons set out above, custody minus sentences coupled with automatic policies of imprisonment if breached are bound to be ineffective and to result in very high rates of breach, but automatic imprisonment sounds tough.

Minimising outrages

The third risk, actually an inevitability, is that an outrageous crime will be committed by an offender for whom the government will widely be perceived as responsible. This would explain the over-breadth and imprecision of the dangerous offender proposals and the general heavy reliance on imprisonment.

The reality is that horrible crimes have always happened and always will and there is no way to assure they won't. No one can fault the taking of serious steps to minimise those risks, so long as the steps are well-considered and respectful of other important values and interests.

The nature of the Criminal Justice Bill's dangerous offender provisions can be seen by comparing them with American three-strikes-and-you're-out laws (Zimring, Hawkins and Kamin 2001). Twenty-seven states and the federal system enacted such laws mandating life or other lengthy prison sentences following a third serious felony conviction. Reasonable people can disagree as to whether mandatory penalties are ever good policy. Assuming they can be, a three-strikes law can be carefully tailored so that it applies only to defined categories of highly dangerous offenders, or they can be drafted broadly so they are potentially applicable to broad categories of offenders. Twenty-six states and the federal government drafted their laws narrowly, and they have in practice seldom been used. California drafted its broadly and it has been used tens of thousands of times including, notoriously, in the case of a man whose 25-year minimum sentence was predicated on a third felony consisting of the theft of two pieces of pizza. A dangerous offender law that authorises extended sentences following convictions of soliciting by men or damaging property feels uncomfortably like California's three-strikes law.

The centralisation of political power in the English executive makes it difficult for others to block changes wanted by the government of the day. The French and the American constitutional systems provide meaningful separation of powers among the executive, legislative and judicial branches of government which means that, at day's end, the executive achieves its goals only by means of persuasion. Policy emerges from competition among occupants of different places of power. The Dutch, the Swedes and the Germans have long-standing traditions of consensus policy-making in which most major changes in their final forms are approved by most or all of the major parties, by affected constituencies and interest groups, and by people of diverse ideological belief. Policy emerges from collaboration among occupants of different places of power.

In England, by contrast, the executive controls the legislature and, save complexly and partially concerning the European Convention of Human Rights, the judiciary defers to the legislature. Resistance to ill-considered legislation must come from the House of Lords who can delay things, and from Commons backbenchers who can be nuisances, but neither possesses the power to stop a government from obtaining the passage of legislation it wants.

Some of what is proposed in the White Paper and the Criminal Justice Bill is sensible, based on credible evidence and likely to improve the workings of the criminal justice system. Some of what is proposed is ill-advised. Many of the proposals if adopted are unlikely to achieve their substantive aims. Some if adopted will fundamentally undermine basic procedural protections against wrongful convictions. Some if adopted will deprive people of their liberty for extended periods not as deserved punishments for their crimes but because judges on the bases of vague and therefore inevitably idiosyncratic criteria decide that they are dangerous. Whatever else it may be, this is not evidence-based policy-making.

References

Ashworth, A. (2000) *Sentencing and Criminal Justice*. London: Butterworths.

Ashworth, A. (2001) 'The Decline of English Sentencing and Other Stories', in Tonry, M. and Frase, R.S. (eds), *Sentencing and Sanctions in Western Countries*. New York: Oxford University Press.

Auld, Sir Robin. (2002) *Review of the Criminal Courts*. London: TSO.

Beckett, K. (1997) *Making Crime Pay: Law and Order in Contemporary American Politics*. New York: Oxford University Press.

Benn, H. (2003) *Stakeholder Consultation: Summary of Responses to Hilary Benn's Letter of 6 September*. London: Home Office, Strategy and Finance Unit.

Bennett, T., Holloway, K. and Williams, T. (2001) *Drug Use and Offending: Summary Results from the First Year of the NEW-ADAM Research Programme*, Home Office Research Findings 148. London: Home Office.

Bottoms, A.E. (1995) 'The Philosophy and Politics of Punishment and Sentencing', in Clarkson, C.M.V. and Morgan, R. (eds), *The Politics of Sentencing Reform*. Oxford: Clarendon Press.

Caplow, T. and Simon, J. (1999) 'Understanding Prison Policy and Population Trends', in Tonry, M. and Petersilia, J. (eds), *Prisons*. Chicago: University of Chicago Press.

Downes, D. and Morgan, R. (2002) 'The Skeletons in the Cupboard: the Politics of Law and Order at the Turn of the Millennium', in Maguire, M., Morgan, R. and Reiner, R. (eds), *The Oxford Handbook of Criminology*, 3rd edn. Oxford: Oxford University Press.

Dunbar, I. and Langdon, A. (1998) *Tough Justice – Sentencing and Penal Policies in the 1990s*. London: Blackstone.

Edsall, T. and Edsall, M. (1991) *Chain Reaction: The Impact of Race, Rights, and Taxes on American Politics*. New York: Norton.

Garland, D. (2001) *The Culture of Control*. Oxford: Oxford University Press.

Harcourt, B. (2001) *Illusion of Order: The False Promise of Broken Windows Policing*. Cambridge, MA: Harvard University Press.

Home Office (2001a) *Criminal Justice: The Way Forward*, CM 7074. London: TSO.

Home Office (2001b) *Making Punishments Work*. London: Home Office Communication Directorate.

Home Office (2002a) *Justice for All*, CM 5563. London: TSO.

Home Office (2002b) *Justice for All – Responses to the Auld and Halliday Reports*. London: Home Office.

Hood, R., Shute, S. and Wilcox, A. (2000) *The Parole System at Work: A Study of Risk-based Decision-making*, Home Office Research Study No. 202. London: Home Office.

Meehl, P.E. (1954) *Clinical Versus Statistical Prediction: A Theoretical Analysis and a Review of the Evidence*. Minneapolis, MN: University of Minnesota Press.

Monahan, J. (1981) *The Clinical Prediction of Violent Behavior*. Washington, DC: US Government Printing Office.

Monahan, J. (forthcoming) 'The Future of Violence Risk Management', in Tonry, M. (ed.), *The Future of Imprisonment: Punishment in the 21st Century*. New York: Oxford University Press.

Petersilia, J. and Turner, S. (1993) 'Intensive Probation and Parole', in Tonry, M. (ed.), *Crime and Justice: A Review of Research*, Volume 17. Chicago: University of Chicago Press.

Sanders, A. and Young, R. (2002) 'From Suspect to Trial', in Maguire, M., Morgan, R. and Reiner, R. (eds), *The Oxford Handbook of Criminology*, 3rd edn. Oxford: Oxford University Press.

Tonry, M. (1987) *Sentencing Reform Impacts*. Washington, DC: US Government Printing Office.

Tonry, M. (1996) *Sentencing Matters*. New York: Oxford University Press.

Tonry, M. (1997) 'Ethnicity, Crime, and Immigration', in Tonry, M. (ed.), *Ethnicity, Crime, and Immigration*. Chicago: University of Chicago Press.

Tonry, M. (ed.) (2001) *Penal Reform in Overcrowded Times*. New York: Oxford University Press.

Tonry, M. (2002) 'Setting Sentencing Policy through Guidelines', in Rex, S. and Tonry, M., *Reform and Punishment: the Future of Sentencing*. Cullompton: Willan.

Tonry, M. and Frase, R.S. (eds) (2001) *Sentencing and Sanctions in Western Countries*. New York: Oxford University Press.

Tonry, M. and Green, D. (2003) 'Criminology and Public Policy in the US and UK', in Ashworth, A. and Zedner, L (eds), *The Criminological Foundations of Penal Policy: Essays in Honour of Roger Hood*. Oxford: Oxford University Press.

US Surgeon General (2001) *Youth Violence: A Report of the Surgeon General*. Washington DC: US Public Health Service.

Wacquant, L. (2001) 'Deadly Symbiosis: When Ghetto and Prison Meet and Merge', *Punishment and Society*, 3(1), 95–134

Walker, N. and Hough, M. (1988) *Public Attitudes to Sentencing*. Aldershot: Ashgate.

Zimring, F. E., Hawkins, G. and Kamin S. (2001) *Punishment and Democracy: Three Strikes and You're Out in California*. New York: Oxford University Press.

Chapter 2

Drug-dependent offenders and *Justice for All*

Mike Hough and Darian Mitchell

This chapter considers the relationship between illicit drug use and crime, and examines the impact that recent government proposals relating to dependent drug users are likely to achieve. These proposals were outlined in the White Paper, *Justice for All* (Home Office 2001) and statutory provision for them was made in the 2002 Criminal Justice Bill that was passing through Parliament at the time of writing in early 2003. They constitute a package of measures designed to identify dependent drug users as they pass through the criminal process and to coerce them into treatment for drug dependency. The rationale is that coerced drug treatment can be effective and that effective drug treatment will reduce levels of offending among problem users.

The proposals raise a number of significant questions. Is the assumption tenable that a significant proportion of crime is drug-related? Is coerced treatment effective? Is it ethical? Can the practical issues in delivering effective treatment be overcome? Can the enterprise command the necessary public support and confidence? This chapter examines some of these issues. To anticipate our main arguments, the assumptions that underpin the government's proposals for coerced treatment are sound enough: there is a demonstrable causal relationship between drug dependency and offending, though it is more complex than is usually recognised. It is also possible to deliver effective treatment to offenders under conditions of coercion. However, limiting factors are to be found in the practical issues relating to resourcing and in the dilemmas that arise when offenders fail to comply fully with the conditions of their treatment order.

The first half of the chapter is given over to an examination of the research evidence about the links between drug dependency and other forms of crime. We then summarise the proposals in the White Paper and discuss the provision for them made in the Criminal Justice Bill. (It is possible that some of these provisions will be subject to amendment by the time that the Bill is enacted, but the expectation is that they will reach the statute book largely as drafted.) Finally we consider whether coerced treatment for drug-dependent offenders is in principle a viable policy option and whether the government proposals are workable in practice.

Drugs and crime – the nature of the problem

That there are links between some forms of illicit drug use and crime is obvious. The precise nature of these links is not. Widely differing claims are made about the extent to which crime is 'drug-driven'. We aim here to summarise research evidence that can shed light on the relationships. We have drawn on key pieces of recent British research but we have also discussed relevant American work.

We have restricted ourselves to an examination of the links between drug use and *property* crime. This is because the government's current proposals relating to dependent drug users are designed largely to tackle the impact of drug use on crimes such as burglary, shoplifting, robbery and other theft which are often committed to fund drug use. We have not given much space to an examination of the links with violent crime. This is not to deny that some specific drugs may facilitate violence – and others may inhibit it (Anglin and Speckart 1988; Dobinson and Ward 1986; Harrison and Backenheimer 1998; Jarvis and Parker 1989). Nor should one ignore the systemic violence associated with some forms of drug distribution (Goldstein 1985); however, we have not examined it here. We have also ignored links between alcohol and crime – but not because we think these unimportant.

Types of link

There is a clear *association* between illicit drug use and property crime. As will be discussed below, there is a large degree of overlap between those using illicit drugs and those who are involved in crime, with a pool of people who both use drugs and offend. But this link can arise in several ways (see Coid *et al* 2000, Best *et al* 2000 and Walters 1998, for fuller discussions):

- Illicit drug use may lead to other forms of crime, e.g. to provide money to buy drugs or as a result of the disinhibiting effects of some drugs.

- Crime may lead to drug use, e.g. providing the money and the contacts to buy drugs or serving as a palliative for coping with the stresses of a chaotic, criminal lifestyle.

- There could be a more complex interaction, whereby crime facilitates drug use and drug use prompts other forms of crime.

- There may be an association arising from a shared common cause – but no causal link at all between offending and drug use.

The fourth possibility deserves as serious consideration as the other three. Surveys of offenders' health show that they are much more likely to smoke nicotine than the general population (e.g. Singleton *et al* 1999). No one would seriously argue that smoking causes crime, however, or that crime causes smoking. Rather, smoking and crime are likely to share *some* causal roots without themselves being causally related. The same is likely to be true of *some* links between illicit drug use and crime. For example, economic deprivation, inconsistent parenting, low educational attainment and limited employment prospects are risk factors not only for chaotic or dependent drug use but also for heavy involvement in crime. It should also be recognised that there is at least a minority of dependent drug users who do not fund their use through crime and who fail to fit popular stereotypes of 'the drug addict'.

Each of these explanations will apply to *some* people. In some cases problem drug use – dependence on drugs such as heroin, crack/cocaine or amphetamines, or heavy binge use of these drugs – does trigger theft as a means of fund-raising. Others would never have become drug-dependent if crime had not provided them with the means to buy large amounts of drugs. Some people will both be involved in crime and also use illicit drugs without there being any causal connection whatsoever between the two. There are four sorts of relevant study:

- those examining illicit drug use and offending in the overall population;
- those examining drug use in the offending population;
- those examining offending among the 'problem drug using' population;
- those examining patterns of drug use and crime among criminally involved problem drug users.

Drug use and offending in the overall population

Illicit drug use is widespread in the young adult population. There are around four million regular illicit drug users in Great Britain. The most commonly used illicit drugs are cannabis and ecstasy. Large minorities of the teenage and young adult population also admit to other forms of offending, though only a very small proportion are persistent or serious offenders. Those who use illicit drugs are more likely than others to be involved to some degree in crime and vice versa. However, in general there is no significant causal link between use of either cannabis or ecstasy and property crime. Only a very small proportion of illicit users report being dependent on drugs.

According to the British Crime Survey (BCS), 34 per cent of the adult (16–59) population have used illicit drugs at some stage in their life, and 11 per cent report using illicit drugs in the previous year. This represents around 3.5 million people in England and Wales, or four million people taking into account Scotland, who use illicit drugs at least once a year. Use is concentrated among the young: 50 per cent of people between the ages of 16 and 29 will have used a prohibited drug at some time in their life and 25 per cent in the last year (Ramsay *et al* 2001). Nine out of 10 users say they have used cannabis; 1 in 10 ecstasy. Use of heroin and crack is rare. However, the BCS conducted in 2000 reports an increase in the proportion of 16 to 24 year-olds using heroin (from 0.3 per cent to 0.8 per cent) and cocaine (from 3.1 per cent to 4.9 per cent) in the previous year when compared with findings from the 1998 BCS, though this is not statistically significant.

The Youth Lifestyle Survey (YLS) makes broadly similar but slightly higher estimates (Flood-Page *et al* 2000). The YLS found that about a fifth of young people admitted to some form of offending and that self-reported drug use was the strongest predictor of serious or persistent offending. However, for the majority of young people, there is no persuasive evidence that there is any direct causal linkage between offending and drug use. The association between drug use and offending in the YLS is best understood in terms of a common cause, which leads to two – not totally dissimilar – forms of hedonistic risk-taking.

Parker and colleagues' longitudinal studies describe evolving patterns of drug use among young people in the North West of England (Parker *et al* 1998; Measham *et al* 2001). Experience of illicit drugs was widespread in their samples and most funded drug use through legitimate means. Respondents made a sharp distinction between acceptable and unacceptable drugs – with heroin and crack in the latter

29

group and use of these drugs was low. There was only a very small minority who were heavily involved in crime, dependent drug use and other forms of delinquency.

Drug use in the known offending population

Illicit drug use is very much more common among known offenders in Britain than among the young population as a whole. Dependent or problematic drug use is also more common. Majorities of offenders are regular users of illicit drugs, and a large minority regard themselves as dependent, describing their offending as a direct consequence of this dependence.

At any one time, there are very roughly 550,000 people in Britain who are persistently involved in crime, of whom slightly more than 100,000 are high-rate persistent offenders (figures from Appendix 3, Home Office 2001, uplifted to take account of Scotland). The majority of these offenders are known to the police. They are much more heavily involved in drug use, and in problematic drug use, than the general population.

The largest relevant research study is the NEW-ADAM survey (Bennett 1998, 2000; Bennett *et al* 2001) which drug-tests and interviews samples of arrestees. The latest sweep of the survey found that 65 per cent of all arrestees tested (1,435) were positive for some form of illicit drug, with 24 per cent testing positive for opiates and 15 per cent for cocaine. The average weekly expenditure on drugs, for heroin and crack/cocaine users, was £290. The main sources of illegal income during the last 12 months were property crime (theft, burglary, robbery, handling stolen goods and fraud/deception) followed by drug dealing and undeclared earnings while claiming social security benefits. Heroin and crack/cocaine users had an average annual illegal income of around £15,000 – compared with an average annual illegal income of £9,000 for all interviewed arrestees. Bennett concludes that these findings suggest that drug use and in particular the use of heroin and crack/cocaine is associated with higher levels of both prevalence and incidence of offending.

This study has some methodological limitations. The samples are small, and given that they are drawn from eight cities per sweep, they are unlikely to be representative of the country as a whole. Participation is voluntary and urine test data are not adjusted to take account of the differences in the half-life of drugs (for example, amphetamines remain testable in urine for two days; opiates, cocaine and benzodiazepines for three days; and cannabis up to a month with chronic users). The results thus need cautious interpretation (see Stimson *et al* 1998). Nevertheless they give a good idea of the 'order of magnitude' of the relationships between illicit drug use, dependence and offending in this population.

Consistent results have emerged from surveys of prison inmates indicating that a significant minority of the adult convicted population are dependent drug users prior to imprisonment (Maden *et al* 1991; Singleton *et al* 1999). Lader and colleagues in their study of psychiatric morbidity among young offenders aged between 16 and 20 years in England and Wales found that 6 out of 10 had used some drug before entering prison (Lader *et al* 2000). Over half were being held for acquisitive crimes, although among women drug offenders these were more common (1 in 5 being held for these offences). A large proportion reported a measure of dependency – 52 per cent of sentenced male offenders, 58 per cent of female offenders and 57 per cent of remanded male prisoners. In particular opiate dependence in the year before coming into prison was reported by 23 per cent of women, 21 per cent of the male remanded and 15 per cent of the male sentenced group.

While many studies have found extensive drug use among persistent offenders, by no means everyone has concluded that there is a simple causal relationship whereby dependent drug use fuels crime – the so-called 'addiction model' of the links between drugs and crime. A Scottish study by Hammersley *et al* (1989) examined opioid use among a group of offenders (in this case, people who had been sent to prison), contrasting them to a group of non-prisoners. They found that involvement in property crime predicted opioid use better than opioid use predicted property crime, and suggested that heavy heroin use could be understood as a function partly of the spending power of persistent offenders and partly of the criminal subcultures within which heroin use took place.

Several researchers have also drawn attention to the ability of many people to use 'drugs of dependence' over long periods in controlled ways which do not amount to addiction. Ditton and Hammersley (1994) have argued this in relation to cocaine, and Pearson (1987) in relation to heroin (also see Zinberg and Jacobson 1976; Harding *et al* 1980).

These studies argue against the adoption of a simple 'addiction model' of the links between drugs and crime, whereby dependence inevitably follows the regular use of drugs and where crime inevitably follows the onset of dependence. However, there is also the need for some realism in taking at face value the way in which a significant proportion of offenders say that they are drug-dependent, say that they commit crime to feed their habit and are prepared to seek treatment to address their drug problems.

A strong association between drug use and known offending has also emerged from US research. However, the American criminal justice system has been actively targeting drug users for many years as part of the 'war on drugs'. It is therefore not surprising that such studies find large numbers of drug users among those arrested, dealt with by the courts or imprisoned (MacCoun and Reuter 1998).

Offending among the 'problem drug using' population

Problem drug users – those dependent on drugs such as heroin, crack/ cocaine or amphetamines, or heavy binge users of these drugs – are a small minority of the total – perhaps around 5 per cent of regular drug users. They are likely to be heavily involved in acquisitive crime, though large minorities of those who seek treatment do not report funding their drug use through acquisitive crime.

Extrapolating from the Home Office Addicts Index in 1996, Edmunds *et al* (1998, 1999) estimated that problematic drug users in England and Wales number somewhere between 100,000 and 200,000 – less than 5 per cent of the four million or so of those who use illicit drugs each year. Numbers of people entering treatment have grown rapidly since then, and more recent estimates of the problem drug-using population suggest that the figure could range between 250,000 and 500,000 (Godfrey *et al* 2002). In any one year there may now be around 50,000 people entering treatment for the first time. Several studies have considered the criminal involvement of those in treatment.

The National Treatment Outcome Research Study (NTORS) was a longitudinal study of 1,100 opiate dependent drug users who had sought treatment. It found high levels of criminal behaviour among the sample (Gossop *et al* 1998). Sixty-one per cent of the sample reported committing crimes other than drug possession in the three months before they started treatment; in aggregate they admitted to 71,000 crimes in this period. The most commonly reported offence was shoplifting.

A smaller study of 221 methadone reduction and maintenance clients found over four-fifths had been arrested for some criminal offence in the past (Coid *et al* 2000). However, offending prior to treatment had not always been undertaken solely to fund drug-taking. Despite this, two-thirds believed there was a strong link between their current offending and their drug habit and half claimed that their current offending served solely to fund their drug habit. Best *et al* (2001) examined 100 people entering drug treatment in London. Consistent with NTORS and Coid *et al* they found slightly more than half of the sample reported funding drug use through acquisitive crime.

Early studies of problem drug users' involvement in crime tended to focus on opiate use as this was the principal drug of dependence being used in Britain. Several studies over the last five years have remarked on the emergence of crack use among problem users and on the convergence of opiate and crack use. Harocopos *et al* (2003) provide the most up-to-date study of chaotic crack users in treatment. They followed up 100 users referred to a crisis intervention centre in London, interviewing them six times each over an 18-month period. While the focus of the study was on the group's experience of treatment, respondents were also asked about their involvement in crime. Most of the sample had criminal records, usually long ones. The start of their criminal career more often than not predated that of the problematic drug career: a minority (36 respondents) said that their criminal careers had been prompted by drug use. Although most were involved in acquisitive crime before they started using crack, the drug led to very steep increases in offending rates and broadened the range of offences they committed. The researchers concluded that crack can sometimes lead to criminal careers, but more often 'crack use will serve to amplify offending behaviour rather than act as a trigger' (p. 37). In months when respondents did not use crack, their offending rates slumped.

There is an extensive research literature in the US which similarly suggests that many problematic users are involved in criminal activity (Nurco *et al* 1995, Anglin and Perrochet 1998, Lurigio 2000, NIJ 2000).

Patterns of drug use and offending among criminally involved problem drug users

Problem users who have recently come to police attention are usually at the more chaotic end of the spectrum of problem drug users. They tend to be poly-drug users, with heroin and crack prominent in their drug repertoires. They are likely to have a long criminal career which often pre-dates their career as a problem drug user. They spend a great deal of money on drugs (often several hundred pounds a week). They are likely to have been arrested for shoplifting, burglary or other acquisitive offences, although drug dealing is also a frequent fund-raising strategy. Treatment has been shown to yield large falls in drug use and consequent reductions in offending.

There is now quite a significant body of research examining patterns of crime and drug use among problem users who are identified as such as they pass through the criminal process. Much of this work has involved evaluations of treatment or referral programmes targeting this group. The studies show that these problem drug users commit large amounts of acquisitive crime. For example, drug using offenders on probation in London were found to be spending an average of £362 per week on drugs prior to arrest, primarily raised by committing acquisitive crime, notably shoplifting. In the month before arrest, over half (51 per cent) of these probationers were using both heroin and crack (Hearnden and Harocopos 2000). The evaluation of a range of 'arrest referral schemes' designed to refer offenders to treatment also found similar levels of expenditure on drugs funded through property crimes such as burglary. Again most reported poly-drug use with 97 per cent using either opiates or stimulants or both (Edmunds *et al* 1999). Turnbull and colleagues described the drug use and offending behaviour of those offenders given Drug Treatment and Testing Orders. Three-fifths of those given the 210 pilot orders had never received any form of help or treatment for their drug use (Turnbull *et al* 2000). Of 132 drug-using offenders interviewed, most (120 or 91 per cent) had been using opiates on a daily basis before arrest. They reported committing several types of property crime on a daily basis in order to fund an average expenditure of £400 per week on drugs. Almost half received their order following a conviction for shoplifting.

An important finding to emerge from both British and North American studies is that the criminal careers of this group usually pre-dated the onset of problematic or dependent drug use. Edmunds *et al* (1999), for example, examining a sample drawn from arrest referral clients and probationers, found that the average age at which illicit drugs were first used was 15 years. The average age at first conviction (for any offence) was 17 years. The average age at which respondents recognised their drug use as problematic was 23 years – six years later.

A review of US research by Deitch *et al* (2000) concluded that roughly two-thirds of drug using offenders report involvement in crime before the onset of drug use. This simple fact has led some to argue that drug use cannot be regarded as a cause; obviously it cannot be the *sole* cause, but as Harrison and Backenheimer (1998) argue, 'addiction to illicit drugs appears to be an amplifier or catalyst which aggravates deviant tendencies'. While dependent drug use may not have triggered the criminal careers of this group, it provides a mechanism by which they are locked into offending and thus fail to mature out of crime in the way that characterises the majority of young offenders.

Both British and US studies point to a preferred hierarchy of fund-raising strategies, with drug dealing and shoplifting at or near the top of the list while burglary and robbery offences also feature prominently.

There are many studies which suggest that treating the drug problems of this criminally involved population has benefit. Both British and US research suggests that drug treatment can work to reduce offending as well as drug use (Gossop *et al* 1998; Coid *et al* 2000; Edmunds *et al* 1998, 1999; Hearnden and Harocopos, 2000; Turnbull *et al* 2000; also see Belenko 1998 and Lurigio 2000 for American reviews). While much of the research can be criticised on methodological grounds (most have relied on urine test data for the period covering the treatment programme, few collected reliable outcome measures relating to re-offending and fewer still have run for periods of time stretching beyond engagement with the programme, comparing treatment groups with comparison samples), cumulatively it offers quite good evidence that appropriate drug services can help reduce drug use and related crime. The studies also have obvious implications about the links between dependent drug use and persistent offending; if reduced dependence results in reduced offending, this provides strong grounds for the existence of a causal link.

The nature of the drugs–crime link: a stocktaking

In summarising what this body of research evidence tells us about the links between drugs and crime, the first point to emphasise is that there are different explanations for the *association* between illicit drug use and crime for different groups of drug user. In considering the links it is essential to be specific about these different groups.

The literature suggests that 'lifestyle' and 'subcultural' factors are important in explaining why those who try illicit drugs are also more likely than others to get involved in other forms of law-breaking. The search for novelty and excitement and enjoyment of the rewards of risk-taking are defining aspects of youth culture. It is hardly a surprise that large minorities of the population engage in the – relatively controlled – risks of both recreational drug use and minor crime at some stage of their adolescence and young adulthood.

For those whose offending – and drug use – is more persistent and less controlled, other explanatory factors also need to be called into play. In the first place, chaotic drug users and persistent offenders – in contrast to controlled drug users and occasional petty offenders – have limited social and economic resources and limited exposure to legitimate 'life opportunities'. The majority are from deprived backgrounds, with in-consistent parenting, poor access to housing and health care, low educational attainment and limited employment prospects. *Controlled* drug use has no obvious association with social exclusion; how could it, given the scale of participation? *Chaotic* or *dependent* use, by contrast, shares that constellation of risk factors that also predict heavy involvement in crime – and exposure to many forms of social exclusion.

If these risk factors *predispose* people both to uncontrolled drug use and to involvement in persistent offending, Walters (1998) and De Li Periu and MacKenzie (2000) have discussed how reciprocal causal relationships can begin to emerge whereby criminal involvement both facilitates and maintains drug use and drug use maintains involvement in crime. While some researchers, such as Hammersley and colleagues (1989), have argued for subcultural explanations of the close linkage, the accounts of the offenders themselves are more consistent with a pathological perspective where dependence provides the motive for acquisitive offending.

A 'war on drugs' is one of the most persistent of political metaphors. In mobilising their troops, drug warriors point to drug-related crime as one of the worst consequences of drug use. The research evidence calls into question the simple 'addiction model' of the relationship between drugs and crime whereby illicit drug use leads inexorably to dependence and thence to crime. The relationships are actually more complex. Most drug users are – and remain – in control of their use; many such users are also involved in crime, but drugs are not to blame for this. There is a small minority of drug users who are dependent in their use and chaotic in their lifestyles; there is a strong probability that these will finance their drug use through property crime. The interrelationships between illicit drug use, problematic drug use and persistent offending are set out schematically in Figure 2.1 This is intended to be illustrative rather than precise.

It makes sense to think of chaotic or dependent drug use and persistent offending sharing causal roots; but it is also important to understand how, once established, the two behaviours can be mutually sustaining. Drug dependence tends to *amplify* the offending rates of people whose circumstances may predispose them to becoming persistent offenders. There are important policy implications here. It makes excellent sense to provide treatment services for drug-dependent offenders; if successful, it should substantially reduce levels of crime. However, to maintain the lifestyle changes which treatment may enable, it will also be necessary to address the factors that drew this group into persistent offending in the first place.

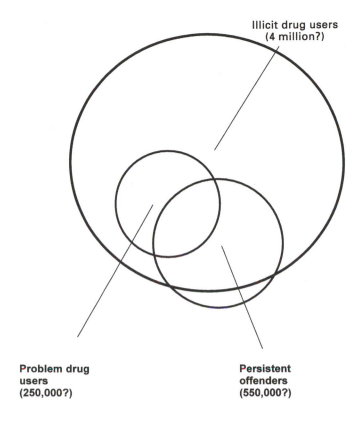

Illicit drug users
(4 million?)

Problem drug
users
(250,000?)

Persistent
offenders
(550,000?)

Figure 2.1 Illicit drug use, problem drug use and persistent offending

The government's proposals for tackling drug-related crime

It should be clear from the discussion so far that drug dependent offenders constitute an important part of the business of the criminal process. As such, many of the proposals in the White Paper *Justice for All* and in the Criminal Justice Bill bear indirectly on them. Here we have restricted ourselves to consideration of those that have an explicit and obvious impact.

The White Paper proposed several measures of fairly direct relevance to drug-related crime:

- a new community sentence, enabling intensive supervision for drug offenders;
- drug treatment as part of community sentences for juveniles;
- custody plus: short sentence plus supervision, totalling 12 months maximum;
- custody minus: suspended prison sentence plus supervision;
- custodial remands for arrestees who test positive to Class A drugs but refuse treatment;
- conditional and deferred cautioning for drug offenders and others (linked to drug testing on arrest);
- extending drug-testing provisions to juvenile offenders.

The 2002 Criminal Justice Bill was passing through Parliament at the time of writing, providing the statutory provisions for these proposals. These were broadly as outlined in the White Paper. Perhaps the most significant, for our purposes, is the new generic community penalty which will allow sentencers to impose one or more requirements in a single order. Thus it will be possible to attach a drug treatment and testing requirement to a community order, making the order equivalent to the current drug treatment and testing order (DTTO). Alternatively, this requirement could be combined with one or more others, such as a curfew requirement, a requirement to do unpaid work or participation in any specified activities. The drug treatment and testing requirement retains the review provisions that were introduced originally for DTTOs, whereby the offender returns to court, initially on a monthly basis, for a review of progress. Other requirements that can be made as part of a community order do not include this provision for review.

The 'custody plus' provisions appear in the Bill much as they were set out in the White Paper. Sentencers will be able to pass a short prison sentence (of up to three months), followed by a period of community supervision where requirements can be imposed analogous to those for community orders. Thus – to use current terminology – a sentencer could use the 'custody-plus' powers to impose a three month sentence (or less) followed by a DTTO.

'Custody minus' will involve the power to impose a short suspended prison sentence, while adding requirements for community supervision that mirror those of 'custody plus'. Thus a sentencer could – to use current terminology – impose a three-month suspended prison sentence in parallel with a DTTO. An interesting feature of these provisions is the inclusion of a review process for offenders subject to a suspended sentence with conditions, regardless of whether these conditions include drug treatment and testing.

The Bill amends the current bail legislation to create a presumption against bail for offenders who have tested positive to a Class A drug at the point of arrest or prior to sentence. Before remanding the offender to custody, the court must satisfy itself not only that the offender has tested positive, but (a) that drug dependency was a factor leading to the offence and (b) that the offender has been offered and refused opportunities presented to him or her to engage in treatment.

The powers to impose conditional cautions allow for the imposition of requirements on cautioned offenders. The requirements must be designed to provide for the offender's rehabilitation or for reparation, or for both. The nature and range of requirements are to be set out in a code of practice, but obviously the requirement to undergo drug treatment will be included in the list. Failure to meet the requirements will result in prosecution and the admission of guilt signed by the offender at the time of the caution will be admissible evidence in court.

Powers are being introduced to allow the police to drug-test young offenders over the age of 14; the current legislation is applicable to those aged 18 or over. The existing legislation imposes a requirement to test provided that the offender has committed a 'trigger offence' (involving drug possession, drug supply or theft offences). The new powers will permit the police to test, regardless of whether the offender has been arrested for a trigger offence if they suspect that the offender has drug problems. A 'responsible adult' must be present where the offender is aged 14–16.

To summarise, the Criminal Justice Bill very substantially extends the powers of the police and the courts to coerce drug dependent offenders into treatment. Until now, the coercive powers have been explicit only in the case of DTTOs (and their precursors, 1A6 probation orders). Clearly some offenders may interpret the offers of help made by arrest referral workers as 'offers they cannot refuse', but the police have not had any powers to coerce dependent drug users into treatment at the point of arrest. Now they will, using the conditional caution. If the offence is too serious to attract a caution, the amendments to the Bail Act mean that offenders who decide against treatment after a positive drug test will face a custodial remand unless they take up offers of assessment for treatment or treatment itself. At the point of sentence there will be three variants of coerced treatment orders:

- the equivalent (or near-equivalent) of a DTTO;
- a DTTO (or similar) preceded by a short prison sentence;
- a DTTO (or similar) underpinned by a suspended prison sentence.

All these provisions will be implemented against the backdrop of the Communities against Drugs initiative, which aims to harness enforcement strategies and those concerned with primary and secondary prevention. The element common to all of them is that drug-related crime can be addressed through coerced treatment. The key issues to examine in assessing the probability of success are:

- whether in principle coerced treatment can 'work';
- whether in practice the proposals will be implemented effectively;
- whether they can command and retain public support.

Does coerced treatment 'work'?

This question has to be answered in two stages. The first is to see whether, in general, drug treatment has successful outcomes. The second is to examine whether success is still possible when people are coerced into treatment. On the first question, several UK reviews – drawing largely on the international research literature (see Hough 1996 for a summary) – show that a variety of treatment modalities can be effective against criteria of reduced drug use and improved health and social functioning. Methadone maintenance prescribing emerges well from the international research literature. There are a number of key elements to successful treatment: getting drug misusers into treatment quickly; using incentives to retain them for as long as possible, and for a minimum of three months; and providing treatment within a positive and supportive environment. However, the research literature has not always made clear exactly how treatment works and which treatment modalities work best with whom.

A note of caution needs to be expressed about the quality of the research evidence. Many of the relevant studies have quite weak experimental designs, relying on 'before and after' interviews (and, more rarely, drug testing) with people passing through treatment. For ethical and practical reasons, random controlled trials are a rarity. Where comparison groups are used, they may not be as comparable as one might wish. And crucially, there is a systemic problem relating to programme drop-outs. The 'successes' of any treatment programme tend to be readily contactable and amenable to interview. The drop-outs are much harder to contact and may be less prepared to talk to researchers. This biases any 'before and after' study towards success. This said, there is a consistency of outcome for research with strong experimental designs and studies with weaker designs. Ethnographic studies also support the general conclusion that 'treatment works'.

Answers to the second question – whether coercion negates the impact of treatment – have traditionally been pessimistic. Received wisdom has been that without motivation to change, dependent drug users will not benefit from coerced treatment. The research evidence does not support this pessimism. While not entirely conclusive or consistent, on balance the international research evidence suggests that coerced treatment appears to be no less effective than treatment entered into voluntarily and those coerced into treatment often remain there longer than those engaging on a voluntary basis. It also suggests that the targeted use of appropriate, well resourced treatment options for criminally involved problem drug users at various stages of the criminal process can act as a viable mechanism for retention in treatment, yielding benefits and reducing harm both for individuals themselves and the wider community.

These findings should not, on reflection, be too surprising. There is an obvious flaw in the argument that motivation is a precondition for effective treatment. This is that it denies the possibility of ambivalence. Obviously those who really want to stop their drug use will do very much better in treatment than those who really want to continue. If problem users fell only into these two categories, then coerced treatment would fail. However, a large proportion – probably the vast majority – of dependent users will see both costs and benefits in their drug use. Most will enter into treatment with a degree of ambivalence. Legal coercion seems likely to offer a means to hold problem users within a treatment programme for sufficiently long to allow drug workers to exploit this ambivalence. It does not appear to be qualitatively different from the other forms of coercion – from partners, family, friends or even employers – to which apparently voluntary clients are exposed. It is helpful to distinguish between all these forms of coercion, on the one hand, whereby people's decisions to engage in treatment are structured by outside pressures, and outright compulsion, on the other hand. Compulsory treatment involves the *removal* of choice and decision-making. It seems an inappropriate way of tackling drug dependency.

In so far as there is a research consensus about coerced treatment, it is argued that coercion provides a viable mechanism for *retention* in treatment, and retention in treatment is, not surprisingly, a pre-condition for success. The evidence is summarised succinctly by Farabee *et al* (1999). Anglin's (1988) study of the California Civil Addict Program (CAP) remains one of the best demonstrations that legally coerced treatment provides long-term benefits.

Will the White Paper's proposals for coerced treatment work in practice?

So far, this chapter has suggested that there is fairly reliable research evidence to show three things:

- There are clear, if complex, links between problem drug use and acquisitive crime.
- A variety of treatments for problem drug use have been shown to be effective.
- Coerced treatment can be no less effective than treatment on a voluntary basis.

Perhaps the key issue is whether the proposals can be implemented in the British context with sufficient commitment, and with sufficient resources, to ensure that offenders are effectively engaged and retained in treatment. So far, the best available evidence comes from the evaluation of the three pilot studies that were set up in Croydon, Liverpool and Gloucestershire in October 1998. We followed up 212 offenders on DTTOs between late 1998 and Easter 2000; we tracked their progress through the order, and did 'exit' interviews with a small proportion of offenders. The findings are set out in Turnbull *et al* (2000). A reconviction follow-up study is forthcoming (Clancy *et al*, in press). The key points are as follows:

- A majority of the group were reconvicted within two years of starting the order.
- A minority completed their order successfully, and the remainder were revoked.
- There were very substantial differences in reconviction rates between those who completed their orders and those whose orders were revoked.
- Those who completed their orders reduced their annual conviction rate to levels well below those of the previous five years.
- There were clear differences between pilot sites in performance.

The key message from the study is that those who can be engaged in DTTO programmes and can be retained on them show marked reductions in their drug use and in drug-related offending. The proportion reconvicted is much lower than for revokees, and the annual number of convictions per year drops substantially. There remains a possibility that these positive results are the result of a 'selection effect' rather than a treatment effect: in other words, those who had in any case decided to address their drug problems naturally did best on their orders. However, this interpretation is inconsistent with the accounts of the offenders themselves which stressed the benefits of being on the order.

If our interpretation is correct, the challenge facing DTTOs and, when implemented, Community Orders with drug treatment and testing requirements is to improve retention rates so that the proportion completing their order rises and the proportion with relatively low reconviction rates increases. To achieve this will involve the provision of more timely, more responsive and more appropriate treatment than was often the case in the pilot projects. This will involve considerably better inter-agency working than occurred in some of the pilot sites. Partnership work often fails. The reason, in short, is that agencies are required to do things which in the short-term advance their partners' organisational goals rather than their own. The mutual trust and commitment needed to pursue shared long-term benefits often proves fragile. It is easily shattered by fundamental conflicts of approach – care versus control, for example – or by conflicts in treatment philosophy – abstinence versus harm reduction (cf. Edmunds 1999; Turnbull *et al* 2000).

It should be stressed that the DTTO pilots were exactly that – challenging and innovative programmes in which some mistakes were inevitably made. In one site, the treatment programme had to be completely redesigned. Since the end of the pilot period many programmes have found their feet, and there are emerging models of good practice. New funding arrangements are also making the 'fast tracking' of treatment a reality for offenders with drug problems in some areas.

Experience with DTTOs since the pilot was carried out has suggested that they have proved inflexible in various ways. They have been targeted at offenders who have committed serious offences; they are genuinely demanding and as a result get taken seriously by sentencers. However, this has meant that many offenders who could benefit from a DTTO are ineligible by virtue of the offence for which they are being sentenced. Those who have severe drug problems but are before the court on a relatively minor charge will not get a DTTO.

There are dilemmas over the enforcement of the conditions of orders. The high levels of non-compliance with DTTOs, at least initially, point to a need to enforce conditions of DTTOs and their successors with a degree of pragmatism. Offenders are exposed to a very much greater risk of non-compliance than most of those serving community punishments, simply because the opportunities for non-compliance are so much greater than for orders that involve relatively little contact. If the probation service continues to apply the same National Standards to DTTOs and Community Orders with drug conditions that apply for 'normal' probation supervision, the breach rate will inevitably be high and it will prove impossible to retain a critical mass of offenders in treatment. There is a clear case for reviewing this feature of enforcement policy.

The element of 'sentencer review' in DTTOs seems to be a feature of the order that is popular with offenders, sentencers and probation officers alike – leaving aside the practical problems relating to scheduling. It appears to impose a greater degree of accountability on the offenders. If there were more flexibility in using review hearings for breach proceedings, some of the dilemmas of enforcement might be more readily resolved.

DTTOs provide a paradigm for court-mandated treatment, and if the problems they face can be resolved then there is room for optimism about cognate disposals. The 'custody-plus' and 'custody-minus' provisions in the Criminal Justice Bill raise precisely the same issues about the need to ensure retention on programmes and the need for pragmatism in response to failure. At the same time, these new sentencing provisions should provide the means to ensure that the sort of community-based treatment that DTTOs can now provide can also be arranged for offenders who have committed more serious offences.

In assessing prospects of success for conditional cautions, similar considerations apply as to court-based coerced treatment. There is plenty of evidence to support the idea of arrest referral schemes and some evidence of effective practice. The weak links, until now, have been in identifying suitable candidates in sufficient numbers and in persuading them to engage with treatment (Edmunds et al 1999). In combination with the drug testing powers introduced in 2000, the conditional caution provides the means to overcome these problems. However, it is likely that the 'devil will lie in the detail'. If drug dependent offenders are coerced into attending drug programmes with long waiting lists or if they are offered inappropriate or unresponsive services, this will achieve little. Offenders will fail to meet the requirements of their conditional cautions and will be returned to the courts for sentence.

A risk that all the new provisions run is that the treatment agencies could lose the confidence of users. Perhaps the worst possible outcome could be that large numbers of drug agencies become associated in the minds of problem users with coerced treatment, and that these drug agencies are insufficiently resourced to provide the quality of service that would justify coercion. Word would quickly get round the community of drug-using offenders that coerced treatment programmes made unrealistic demands on those involved.

Securing public support

One of the dilemmas of court-mandated community treatment relates to non-compliance and public support. The reality of dealing with very persistent drug-dependent offenders under Community Orders is that a degree of continued drug use and continued drug-related offending can be expected. Many report committing several offences a day in the period immediately before their arrest. Cutting their offending rate back to a few crimes per month may seem like a significant achievement for those familiar with drug dependence among persistent offenders. It is a commonplace among probation officers and sentencers that relapse is frequent and that offenders often take two steps forward and one step back. To the tabloid press, however, and indeed to sectors of the public, a Community Order which tolerates a much reduced rate of drug use and offending may seem like an unacceptable form of collusion with crime.

The viability of orders such as the DTTO and its successors may eventually depend on the completion rates that can be secured and on the skill with which the outcomes can be explained to the media and the public. Drug-dependent persistent offenders have exceptionally high rates of reconviction. With an average number of previous convictions of 30–50, their risk of getting a further conviction within a two-year period is well over 90 per cent, according to the Offender Group Reconviction Scale (OGRS). Success, in realistic terms, for DTTOs and similar orders might look like retention rates of 50 per cent and reconviction rates for 'completers' of 50 per cent. Getting key audiences to understand why this counts as success could prove an uphill battle.

Ethical issues

Coerced treatment raises ethical issues. These are not the same as ones relating to compulsion, where choice is removed from the person in need of treatment. The main ethical concern is that the intrusiveness of court-mandated treatment should not exceed that of a conventional punish-ment. This has not proved a significant concern for DTTOs, as the orders have been reserved for offenders who have committed offences serious enough to put them at risk of custody. However, the community order should allow for more flexibility with scope for imposing conditions of drug treatment for less serious offences. It is here that significant risks of over-intrusiveness emerge – where, for example, a problem drug user is coerced into an extensive treatment programme for a minor shoplifting offence. These ethical dilemmas become more acute when the risk of failure is known to be significant, and where the consequences of failure can be very serious for the person who accepts the offer. The general principle that should be followed is that the overall intrusiveness of an order, including sanctions for non-compliance, should be no greater than the sort of punishment that the offence might have attracted were treatment not a consideration.

Coerced treatment also raises another completely separate set of ethical issues relating to distributive justice. Resources for treatment are inevitably limited, and thus those in need of treatment are in competition for these resources. Any system of coerced treatment needs to ensure that it does not displace needy people from the treatment queue by virtue of their lack of involvement in crime.

Prospects

Many social policies are worth doing half-well if that is all that can be afforded. Some investment is usually better than none. However, there are some unusual characteristics of dependence on illicit drugs that means that anything except top-quality treatment programmes will achieve little. In a sense, treatment services are in competition with illicit drug markets. The latter offer attractive goods at a price, while the former offer less attractive goods – or goods carrying only long-term benefits – for free. People who are ambivalent about their illicit drug use will require a lot of persuasion to opt for the latter rather than the former, even when the choice is to some degree coerced.

There is a real risk that the current and promised initiatives relating to drug-dependent offenders will be financed on a shoestring. For all the government's commitment to strengthening community penalties, it seems uncertain whether there will be significant extra investment in the probation service, at least in the short term. Provision for drug dependent offenders *may* prove the exception, but pessimism is probably the more realistic stance. If this pessimism proves justified, the strategy of using the criminal process as a conduit to treatment could turn out to be an avoidable failure.

Nevertheless we retain a degree of optimism about the overall strategy of using drug treatment as a way of achieving a significant impact on crime and disorder. After all, the government appears to have recognised that treatment needs serious investment and there are signs that the necessary money is being found. This may allow for a fairly comprehensive system for locating problem drug users at all stages of the criminal justice system and for forcing or cajoling them into treatment. We also draw some optimism from the rate of increase in treatment budgets and in the experience of working with pooled treatment budgets. These have proved challenging to manage but force all the stakeholders to plan together and negotiate with one another and have helped create much firmer partnerships.

The provisions in the Criminal Justice Bill also introduce rather more flexibility into the systems for responding to drug-dependent offenders. The integration of DTTOs into a generic community order should prove a benefit, allowing drug treatment of varying intensity to be offered to offenders either as a 'stand-alone' programme or in combination with other interventions. There will always be a proportion of problem drug users who will prefer to continue to take drugs regardless of the consequences, but at least we now face the prospect whereby it will be quite hard for criminally involved problem users to pass through the criminal process without being exposed to offers of treatment. Although many will refuse the offer – and live with the consequences – others will certainly will take up the opportunity, and if the treatment is of a good standard they will stay in treatment and reap the benefits.

References

Anglin, M.D. (1988) 'The Efficacy of Civil Commitment in Treating Narcotic Addiction', in Leukfield, C.G. and Tims, F.M. (eds), *Compulsory Treatment of Drug Abuse: Research and Clinical Practice*, NIDA Research Monograph No. 86. Rockville, MD: National Institute on Drug Abuse.

Anglin, M.D. and Perrochet, B. (1998) 'Drug Use and Crime: a Historical Review of Research Conducted by the UCLA Drug Abuse Research Center', *Substance Use and Misuse*, 33(9),1871–914.

Anglin, M.D. and Speckart, G. (1988) 'Narcotics and Crime: a Multi-Sample, Multi-Method Analysis', *Criminology*, 26(2), 197–233.

Belenko, S. (1998) *Research on Drug Courts: a Critical Review*. New York: National Centre on Addiction and Substance Abuse at Columbia University.

Bennett, T. (1998) *Drugs and Crime: the Results of Research on Drug Testing and Interviewing Arrestees*, Home Office Research Study 183. London: Home Office.

Bennett, T. (2000) *Drugs and Crime: the Results of the Second Development Stage of the NEW-ADAM Programme*, Home Office Research Study 205. London: Home Office.

Bennett, T., Holloway, K. and Williams, T. (2001) *Drug Use and Offending: Summary Results of the First Year of the NEW-ADAM Research Programme*, Home Office Research Findings No. 148. London: Home Office.

Best, D., Sidwell, C., Gossop, M., Harris, J. and Strang, J. (2001) 'Crime and Expenditure Among Polydrug Misusers Seeking Treatment', *British Journal of Criminology*, 41, 119–26.

Clancy, A., Hough, M., Turnbull, P.J. and McSweeney, T. (in press). *The Impact of Drug Treatment and Testing Orders on Offending*. Home Office Research Findings. London: Home Office.

Coid, J., Carvell, A., Kittler, Z., Healey, A. and Henderson, J. (2000) *Opiates, Criminal Behaviour, and Methadone Treatment*. London: Home Office.

Deitch, D., Koutsenok, I. and Ruiz, A. (2000) 'The Relationship between Crime and Drugs: What We Have Learned in Recent Decades', *Journal of Psychoactive Drugs*, 32(4), 391–7.

De Li Periu, H. and MacKenzie, D. (2000) 'Drug Involvement, Lifestyles and Criminal Activities among Probationers', *Journal of Drug Issues*, 30(3), 593–620.

Ditton, J. and Hammersley, R.H. (1994) 'The Typical Cocaine User', *Druglink*, 9, 11–12.

Dobinson, I. and Ward, P. (1986) 'Heroin and Property Crime: an Australian Perspective', *Journal of Drug Issues*, 16(2), 249–62.

Edmunds, M., Hough, M., Turnbull, P.J. and May, T. (1999) *Doing Justice to Treatment: Referring Offenders to Drug Services*, DPAS Paper 2. London: Home Office.

Edmunds, M., May, T., Hough, M. and Hearnden, I. (1998) *Arrest Referral: Emerging Lessons from Research*. Home Office: Drugs Prevention Initiative Paper No. 23.

Farabee, D., Prendergast, M. and Anglin, M.D. (1998) 'The Effectiveness of Coerced Treatment for Drug-Abusing Offenders', *Federal Probation*, 62(1), 3–10.

Flood-Page, C., Campbell, S., Harrington, V. and Miller, J. (2000) *Youth Crime: Findings from the 1998/99 Youth Lifestyles Survey*, Home Office Research Study 209. London: Home Office.

Godfrey, C., Eaton, G., McDougall, C. and Culyer, A. (2002) *The Economic and Social Costs of Class A Drug Use in England and Wales, 2000*, Home Office Research Study 249. London: Home Office.

Goldstein, P. (1985) 'The Drugs/Violence Nexus: a Tripartite Conceptual Framework', *Journal of Drug Issues*, 15(4), 493–506.

Gossop, M., Marsden, J. and Stewart, D. (1998) *NTORS at One Year. The National Treatment Outcome Research Study. Changes in Substance Use, Health and Criminal Behaviour at One Year after Intake*. London: Department of Health.

Hammersley, R.H., Forsyth, A., Morrison, V. and Davies, J.B. (1989) 'The Relationship between Crime and Opioid Use', *British Journal of Addiction*, 84(9), 1029–43.

Harding, W.M., Zinberg, N.E., Stelmack, S.M. and Barry, M. (1980) 'Formerly-Addicted-Now-Controlled Opiate Users', *International Journal of the Addictions*, 15, 47–60.

Harocopos, A., Dennis, D., Turnbull, P.J., Parsons, J. and Hough, M. (2003) *On the Rocks: A Follow-up Study of Crack Users in London*. London: South Bank University.

Harrison, L.D. and Backenheimer, M. (1998) 'Research Careers in Unravelling the Drug–Crime Nexus in the U.S.', *Substance Use and Misuse*, 33(9), 1763–2003.

Hearnden, I. and Harocopos, A. (2000) *Problem Drug Use and Probation in London*, Home Office Research Findings No. 112. London: Home Office.

Home Office (2001) *Making Punishments Work. Report of a Review of the Sentencing Framework for England and Wales* (The Halliday Report). London: Home Office.

Home Office (2002) *Justice for All*, Cm 5563. London: TSO.

Hough, M. (1996) *Problem Drug Use and Criminal Justice: A Review of the Literature*, Drug Prevention Initiative Paper No. 15. London: Home Office Central Drugs Prevention Unit.

Jarvis, G. and Parker H. (1989) 'Young Heroin Users and Crime: How Do The "New Users" Finance Their Habits?', *British Journal of Criminology*, 29(2), 175–85.

Lader, D., Singleton, N. and Meltzer, H. (2000) *Psychiatric Morbidity among Young Offenders in England and Wales*. London: ONS.

Lurigio, A. (2000) 'Drug Treatment Effectiveness and Availability', *Criminal Justice and Behaviour*, 27(4), 495–528.

MacCoun, R.J. and Reuter, P. (1998) 'Drug Control', in Tonry, M. (ed.), *The Handbook of Crime and Punishment*. New York: Oxford University Press.

Maden, A., Swinton, M. and Gunn, J. (1991) 'Drug Dependence in Prisons', *British Medical Journal*, 302 (6781), 880.

Measham, F., Aldridge, J., and Parker, H. (2001) *Dancing on Drugs. Risk, Health and Hedonism in the British Club Scene*. London: Free Association Books.

National Institute of Justice (2000) *1999 Annual Report on Drug Use Among Adult and Juvenile Arrestees*, Arrestee Drug Abuse Monitoring Program (ADAM). Washington, DC: National Institute of Justice, NCJ 181426.

Nurco, D.N., Kinlock, T.W. and Hanlon, T.E. (1995) 'The Drugs–Crime Connection', in Inciardi, J. and McElrath, K. (eds), *The American Drug Scene: an Anthology*. Los Angeles: Roxbury.

Parker, H., Aldridge, J. and Measham, F. (1998) *Illegal Leisure: The Normalisation of Adolescent Recreational Drug Use*. London: Routledge.

Pearson, G. (1987) *The New Heroin Users*. Oxford: Basil Blackwell.

Ramsay, M., Baker, P., Goulden, C., Sharp, C. and Sondhi, A. (2001) *Drug Misuse Declared in 2000: Results from the British Crime Survey*, Home Office Research Study 224. London: Home Office.

Singleton, N., Farrel, M. and Meltzer, H. (1999) *Substance Misuse Among Prisoners in England and Wales*. London: ONS.

Stimson, G.V., Hickman, M. and Turnbull, P.J. (1998) 'Statistics on Misuse of Drugs Have Been Misused', *British Medical Journal*, 317, 1388

Turnbull, P.J., McSweeney, T., Hough, M., Webster, R. and Edmunds, M. (2000) *Drug Treatment and Testing Orders: Final Evaluation Report*, Home Office Research Study 212. London: Home Office.

Walters, G. (1998) *Changing Lives of Drugs and Crime*. Chichester: Wiley & Sons.

Zinberg, N.E. and Jacobson, R.C. (1976) 'The Natural History of "Chipping", *American Journal of Psychiatry*, 133, 37–40.

Chapter 3

Unprincipled sentencing?
The policy approach to
dangerous sex offenders

Amanda Matravers and Gareth V. Hughes

Today, there is a new and urgent emphasis upon the need for security, the containment of danger, the identification and management of any kind of risk. Protecting the public has become the dominant theme of penal policy.

David Garland, *The Culture of Control* (2001: 12)

Introduction

The protection of the public from dangerous offenders has dominated the criminal justice agenda for more than ten years. Reflecting a tough, populist stance inherited from the Conservative government, New Labour's crime policy has singled out groups of serious offenders for 'special treatment' in the form of extended prison sentences and supervision and surveillance in the community. Although these groups include violent and drug offenders, it is on sex offenders that political and popular attention has increasingly come to focus. In part this reflects the unique repugnance which sex crime provokes, which in turn may be a product of knowledge about the severe long-term physical and psychological damage endured by victims. However, the term 'sex offence' is a vague one that is applied to a wide range of offences, some of which provoke conflicting emotions. The central argument of this chapter is that policy-makers ignore the complexity of sex offending at their – and the public's – peril.

At present, two contrasting approaches characterise policy-making in this area. One is exemplified by many (though not all) of the proposals in the Review of the Sentencing Framework, *Making Punishments Work* (Home Office 2001) that fed into the White Paper, *Justice for All* (Home Office 2002a), and the Criminal Justice Bill 2002. The other may be seen in the Review of Sex Offences, *Setting the Boundaries* (Home Office 2000), the sex offences White Paper, *Protecting the Public* (Home Office 2002b), and the Sex Offences Bill which it informed. The former focus on a small number of violent, predatory individuals and offer proposals designed to punish them more severely and for longer periods. The latter acknowledge the variety of sex offences and the need to balance public protection with the rights of defendants. The second approach is much the more promising.

On the face of it, the development of a robust sentencing framework to deal with dangerous sex offenders needs little justification. Sex offenders have long been a focus of fear and opprobrium, and not without good reason. Sex crime is the only offence that involves primarily child victims, and the harmful long-term physical and psychological effects of sexual violence are well documented (see, for example, Salter 1988; Harris and Grace 1999). Victim surveys indicate that child sexual abuse is as prevalent in the UK as elsewhere, and tabloid newspaper campaigns dwell on the risks posed to children by unconvicted and post-release paedophile offenders in the community. It is hardly surprising that punitive responses to sex offenders command public support (see Hough *et al* 1996).

As part of a wider government strategy with the stated aim of protecting the public from sex offenders, *Justice for All* sets out proposals for new sentencing arrangements in the form of a 'special' determinate sentence and an indeterminate 'public protection' sentence. Both are aimed at offenders who are considered to be 'dangerous' and for both sentences release is contingent on positive risk assessment. Although the provisions apply to the dangerously violent as well as sex offenders, it is clear that the latter are the main target. The supposition that sex offenders may pose higher risks of reoffending is linked to the imposition of a lower threshold for the use of the proposed 'special' sentence in their case (see Home Office 2001: 33, para. 4.33).

However, the creation of yet another 'special' provision involves a number of assumptions about sex offenders (that they present an increasing problem; that significant numbers of them are 'dangerous'; that they reoffend at uniquely high rates) and about existing legislation (that it is insufficiently punitive; that it leaves the public 'unprotected'; that it fails to address the problem of the offenders who present the greatest danger to the community). None of these assumptions is supported by empirical evidence; indeed, the more we consult what we know about sex offending, the more mysterious the rationale for the current proposals becomes.

Firstly, there is no reason to suppose that sex offenders present an increasing problem. Sex offences continue to account for less than 1 per cent of all recorded crime and the number of offenders found guilty or cautioned for sex offences has been falling for a decade (Home Office 2002d). In particular, there has been no increase in the sorts of offences that worry the public most: murders of children by sexual predators have remained remarkably constant and mercifully rare, at some five or six per year since 1980. Although recorded rapes have doubled since 1987, this is generally attributed to a greater willingness by victims to report, particularly among complainants whose accounts do not follow the contours of the 'classic' stranger rape, and of the police to record (see Harris and Grace 1999).

Secondly, 'dangerous', that is predatory, violent individuals form a tiny minority of sex offenders. While public and media attention focus on serious crimes committed by offenders who are strangers to their victims, some 80 per cent of sex offences against children take place in the home of the victim or the offender. It is estimated that between 25–40 per cent of offenders have a fixated sexual attraction to children and therefore fit within the category of 'paedophiles'. The majority of child molesters, however, are people who are known to their victims, in many cases fathers, stepfathers and other family members (Grubin 1998).

Thirdly, it is not the case that sex offenders as a group are reconvicted at higher rates than other offenders. Of course, reconviction is not synonymous with reoffending, and as with other offences a proportion of sex crime is bound to remain undetected. Research does indicate that sex offender sub-groups are reconvicted at different rates, and that a small group of paedophile offenders have substantially higher rates of recidivism. However, among offenders against children, some 20 per cent are reconvicted of similar offences, a rate that is substantially lower than that for offenders generally.

A fourth and more complex question relates to the effectiveness of existing legislation. In so far as the proposals in *Justice for All* and the Criminal Justice Bill are justified at all, they are linked to the restoration of public confidence in a system that 'does not make sense', that allows sexual and other serious offenders to 'get off lightly' and that doesn't keep them in prison long enough (Home Office 2002a: 86, para. 5.2). As we discuss below, the last decade has seen the introduction of a plethora of preventive and increasingly punitive legislation aimed at serious violent and sexual offenders. These measures include longer custodial sentences, extended post-release supervision, and registration and surveillance within the community. This doesn't sound like a system that lets dangerous offenders off lightly.

Of course, this could still be the case if the legislation existed but was not used or was for some reason not working. However, there is ample evidence that the probability and severity of sentencing for sexual offences have increased since 1989. In 1999, the percentage of sex offenders receiving a custodial sentence rose from 35 to 66 per cent and the average sentence length increased by 25 per cent from 13.4 to 16.6 months. Meanwhile, an evaluation of the registration proposals required by the Sex Offenders Act 1997 found a high rate of compliance and a police service that expressed confidence in the legislation and its positive contribution to policing (Plotnikoff and Woolfson 2000).

The problem for *Justice for All* is that even if it put up a spirited argument against the effectiveness of existing legislation (which it doesn't), this still wouldn't justify the introduction of still more punitive measures along similar lines and with significant implications for the rights of individual offenders. The explanation for the 'special provisions' falls short of a justification for them, but lies in a political failure to resist tying the 'sex crime problem' to the need to protect children from dangerous sexual predators. As long as 'public protection' and effective sentencing remain harnessed to the prevention of exceptionally horrific, high-profile but essentially unpredictable offences, each new case will be taken as proof of the failure of the system as a whole and of the need for still more 'special' measures.

Violent, predatory sex offenders, while undoubtedly the easiest group to imagine and to fear, are not the best target for public protection strategies. A better target would be the promotion of a more nuanced understanding of sex offending, one that emphasises its variety and makes explicit the dangers posed to children and vulnerable individuals by family members and acquaintances. This is broadly the line taken in *Setting the Boundaries*, which describes its task as the development of a set of proposals that would be 'fair, just and fit for the twenty first century' (Home Office 2000: ii). Although *Protecting the Public* and the Sex Offences Bill reveal a continuing preoccupation with mobile anonymous sex offenders in the form of amendments to the Sex Offenders Register, restrictive orders and a new offence of 'sexual grooming', they also focus on the management (via multi-agency partnerships) of sex offenders in the community, clarify the law on rape and introduce new offences relating to sexual abuse within families and by adults in positions of trust. The point is not that these are all exemplary proposals, but that they give a sense of the range and variety of sexual offending in ways that the other documents do not.

Although penalising sex offenders will never be unpopular, the continuing focus on a very small group of predatory paedophile offenders indicates a political willingness to allow the public to believe that their children are at greater risk than they are. In addition to increased fear of crime, this leads to over-inclusive legislation and professional anxiety among those charged with the duty of managing sex offenders in custody and the community. Politicians would be better advised to counter the public's preoccupation with a small group of dangerous offenders than to fuel it. This is more difficult than it sounds, because the idea of the predatory offender as a ubiquitous threat is a key component of contemporary understandings of the 'sex crime problem'. Changing this will involve a commitment to the development and implementation of effective strategies for assessing and managing offenders who present varying levels of harm to the public. Importantly, it will also involve communicating information about risk to communities in ways that foster empowerment rather than provoke fear and resentment.

In this chapter we explore the ability of current legislation to deliver the public protection that preoccupies contemporary penal policy in general and sex offender statutes in particular. We divide our observations into three sections. In section I we describe recent policy proposals and set them in the contexts of heightened public and media concern about sex offenders and a decade of legislative changes and evolving practices. In acknowledgment of the central place that the concept of 'risk' has come to occupy in attempts to address the problem posed by sex offending, section II surveys recent trends in dispositions of sex offenders and research on their reoffending before focusing on the strengths and weaknesses of the risk assessment process. In section III we draw on the work of sociologist David Garland to discuss some of the cultural backdrop to current concerns about sex offenders and end by sketching out a broad agenda for the creation of a comprehensive and principled approach to the problem of sex offenders.

I. Sex offender legislation and its context

While public concerns about 'dangerous' offenders have a long pedigree, current approaches to sex offenders are illustrative of the intertwining of criminal justice discourses with popular understandings. These understandings involve a belief in the 'special' nature of sex offending and the corresponding need for 'special' measures in order to address it. In crime perpetration as in other areas of life, it is not a good thing to be singled out as 'special'. The 1990s saw the introduction of a welter of punitive and preventive legislation, aimed in theory at a range of so-called 'dangerous' offenders but in reality designed to address public fears about predatory paedophiles (see Kemshall and Maguire 2001).

The legislative background, 1991–2000

The development of a distinct set of policies aimed at dangerous offenders may be traced back to the 1980s and a trend towards a twin-track approach to sentencing that sought to reduce the use of custody for less serious offenders while increasing prison sentences for those deemed to present a risk of harm to the public. The current statutory framework for sentencing is grounded in the concept of 'just deserts', which requires sentencers to determine levels of punishment primarily in accordance with the seriousness of the offence or offences committed. The Criminal Justice Act 1991 made sex offenders (along with violent and drug offenders) an exception to this overall 'just deserts' approach, allowing for the imposition of longer than commensurate sentences and extended parole supervision in the name of 'public protection' (section 44). While in general a custodial sentence may only be imposed where the offence is deemed to be so serious that such a sentence is justified, violent and sexual offenders may be sentenced to custody if the court is persuaded that this is necessary to protect the public from serious harm.

Continuing the public protection theme, the Crime (Sentences) Act 1997 extended the sentencing powers available on the grounds of seriousness, incorporating rape, attempted rape and intercourse with a girl under 13 among the offences attracting a mandatory life sentence when committed a second time. The Crime and Disorder Act 1998 gave the courts the power to impose a discretionary life sentence for a second serious violent or sexual offence, and to add an extended period of post-release supervision in cases where the offender posed a continuing risk of harm to the public.

The segregation of sex offenders from general offenders – memorably described by Soothill and Francis (1998) as a form of 'criminal apartheid' – is most apparent in legislation relating to control measures within the community. The Sex Offenders Act 1997 (SOA) requires all offenders cautioned or convicted in respect of an offence outlined in Schedule 1 to the Act to notify the police of their address and any subsequent changes. Although popularly known and referred to as a 'register', the Act makes no provision for a separate register; relevant offenders are flagged on the Police National Computer and on local police databases.[1]

Two key criticisms of the SOA relate to its scope and application (Thomas 2000). Firstly, because the Act was not retrospective, many thousands of offenders cautioned or convicted prior to its implementation fell outside the registration arrangements. Secondly, although the SOA was clearly designed to track the movements of recidivist sex offenders, it offered no direction to the police as to how they should act on the information they were receiving. In particular, it was not clear how the police were to determine the nature of the harm individual offenders posed to the public or in what circumstances it might be acceptable to disclose information to other organisations or members of the public. Subsequent legislation has addressed these omissions, and in so doing, imposed significant controls on the behaviour of sex offenders in the community.

The Crime and Disorder Act 1998 introduced the Sex Offender Order (SOO), a civil order, breach of which constitutes a criminal offence and attracts a maximum penalty of five years' imprisonment. Applications for SOOs are the responsibility of senior police officers and may be made in relation to convicted sex offenders and others in order to protect the public from serious harm. The SOO closes the gap left by the SOA, since offenders made subject to an Order must register under the Act within the specified time period.

Critics of the SOA were concerned that registration as conceived in the legislation consisted of no more than the compilation of a list of names and addresses. Home Office guidance issued in 1997 emphasised the proactive nature of the registration process, focusing on three themes which have remained at the centre of public and political debate, namely risk assessment and management, community notification and shared working with other agencies (specifically the probation service). This led to the organisation of informal working arrangements between the police, the probation service and other local agencies to assess and manage the risk posed by sex offenders in their local areas. These arrangements generally consisted of some sort of working group or public protection panel (PPP) that met at intervals to exchange information and draw up risk plans for identified offenders (see Maguire *et al* 2001). The work of multi-agency protection panels was formalised in sections 67 and 68 of the Criminal Justice and Court Services Act 2000, which places a joint statutory duty on the police and probation services to establish arrangements for assessing and managing high-risk sexual and violent offenders.

The immediate backdrop

Public concerns about predatory paedophiles were galvanised in 2000 by the murder of eight-year-old Sarah Payne. More than any political strategy or legislative provision it is the response to this event that has dictated the style and tone of subsequent debates about sex offenders in the community. Following Sarah's murder, a tabloid newspaper, *The News of the World*, published the names and addresses of some 50 alleged 'paedophiles' as part of a crusade dedicated to the 'naming and shaming' of known or suspected sex offenders. This was followed, unsurprisingly, by a rash of vigilante attacks, together with a campaign – again orchestrated by the tabloid press – for public access to the Sex Offender Register.

In the US, sexual offender community notification laws were implemented following the abduction and murder of seven-year-old Megan Kanka by a sex offender with previous convictions. So-called 'Megan's Laws' mandate the compilation and release of information about convicted sex offenders (including those whose victims are adults). Notification may be 'active' (meaning that information will be supplied whether or not it is requested) or 'passive' (meaning that a specific request may be made on behalf of an individual or institution).

In spite of an emotive campaign supported by Sarah Payne's parents for a 'Sarah's Law', the UK government has consistently – and un-characteristically – resisted populist calls for widespread community notification on the American model. While revenge attacks on suspected paedophiles have taken place in the absence rather than the presence of a community notification statute, such activity has reinforced fears (shared by many police and probation professionals) that widespread notification would increase vigilantism and public disorder while decreasing compliance with registration (see Thomas 2000). In a reversal of the usual formula, the 'risk discourse' has been harnessed to a decision not to legislate, through the assertion that notification would put children at risk by 'driving sex offenders underground'.

In lieu of community notification, the government introduced some refinements to its existing registration arrangements and engaged in discussions about the introduction of (even) tougher sentencing. More imaginatively, it also announced a package of measures designed to strengthen existing legislative arrangements for public protection. These centred round the designation of the police and probation services as 'responsible authorities' with a duty to assess and manage the risks posed by serious sexual and violent offenders who have been released into the community. In addition to providing a statutory framework for the management of high-risk offenders, these measures (laid out in the Criminal Justice and Court Services Act 2000) incorporate a commitment to working with victims (including the disclosure of information where this is deemed necessary for the protection of the public). However, the limited capacity of registration and community risk management to guarantee public protection was vividly demonstrated in 2001 when a registered sex offender was convicted of Sarah Payne's murder.

Making Punishments Work: The Halliday Report

Those are the policy and legislative contexts in which policy proposals since 2000 were developed. We continue with a discussion of the Review of the Sentencing Structure undertaken by John Halliday, whose recommendations relating to 'dangerous' offenders received the unconditional acceptance of the government (Home Office 2002c). Halliday's recommendations are characterised by the development of an approach that distinguishes 'dangerous' sex offenders even from other 'dangerous' offenders and continues a tendency to introduce punitive sanctions whose contribution to public safety is, at best, unclear. In addition, the definition of offenders as 'dangerous' on the basis of a risk assessment implies a level of certainty that cannot be guaranteed by existing risk assessment procedures.

The Halliday Report addresses itself to clarifying the 'muddled legacy' of the just deserts approach to sentencing, although, as we have seen, this has long been abandoned as a guiding principle for the sentencing of sex offenders. In a section entitled 'Principled Sentencing' (Home Office 2001: iii, para. 0.6), Halliday argues for the introduction of a modified proportionality principle that would take more explicit account of previous convictions with the combined intention of reinforcing denunciation and increasing the opportunities for reform and rehabilitation. This principle is augmented in the case of 'dangerous' offenders whose sentences are to take into account not only previous convictions but potential future ones.

One of Halliday's main proposals is that prison sentences of more than 12 months be made more transparent and 'real' by requiring them to be served in full, half in prison and half in the community under supervision and conditions, any breach of which would render the offender liable to recall to prison. An exception to this would be made, however, for dangerous sexual and violent offenders. In addition to retaining the existing provision which allows for the extension of the post-sentence supervision of sex offenders for up to ten years (Courts (Sentencing) Act 2000), Halliday recommends the introduction of a new 'special' sentence for violent or sexual offenders deemed to present a risk of serious harm to the public. The new sentence is aimed at the (increasingly small) group of offenders who are not caught by existing provisions allowing for the imposition of a life-time penalty. Although it would not alter the length of the sentence, the new provision would change its effect by making release during the second half of the sentence dependent on a decision by the Parole Board. Used to its maximum extent, the proposed new sentence would double the length of time spent by an offender in custody.

Halliday's recommendation that discretionary release be reserved for 'dangerous' prisoners reflects his belief that such a system carries with it a number of disadvantages (time and resource intensity; the likelihood of over- and under-estimation of risk; interference with the original sentencing decision with implications for public confidence) that can presumably be set aside in the case of these offenders. It is certainly true that the public is unlikely to lack confidence in any measure that lengthens the time spent by sex offenders in custody. However, the arguments about risk inflation are less easily countered and depend upon the ability of those charged with the decision whether or not to recommend release accurately to assess the risk presented by individual offenders.

'Harm', Halliday suggests, could be defined as currently in section 161 of the Powers of Criminal Courts (Sentencing) Act 2000 in terms of death or serious physical or psychological injury. While he does not discuss risk assessment beyond a reference to 'the pre-sentence report and any other available information (e.g. a psychiatrist's or psychologist's report)' (p. 32, para. 27), the implication is that such risk assessments will give precedence to individual and clinical assessments over statistical tools. In recommending that discretionary release decisions be made by the Parole Board rather than being transferred to the courts, Halliday makes reference to the 'special importance of decisions in these cases, and the need for time and expertise in weighing up the risks and options, while keeping the needs of the public in mind'. These are responsibilities, he suggests, to which the Parole Board, with its existing role in release decisions in relation to life sentence prisoners, is 'well-suited' (p. 32, para. 4.28).

Recognising the 'potentially very onerous and punitive' nature of the proposed new sentence, Halliday emphasises the importance of setting a threshold that will ensure that it is not used inappropriately. The approach adopted in the Criminal Justice and Court Services Act 2000 is advocated as a starting point. For sex offenders only, Halliday suggests that eligibility might be tied in with the list of sex offences deemed to carry sufficient risk to justify registration as a sex offender. Noting that Part 1 of the Sex Offenders Act (as well as policies concerning sex offences in general) is currently under review, Halliday declines to make a firm recommendation in this respect. He does, however, admit of the possibility of divergent thresholds for sexual and violent offenders, on the grounds that '[s]ex offenders as a group may pose higher risks of reoffending, which could justify a lower threshold for them' (p. 33, para. 4.33). In line with other measures relating to sex offenders, Halliday makes no recommendations relating to sentence management or treatment during this extended term of imprisonment, although risk management in the community features in the White Paper.

Halliday ends his consideration of the provisions for 'dangerous' offenders by suggesting that more thought needs to be given to the options 'than has been possible in this review' (p. 33, para. 4.35). Unfortunately, the White Paper seems to have given them less thought rather than more.

Justice for All

The White Paper *Justice For All* commits itself to 'rebalanc[ing] the system in favour of victims, witnesses and communities'. Increased prison sentences are presented as the key to enhanced public protection. Among other proposals, *Justice for All* introduces the latest 'special' initiative in the form of the 'special sentence'. The new measures give discretion for release under the second half of the sentence to the Parole Board and retain the provision allowing for the extension of post-release supervision up to a maximum period of ten years (see Home Office 2001: 33; 2002a: 95).

The mantra of public protection is the closest *Justice for All* comes to justifying these harsh new measures. The protection of the public is seen as the 'paramount' purpose of sentencing (p. 87, para. 5.8). The White Paper declares its intention to 'ensure that dangerous violent and sexual offenders can be kept in custody for as long as they present a risk to the public' (p. 13, para. 0.0). This is a different message from that given in Halliday, in that those subject to the 'special' sentence would not receive a sentence that was longer but only one that might be served in its entirety in prison.

In its more detailed exposition of sentences for violent and sexual offenders, *Justice for All* explains that:

> We want to ensure that the public are adequately protected from those offenders whose offences do not currently attract a maximum

penalty of life imprisonment but who are nevertheless assessed as dangerous. We believe that such offenders should remain in custody until their risks are considered manageable in the community. For this reason we propose to develop an indeterminate sentence for sexual and violent offenders who have been assessed and considered dangerous. The offender would be required to serve a minimum term and would then remain in prison beyond this time, until the Parole Board was completely satisfied that the risk had sufficiently diminished for that person to be released and supervised in the community. The offender could remain on licence for the rest of their life.

(p. 95, para. 5.41)

What is not clear is what happens to individuals who do not elicit the complete satisfaction of the Parole Board by the end of the second half of their sentence. If they remain in prison, this constitutes a much more 'special' sentence than the one envisaged by Halliday which he states explicitly does not involve the imposition of a longer sentence in relation to those who meet the criteria. If they are released into the community, this suggests that their risk, though unchanged, is somehow now 'manageable' in the community in a way that it was not before.

The invocation of public protection as a justification for harsh treatment re-emerges in a section that discusses the proposed arrangements for the supervision of sexual and violent offenders in the community. This is a tricky moment for the White Paper, which is forced to concede that the 'vast majority' of the dangerous offenders that it pledged to keep in prison in an earlier section will in fact, eventually, be released. It must, in addition, introduce improvements to the existing public protection procedures without seeming to suggest that they were in need of improvement (and thereby leaving the public vulnerable to risk).

The refinements the sentencing White Paper proposes to the 'currently stringent procedures for risk assessment and supervision' relate to the mandated co-operation of a wider range of agencies (including local authority housing and social services) in multi-agency public protection panels (MAPPPs), as well as, for the first time, lay members (whose role will be a restricted supervisory one as members of the strategic boards that oversee MAPP panels). The White Paper alludes to the UK's 'strong civic tradition of public engagement in criminal justice'. Unfortunately, in relation to sex offenders in the community, the government treads a difficult (and narrow) line between encouraging people to be vigilant and seeming to endorse their becoming vigilantes (see Hughes 1998).

In spite of their rhetorical commitment to public protection there is a vacuum at the centre of the White Paper's proposals for the management of the risk posed by so-called 'dangerous' sex offenders in the community. Although the local arrangements are designed to include information-sharing, risk assessment and the development of jointly agreed risk management plans, it is difficult to get a sense of what risk management means beyond these administrative procedures. It is also unclear to what extent personal anxiety and the maintenance of agency credibility will affect the ability of multi-agency panels to avoid net-widening in their classification of sex offenders as 'high risks'.

The Criminal Justice Bill introduced in the House of Commons on 21 November 2000 draws on the reviews of the courts and the sentencing framework carried out by Auld (2001) and Halliday (Home Office 2001). Included among the purposes of sentencing (set down in statute for the first time) is 'public protection' alongside the more familiar themes of punishment, crime reduction and reparation. Clearly, the public protection rationale is uppermost in the new sentences for dangerous offenders – a life sentence and an indeterminate sentence of 'imprisonment for public protection' to be applied in cases where: 'The court is of the opinion that there is a significant risk to members of the public of serious harm occasioned by the commission by him of further specified offences' (Part 12, Ch. 5, s. 207).

The 'proper protection' of the public from sex offenders involves a very selective notion both of protection and of sex offenders. The government's willingness to base public policy on high-profile but extremely atypical cases of children murdered by strangers is indicated by the admission that '[o]ur overhaul of the system began with the special measures we put in place after the tragic murder of Sarah Payne' (*Justice for All*: 95, 5.39). Although the implicit message is that these measures would or could have saved Sarah and may save victims in the future, there is no justification made of the new procedures on these grounds for the very good reason that it is unclear that they add anything to the measures that already exist.

Setting the Boundaries: The Review of Sex Offences

The Halliday Report, though sensitive to civil liberties concerns and dangers of over-reaction, is concerned primarily with punitive responses to the most threatening sex offenders. Another pair of policy reviews, however, more narrowly focused on sex offenders and offences, bring broader concerns to bear and contemplate a wider range of policy responses. Following the Review of Sex Offenders (interrupted, significantly, by the murder of Sarah Payne in July 2000), the Home Secretary established a Review of Sex Offences that is distinguished by a recognition of the complexity of this form of offending and the very different emotions to which it gives rise. The proposals on sex offences that were developed from the Review are presented in the White Paper *Protecting the Public*.

Based on wide consultation and a commitment to an evidence-based approach, *Setting the Boundaries* generated 62 recommendations and a list of consultation points. Taking as its task 'the development of a set of proposals which are fair, just and fit for the twenty-first century' (p. ii), the Review of Sex Offences addresses itself to the problem of balancing public protection, what it calls 'appropriate punishment' and individual freedoms. Its laudable aim, taking into account the incorporation of the European Convention of Human Rights (ECHR) into domestic law, is the creation of a 'safe, just and tolerant society' (p. iii). Recognising the 'archaic' nature of some existing laws, the Review recommends the repeal of gender-specific offences such as soliciting by men and out-of-date ones such as those criminalising consensual sexual activity between adults. It also addresses the difficult issue of vulnerable adults, some of whom may be capable of consenting to sexual activity as well as in need of protection from exploitation.

The discussion of sexual offending in *Setting the Boundaries* differs from Halliday and *Justice for All* in content as well as style. Beginning with rape, which it describes as 'the most serious, the most feared, and the most debated' (p. 9) of all sex offences, *Setting the Boundaries* argues powerfully for its proposals, making reference to wide consultation, research evidence and cross-national policy development. It advocates an extension of the existing law to include oral penetration and proposes a new offence of 'sexual assault by penetration' to include all non-penile penetrative assaults. In considering the redefinition of rape, the Review rejects the concept of 'lesser rape' based on a pre-existing relationship between the victim and the offender. Although this does not solve the problem of low conviction rates (sometimes attributed to the un-willingness of juries to convict where victims knew or were intimate with their attackers), it does accord with research findings and the views of advocacy groups (see Harris and Grace 1999).

Reflecting what we know about the characteristics of child sexual abuse, *Setting the Boundaries* focuses on the protection of children not from strangers, but from family members, caretakers and other trusted adults. It proposes two new offences. The first, an offence of 'persistent sexual abuse of a child', recognises the long-term nature of much intrafamilial sex offending and is intended to reflect a continuing course of conduct as opposed to specific, isolated instances of abuse. The second seeks to replace existing incest prohibitions with an offence of 'familial sexual abuse' that applies to children under the age of 18, and to adoptive and step as well as natural parents. The risk posed to the young and vulnerable by known individuals in positions of care and authority is recognised in the existing offence of 'abuse of trust' and a new offence of 'breach of a relationship of trust'.

Another refreshing element in *Setting the Boundaries* is the consideration, under the rubric of 'effective punishment', of sex offender treatment programmes in prison and the community. With some sensible reservations about treatment effectiveness, the Review argues that suitability assessments should be an integral part of the sentence – which, as it notes, is likely to include extended periods of community supervision.

The preventative function of treatment is of particular relevance to young abusers, an often-overlooked but significant sex offender sub-group who may be responsible for some one-third of all sex crime (Grubin 1998). The Review's proposals relating to young perpetrators avoid the demonisation that too often accompanies media stories about juvenile sex offenders. It calls for a more minor offence of sexual activity between children, to reflect the fact that while some children actively abuse others, some older children engage in sexual experimentation that may or may not be coerced. The Review also suggests that there should be discussion of the issues of child registration and diversion from the criminal justice system.

Protecting the Public

The sex offences White Paper *Protecting the Public* perhaps not surprisingly contains a sprinkling of overheated rhetoric, tempered by the cooler style of *Setting the Boundaries*. The foreword combines a description of sex offending as a heinous crime that can 'tear apart the very fabric of our society' with an acknowledgment of the complexity and sensitivity of the issues raised by law reform in this area. The document makes it clear that it owes its existence to high-profile cases that have generated public concern about danger to children; however, it makes the point that legislators 'cannot hope to provide 100 per cent safeguards and protection' (p. 5). With a nod to the ECHR, *Protecting the Public* sets itself the task of presenting a set of laws that uphold the interests of justice and private individuals; it's not clear though that dangerous offenders are among those whose right to a fair trial and a private life (and, indeed, protection from degrading treatment – Article 5, ECHR) is to be respected.

For anyone seeking evidence of the tempering of punitive sanctions with more systematic if bureaucratic solutions, the emphasis given in the paper to multi-agency protection arrangements looks promising. The involvement of members of the public in the management process is limited here to the extension of a pilot scheme as part of which civilians are invited to sit on the strategic management boards that oversee the work of MAPPPs in local areas. The government still seems committed to keeping the public at arm's length from the actual business of decision-making and information exchange; however, the publication of annual reports by the 'responsible authorities' is intended to inform communities about sex offender management in their locality.

The proposal in *Setting the Boundaries* for an offence of persistent sexual abuse was not supported by the government, partly on the grounds that existing provisions allow judges to pass higher sentences in cases where abuse has taken place over long periods. It did, however, support the proposal for other offences relating to sexual activity within the family, including an offence of 'adult sexual activity with a child' to cover consensual activity between family members, and an offence of 'familial sexual abuse of a child' to apply to abusive and exploitative behaviour. However, the paper also contains several measures aimed at paedophile offenders, including changes to the arrangements for registration and a new 'risk of sexual harm order' to apply to adults acting in such a way as to present a risk of sexual harm to a child, whether or not the individual has previously been convicted of a sex offence. Another provision that applies to prospective rather than actual offending is the controversial new offence of 'meeting a child following sexual grooming' (Sexual Offences Bill 2003, clause 17). Although the grooming process has long been recognised as a facet of child sexual abuse (Salter 1988), the new offence is designed to address the much-publicised problem of sex offenders who use the Internet to befriend children and arrange meetings with them.

The policy documents described above reveal contradictory responses to the problem of sex offenders. On the one hand, public safety is directly associated with punitive and protective measures aimed at a small minority of dangerous offenders. On the other, sex offending is recognised as a complex and multi-faceted phenomenon that requires a range of strategies including treatment programmes and multi-agency management. In spite of the often reiterated observation that sex offenders – paedophiles in particular – are a universally reviled group for whom no punishment could be too great, a number of dissenting voices have been raised in relation to various aspects of recent legislation. Some critics focus their attention on the human rights implications of provisions that rely on assessments of future rather than actual offending (Power 1999). Others note the divergence between empirical data about the nature of the risks posed by sex offenders and the strategies devised by governments in the name of 'public protection' (Soothill, Francis and Ackerley 1998; Grubin 1998).

The key question is whether there is a criminal justice rationale for further sentencing provisions relating to dangerous sex offenders and, if not, how we should understand their introduction. We return to this question in section III, where we examine the cultural role that has been assigned to these offenders in contemporary society. First though, we review recent work on sex offender recidivism and risk management. The efficacy of indeterminate sentences for a small group of especially dangerous offenders depends on our ability accurately to distinguish these offenders from the majority of sex offenders who present lower levels of risk. The unpredictability of serious violent sex offending suggests that a more comprehensive strategy focused on multi-agency risk management presents a more plausible way forward for the protection of the public.

Risk management and recidivism

In this section, we look at what the statistics tell us about sex offences and sex offenders as well as how well we can predict serious sexual offending. We suggest that not all sexual offences should be construed as serious. Nor can all or even most sex offenders be categorised as 'dangerous'. We also suggest that the prediction of who will commit a serious and dangerous sexual offence is fraught with difficulty. In the following discussions of recidivism and risk assessment, it is important to note that there is no widely accepted definition of a serious sexual offence or of a dangerous sexual offender.

Trends in dispositions of sexual offences and offenders

Sex offences range widely from non-contact offences such as indecent and lewd behaviour (exhibitionism) through to rape with serious physical assault and sexual murder. The details of offences such as indecent assault vary widely from rubbing up against a victim in a crowd (frotteurism) to acts of violent attempted rape. Indecent exposure is a summary offence in the UK and little information regarding this offence is provided in the Home Office Annual statistics for England and Wales. The cautioning rate for sexual offences in 2000, reported by the Home Office, was 25 per cent, roughly similar to the rates for burglary, fraud and criminal damage. Interestingly, the cautioning rate for violent offences was substantially higher at 36 per cent. Clearly, police and other criminal justice system officials do not consider all sex offenders to be dangerous.

The use of custody for those convicted of a sexual offence in 2000 in England and Wales was noted as 62 per cent. This rate is not dissimilar to other jurisdictions such as Canada that reported a 57 per cent rate of custodial sentences for sex offenders in 1997. Both are substantially higher than the 41 per cent rate reported by Radzinowicz (1957) some four decades ago in England and Wales. Percentage use of custody varies widely depending on whether the offender was under or over 21 years of age and whether the offence was adjudicated in a magistrate's court or Crown Court. The use of custody for the under 21s is approximately half that for those over 21, at 11 per cent by magistrates' courts (against 24 per cent) and 43 per cent by Crown Courts (against 78 per cent). For the over 21s, the percentage use of custody was only outstripped by that used for offences of burglary and robbery.

Sentence length for sex offences, as with other offences, is influenced by the offender's plea. Sentence length is invariably increased by a not guilty plea (with the exception of motoring offences). Persons convicted of sex offences registered the lowest number of guilty pleas at 33 per cent, with violent crimes next lowest at 50 per cent. Sentence length (excluding those given a discretionary life sentence) was the second highest, for the categories of crime reported in the 2000 figures from the Home Office, at 34 months for a guilty plea (cf. 36 months for robbery) and 50 months for a not guilty plea (cf. 58 months for drug offences).

Thus, while some sex offences are punished more severely than other types of offence (including non-sexual crimes of violence), there are substantial numbers of sex offences (approximately one-third) that are not viewed by police or magistrates and judges as serious and earn either a caution or a non-custodial sentence. While it may be a relatively straightforward matter to judge each sexual offence as more or less dangerous and warranting a custodial penalty or not, it is not so simple to judge each sex offender as more or less dangerous and potentially warranting a lengthy period of custody followed by strict supervision. This brings us to the first important point we wish to make. It is difficult to categorise sex offenders and there are few readily available and accurate predictors of who will go on to commit a serious sexual offence.

Predicting reoffending

A recent study for the Scottish Office (Fisher and Mair 1998) concluded that none of the classification schemes available for sex offenders was immediately usable. This is hardly surprising in light of recent work by Soothill and his colleagues (2000) that suggests, while some sex offenders specialise in particular sexual crimes, others can be generalists in terms of ranging across a wide array of sexual offences. For example, those convicted of an indecent assault on a male were more likely (26.7 per cent) to be subsequently convicted of the same offence yet 12 per cent were later convicted of an indecent assault against a female and 9 per cent of gross indecency with a child. Similarly, Abel and Rouleau (1990) reported that 54 per cent of a sample of 153 offenders who admitted to non-incestuous paedophilic acts with male children reported three or more different deviant or offending sexual behaviours. This would suggest that there are many sex offenders who do not specialise and may commit a variety of sex offences ranging from the less serious to the highly dangerous. Indeed, other research by Abel *et al* (1987) found that good predictors of sexual offence recidivism included a lack of speciali-sation. He notes, for example, paedophilic assaults on both boys and girls, evidence of both contact and non-contact sexual offences, and assaults of both familial and non-familial victims.

Predicting which offenders pose unacceptable risks of committing serious sexual offences, or in the words of the Halliday Report, identifying those '… having a high risk of committing a further offence that would cause serious harm to the public' (section 4.25), from among those who have already committed a sexual offence is problematic for other reasons. The first problem pertains to the low base rate of sexual offence recidivism. Sexual offence recidivism rates for sex offenders, as measured by official statistics of criminal conviction, are remarkably lower than those for offending in general. Grubin (1998) notes that the 20-year sex offence reconviction rate for those convicted of sexual offences against children is approximately 20 per cent. In contrast, the Home Office (1999) reports the two-year recidivism rate for all offenders in 1994 as 54.9 per cent. The New Zealand Ministry of Justice (2002) reported that the sexual reconviction rate for all imprisoned sex offenders varies from 2.3 per cent at one year to 6.7 per cent at five-year follow-up. Sipe *et al* (1998) recorded a 10 per cent sexual reconviction rate over six years for a selected sample of non-violent adolescent paedophiles.

While there are clearly differences in reconviction rates depending on the type of offence both within all crimes and between particular types of sexual crime, the lower recidivism rates for sexual crimes remains true even with lengthy follow-up periods or by taking small samples of highly selected groups of sex offenders. The Soothill *et al* (2000) study demonstrates that over a 32-year period the overall sexual recidivism rate was 25.8 per cent. Broken down into categories of sexual offence, rates ranged from 19.3 per cent for those convicted of unlawful sexual intercourse with a girl under 16 to a rate of 41.2 per cent for indecent assault on a male.

Marshall and Barbaree (1990) argue that official reconviction rates for sexual crimes underestimate by a factor of almost three and are, therefore, unreliable measures of sexual crimes committed. Similarly, Falshaw, Friendship and Bates (2003) believe that actual sexual offending rates are over five times greater than the reconviction rate obtained from official public records. Abel and Rouleau (1990) found that a sample of 561 sex offenders, granted immunity from prosecution for revelations of their sexual offending activity, reported multiple paraphilic activities. These ranged from innocuous homosexual and transvestite activities through the relatively minor offences of public masturbation to more serious sexual assaults often with multiple victims, sometimes running into the hundreds. For example, the sample of 153 offenders who admitted to non-incestuous paedophilic acts with male children reported 43,100 acts with some 23,000 victims. Other studies have found similar, if not such spectacular, results. All accord with estimates of the 'dark figure' of sex offending as approximately nine out of ten offences not reported. It is difficult to see, though, how a more reliable estimate of actual offending behaviour can be obtained at the point at which someone is charged with a sexual crime. The offender has every reason to minimise or deny any previous offending behaviour and information from others (especially victims who have not reported crimes) may not be forthcoming. Much of the research cited is based on detailed interviews and often privileged knowledge of the offender that is rarely available in the routine processing of offenders.

The Soothill *et al* (2000) study also raises a second problem in predicting serious sexual offending from previous sexual offences. The highest group of sexual recidivists (i.e. indecent assault on a male) were almost as likely (38 per cent) to be reconvicted of theft or handling stolen goods. In the case of those convicted of unlawful sexual intercourse with a girl under 16, they were over three times more likely and those convicted of indecent assault on a female were twice as likely to be reconvicted of theft and handling stolen goods than they were to be reconvicted of any sexual offence.

A third problem is that the majority of sex offenders are, at least from an official record perspective, first-time sex offenders. A New Zealand Ministry of Justice (2002) report notes that 82 per cent of sex offenders released from prison had not previously been convicted for a sexual offence. Interestingly, Radzinowicz's (1957) seminal study of sex offenders also found that 83 per cent had been convicted for the first time. A US Department of Justice (1997) study reported that, of those sex offenders serving sentences for rape and sexual assault (including crimes against children), approximately 55 per cent had no previous convictions for either violence or serious sexual offences. Only 17 per cent had a prior conviction for a serious sexual assault. The report notes that '... rapists and sexual assaulters ... were less likely to have a prior conviction history or a history of violence than other incarcerated violent offenders'. More recently, Soothill et al (2002) provided data on a large sample of serious sexual offenders (against women over 16). These researchers showed that over a third of their sample of serious sexual offenders had no previous convictions of any kind. Thus there is limited opportunity for the criminal justice system to identify a substantial proportion of those who commit serious sexual offences.

A fourth problem is the sheer variety of crimes found in the backgrounds of those who go on to commit a serious sexual assault. A New Zealand Ministry of Justice study (2002) found that 10 per cent of those released from a prison sentence for aggravated burglary were convicted of a sex offence within five years. Soothill et al's (2002) data indicate that of those serious sexual offenders who do have previous convictions, only 7 per cent had previous convictions for sexual offences while some 50 per cent had a previous conviction for a crime of violence and 75 per cent had previous convictions for theft or handling stolen goods. Soothill et al (2002) propose that not only serious sexual assaults but also cruelty and neglect of children as well as conviction for kidnap are pertinent to the prediction of serious sexual crimes. Soothill and his colleagues note that their '... findings reinforce the heterogeneity of the criminal backgrounds of those convicted of serious sexual offences and the range of "offending pathways" that exist' (p. 26).

Thornton and Travers (1991), in an unpublished paper, attempt to demonstrate that there are many different patterns of reoffending and attempt to show that prior sexual convictions and violence are associated with sex offender recidivism. Phillpotts and Lancucki (1979) specifically showed that having one previous sexual offence conviction increases the recidivism rate to 10 per cent from 1.5 per cent with no priors, and to 22 per cent with two previous convictions. On the other hand, Barbaree and Marshall (1988) reported that the actual number of previous convictions for sexual offences does not predict reoffending.

Firestone *et al* (1998) showed that, in comparison with a sample of incest offenders, homicidal sex offenders were more likely to have been charged or convicted of more violent and non-violent offences, to have greater deviant sexual arousal (e.g. sexual sadism) and to have greater levels of psychopathology including substance abuse, mental illness and personality disorder. This introduces yet another problem in identifying those who are potentially dangerous but by reason of mental disorder are diverted into the mental health system prior to any charges being laid or useful information recorded by the criminal justice system. Most mental health services are reluctant to provide what they consider to be confidential medical information to assist the criminal justice system in the prediction of risk of dangerous sexual offending.

Thus we can conclude that previous convictions are associated with sex offender recidivism. However, there is little evidence that specific unusual crimes or the volume of other violent and sexual crimes in general help us to predict 'dangerous sexual offending' other than in combination with serious and dangerous offences already committed and for which a discretionary life sentence is already available. Should we then propose to widen the net even further to create a potential sex offender register (a register now approaching some 19,000 names) containing all offenders who have an increase in likelihood of going on to commit a sexual crime? Such a register would amount to no more than a list of all known offenders and be of little help in predicting which of them will go on to 'cause serious harm to the public'.

Risk assessment instruments

Much is made in the Halliday Report of establishing or assessing risk, since this is the crucial issue in deciding how to best manage sexual and violent offenders. However, Hanson and Bussiere (1998) demonstrated that 'unguided clinical assessment of sexual offenders' was of little value and barely surpassed chance predictions. Actuarial methods did provide more accurate predictions. It is instructive to look at a few of the more widely used and well researched statistical methods of risk prediction for sex offenders.

The Violence Risk Assessment Guide (VRAG), developed by Webster *et al* (1994), uses a weighted scoring system applied to 12 features of the offender. These range from simple – to obtain facts about the offender's previous offence history – to more complex judgments about the offender's level of school adjustment and a measure of psychopathy that requires an intensive interview and file review by a trained clinician. This instrument is reported as having a high level of reliability in predicting violent recidivism, including sexual offending with violence.

The Rapid Risk Assessment for Sexual Offence Recidivism (RRASOR) developed by Hanson (1997) is based on four relatively easy to obtain variables, namely prior sexual offences, age at risk, victim gender and relationship to victim. Its predictive reliability is half that of the VRAG. Hanson and Bussiere (1998) note that the original research demonstrated that the strongest predictors were measures of sexual deviancy and phallometric assessment of sexual interest in children. Neither of these variables are readily available in the routine processing of sex offenders by the criminal justice system.

Risk Matrix 2000, developed by David Thornton for the British Prison Service, is a weighted score of three items based on age and criminal history, modified by four further items. The latter include three features of the index sexual offence and whether the offender has had a stable live-in relationship lasting more than two years. This has the advantage of simplicity and ease of scoring, but produces a prediction of 20-year sexual reconviction rates. Recent research by Hood *et al* (2002) suggests that an earlier version of this instrument (Static 99) produced over 50 per cent false negatives over a follow-up period of four years.

Sexual Violence Risk – 20 is a combined clinical and actuarial instrument developed by Boer *et al* (1997) that looks at 20 factors relating to psychosocial adjustment, the offender's future plans and character-istics of his sex offending behaviour and related attitudes. Once again, the instrument requires a detailed knowledge of the offender and analysis by skilled and trained clinicians.

It would appear that the best risk prediction instruments require lots of information and detail. The simplest ones are likely to offer massively high rates of false positives and, potentially, an unacceptable number of false negatives. It is also worth pointing out that the easy to administer risk assessment instruments are predictive of repeat sexual offending in general and do not predict whether the offender will commit a minor or a 'dangerous' sexual offence. It would appear that we can only know that someone is exceedingly dangerous to the public on the basis of their already having committed a wide range of known serious violent offences and on the basis of detailed knowledge and clinical assessment of their lives.

Those charged with the task of risk assessment are operating in a climate of anxiety and high public expectations. It is important that these professionals are able to stand back from the political context and to base their decisions on detailed assessment and information from as wide a range of sources as possible. We do know a significant amount from the research evidence about sex offences and offenders that can inform policy. Much of what we know refutes commonly-held stereotypes. Two broad lessons stand out. First, the stereotype of sex offenders as violent, chronic and predatory obscures efforts at sensible informed policy-making. There are many types of offences and offenders, most of those prosecuted are first-time offenders (and therefore almost impossible to identify in advance) and recidivism rates for subsequent sex offences are low. Second, risk prediction in this area is fraught with difficulty and with dangers of over-prediction. Since the label of 'dangerousness' carries with it the forfeiture of rights, it is crucial to ensure that the complexities of assessment and prediction are not glossed over in the name of public protection. What we know about sex offenders and risk prediction suggests that public safety will be more effectively advanced through methodical, multi-agency efforts to taxonomise and manage risks than through the adoption of symbolic (and real) policies of ever-greater punitiveness.

III. Understanding and improving policy-making

We began this chapter by identifying contrasting approaches to the problem of sexual crime. Since much recent legislation does not appear to reflect empirical evidence about sex offenders, many commentators have regarded it as a cynical attempt to curry favour with a punitive public. However, we suggest that the government's response to sex offenders is neither so monolithic nor so uniformly malign as it sometimes appears. Rather than being driven exclusively by 'popular' (for which read 'uninformed') opinion, the policy documents described above reflect tensions that are associated with broader trends in responses to crime and punishment.

In a penetrating analysis of crime control, Garland (2001) suggests that the most significant features of contemporary or 'late modern' society are the prevalence of high crime rates and the acknowledgment that the state has a limited ability to control crime and thereby deliver security to its citizens. The key problem facing governments is the need simultaneously to withdraw and reassert their authority as the provider of crime control and public safety. Garland argues that the state's efforts to adapt to or avoid this problem have resulted in a set of contradictory policies that in themselves represent a schizophrenic adherence to polarised criminological frameworks. The first of these invokes a 'criminology of the self' that constructs offenders as ordinary, rational individuals and crime as a routine risk to be managed. This in turn generates pragmatic policies that recognise the need to transfer some of the responsibility for the prevention of crime to the community via organisations and individuals beyond the formal criminal justice system. The second framework involves a 'criminology of the other' that constructs offenders as dangerous others and their crimes as 'evil' and difficult both to predict and understand. This leads to the adoption of punitive strategies involving the exclusion and monitoring of demonised groups and individuals. While such strategies tend to increase support for state punishment, they are less concerned with effective crime control than with acting out popular fears.

Garland's analysis explains the contrasting approaches to sex offending that characterise contemporary legislation. For some time now, the approach implied by the 'criminology of the other' has dominated policy-making. Measures such as the registration process, the Sex Offender Order and the new offence of sexual grooming are clearly designed to counter public fears about predatory sex offenders who target children. However, such policies have the unintended consequence of increasing public anxiety by encouraging a perception that all sex offenders are roaming and unpredictable. The indeterminate sentencing that is proposed in the Criminal Justice Bill 2002 is the inevitable next step in a legislative framework based on a construction of sex offenders as ubiquitous and incorrigible. If this approach prevails, we may cheerfully anticipate the extension of exceptional penalties to a larger percentage of sex offenders, even perhaps to other groups of offenders who appear impervious to existing measures designed to curb their criminality.

It would be overdoing it to present the Review of Sex Offences or the development of multi-agency risk management as evidence of a wholesale conversion to Garland's 'criminology of the self'. However, it is clear that if the government want the public to accept that sex offenders present different levels of risk, they will need to counter the image of the predatory paedophile as a perpetual threat to children. Although this will not be an easy task, there are things that can be done to facilitate the development of a more comprehensive approach to sex offending, and we discuss some of these in brief by way of conclusion.

Firstly, steps should be taken to inform the public about successes as well as failures. The swift introduction of new and ever-more punitive measures suggests that existing measures have 'failed' in some important sense. However, as we show above, the perception that sex crime is an increasing problem is not borne out by empirical evidence.

Secondly, the belief that public protection may be achieved by the incapacitation of a small number of dangerous sex offenders should be replaced by an understanding of the different kinds of risks posed by different kinds of offenders to different kinds of victims. As research has shown, children are in greater danger from known adults than from strangers. This might also open up debate about other significant policy failures – for example, the unacceptably low rates at which rape convictions are secured.

Thirdly, the unreliability of risk prediction instruments suggests that we would be unwise to place too much confidence in their assessments of individual offenders. Rather, current moves towards the involvement of a range of professionals in ongoing, multi-agency management of identified offenders should be developed and supported. In the light of the implications for the rights of individuals labelled as 'dangerous' or 'high risk', however, it is crucial that clear thresholds be established for inclusion in these categories.

Fourthly, in addition to strategies based on the exclusion of sex offenders from society, some thought should be given to their rehabilitation and reintegration. Sex offender management should not be confined to assessment and surveillance, but include referral to treatment programmes where suitable. Some sex offenders – such as adolescent perpetrators – may be more effectively managed via more holistic and less punitive strategies.

Fifthly, while the government is right to resist calls for widespread community notification on the American model, the public could be given a less passive role in the debate about the management of sex offenders in the community. Better communication might meet the requirements of public reassurance in ways that even the most extended sentence cannot do. A range of communication strategies could be explored including work in schools, workshops involving agencies and communities and other local and national educational campaigns and initiatives.

Lastly, it is important to end the cyclical process by which popular fears give rise to populist public policies which reinforce popular fears. Responsible risk management requires government policy to shape as well as be shaped by public opinion. *Setting the Boundaries* shows that policy can be developed in ways that reflect the complexity of this form of offending and embody a concern with the rights of offenders as well as victims.

Note

1. A government-funded national database known as ViSOR (Violent and Sex Offender Register) is currently under development. The new database will include a range of information about dangerous and sexual offenders, allowing police and probation staff to carry out targeted searches.

References

Abel, G.G. and Rouleau, J.-L. (1990) 'The Nature and Extent of Sexual Assault', in Marshall, W.L., Laws, D.R. and Barbaree, H.E. (eds), *Handbook of Sexual Assault: Issues, Theories, and Treatment of the Offender*. New York: Plenum.

Abel, G.G., Becker, J.V., Cunningham-Rathner, J., Mittelman, M.S., Rouleau, J.-L. and Murphy, W.D. (1987) 'Self-Reported Sex Crimes of Non-incarcerated Paraphiliacs', *Journal of Interpersonal Violence*, 2, 3–25.

Auld, Sir Robin (2001) *Report of the Review of the Criminal Courts of England and Wales*. London: TSO.

Barbaree, H.E. and Marshall, W.L. (1988) 'Deviant Sexual Arousal, Demographic and Offence History Variables as Predictors of Reoffence Among Child Molesters and Incest Offenders', *Behavioral Sciences and the Law*, 6, 267–80.

Boer, D.P., Hart, S.D., Kropp, P.R. and Webster, C.D. (1997) *Manual for the Sexual Violence Risk – 20: Professional Guidelines for Assessing Risk of Sexual Violence*. Vancouver, BC: BC Institute against Family Violence.

Falshaw, L., Friendship, C. and Bates, A. (2003) *Sexual Offenders – Measuring Reconviction, Reoffending and Recidivism*, Research, Development and Statistics Directorate Findings No. 183. London: Home Office.

Firestone, P., Bradford, J.M., Greenberg, D.M. and Larose, M.R. (1998) 'Homicidal Sex Offenders: Psychological, Phallometric, and Diagnostic Features', *Journal of the American Academy of Psychiatry and Law*, 26(4), 537–52.

Fisher, D. and Mair, G. (1998) *A Review of Classification Schemes for Sex Offenders*. Edinburgh: Scottish Office Central Research Unit.

Garland, D. (2001) *The Culture of Control*. Oxford: Oxford University Press.

Grubin, D. (1998) *Sex Offending Against Children: Understanding the Risk*. Police Research Series Paper 99. London: Home Office Research, Development and Statistics Directorate.

Hanson, R.K. (1997) *The Development of a Brief Actuarial Risk Scale for Sexual Offence Recidivism* (User Report 1997–04). Ottawa: Department of the Solicitor General of Canada.

Hanson, R.K. and Bussiere, M.T. (1998) 'Predicting Relapse: A Meta-analysis of Sexual Offender Recidivism Studies', *Journal of Consulting and Clinical Psychology*, 66(2), 348–62.

Harris, J. and Grace, S. (1999) *A Question of Evidence? Investigating and Prosecuting Rape in the 1990s*, Home Office Research Study No. 196. London: Home Office.

Home Office (1999) *Digest 4: Information on the Criminal Justice System in England and Wales*. London: Home Office Research, Development and Statistics Directorate.

Home Office (2000) *Setting the Boundaries*. London: Home Office.

Home Office (2001) *Making Punishments Work*, Report of a Review of the Sentencing Framework for England and Wales (July 2001). London: Home Office.

Home Office (2002a) *Justice for All*, CM 5563. London: TSO.

Home Office (2002b) *Protecting the Public*, CM 5668. London: Home Office.

Home Office (2002c) *Justice for All: Responses to the Auld and Halliday Reports*. London: Home Office.

Home Office (2002d) *Criminal Statistics in England and Wales 2001*. London: Home Office.

Hood, R., Shute, S., Feilzer, M. and Wilcox, A. (2002) *Reconviction Rates of Serious Sex Offenders and Assessment of Risk*, Home Office Research Findings No. 164. London: Home Office Research, Development and Statistics Directorate.

Hough M. (1996) 'People Talking about Punishment', *Howard Journal*, 35(3).

Hughes, G. (1998) *Understanding Crime Prevention: Social Control, Risk and Late Modernity*. Milton Keynes: Open University Press.

Kemshall, H. and Maguire, M. (2001) 'Public Protection, Partnership and Risk Penality: the Multi-agency Risk Management of Sexual and Violent Offenders', *Punishment and Society*, 3(2), 237–64.

Maguire, M., Kemshall, H., Noaks, L. and Wincup, E. (2001) *Risk Management of Sexual and Violent Offenders: The Work of Public Protection Panels*, Police Research Series Paper 139. London: Home Office.

Marshall, W.L. and Barbaree, H.E. (1990) 'Outcome of Comprehensive Cognitive-Behavioral Treatment Programs', in Marshall, W.L., Laws, D.R. and Barbaree, H.E. (eds), *Handbook of Sexual Assault: Issues, Theories, and Treatment of the Offender*. New York: Plenum.

New Zealand Ministry of Justice (2002) 'Reconviction and Re-imprisonment Rates for Released Prisoners', <http://www.justice.govt.nz/pubs/reports/2002>.

Phillpotts, G.J.O. and Lancucki, L.B. (1979) *Previous Convictions, Sentence, and Reconviction*. London: TSO.

Plotnikoff, J. and Woolfson, R. (2000) *Where Are They Now? An Evaluation of Sex Offender Registration in England and Wales*, Police Research Series Paper 126. London: Home Office.

Power, H. (1999) 'Sex Offenders, Privacy and the Police', *Criminal Law Review*, 3–16.

Radzinowicz, L. (1957) *Sexual Offences: A Report of the Cambridge Department of Criminal Science*. London: Macmillan.

Salter, A.C. (1988) *Treating Child Sex Offenders and Victims: A Practical Guide*. Newbury Park, CA: Sage.

Sipe, R., Jensen, E.L. and Everett, R.S. (1998) 'Adolescent Sexual Offenders Grown Up: Recidivism in Young Adulthood', *Criminal Justice and Behavior*, 25(1), 109–24.

Soothill, K. and Francis, B. (1998) 'Poisoned Chalice or Just Deserts?' (The Sex Offenders Act 1997) *Journal of Forensic Psychiatry*, 9(2), 281–93.

Soothill, K., Francis, B. and Ackerley, E. (1998) 'Paedophilia and Paedophiles', *New Law Journal*, 12 June 882–83.

Soothill, K., Francis, B., Ackerley, E. and Fligelstone, R. (2002) *Murder and Serious Sexual Assault: What Criminal Histories Can Reveal About Future Serious*

Offending, Police Research Series Paper 144. London: Home Office Research, Development and Statistics Directorate.

Soothill, K., Francis, B., Sanderson, B. and Ackerley, E. (2000) 'Sex Offenders: Specialists, Generalists – or Both?', *British Journal of Criminology*, 40, 56–67.

Statistics Canada (1999) 'Juristat: Sex Offending 1997' (Paper 85-002-XIE), <http://www.statscan.ca/english/indepth>.

Thomas, T. (2000) *Sex Crime: Sex Offending and Society*. Cullompton: Willan.

Thornton, D. and Travers, R. (1991) 'Longitudinal Study of the Criminal Behaviour of Convicted Sex Offenders'. Unpublished.

US Department of Justice (1997) 'Sex Offences and Offenders: An Analysis of Data on Rape and Sexual Assault', <http://www.ojp.usdoj.gov/bjs>.

Webster, C.D., Harris, G.T., Rice, M.E., Cormier, C. and Quinsey, V.L. (1994) *The Violence Prediction Scheme: Assessing Dangerousness in High Risk Men*. Toronto: Centre of Criminology, University of Toronto.

Chapter 4

Nuisance offenders: scoping the public policy problems[1]

Rod Hansen, Larry Bill and Ken Pease

The *Concise Oxford English Dictionary* defines nuisance as 'anything injurious or obnoxious to the community or member of it for which legal remedy may be had'. It is worth dwelling on the verbal decoration of this corner of crime and disorder regulation since it has interesting nuances. Linked with 'offender', the word nuisance takes on a resonance of seriousness which, when standing alone, it lacks. Linked with nuisance, the word offender takes on overtones of triviality. The phrase is oxymoronic (or at least Janus-faced) as to implied seriousness. What are the advantages of terms like 'nuisance offender' or its fellow traveller, 'antisocial behaviour'? The political usefulness of the term is that it permits a different 'take' on behaviour according to the element which is emphasised. The offending is merely a 'nuisance', so the legal safe-guards and standards of proof attending ordinary crime may be dispensed with. However, the actions are offences, so to persist in that behaviour merits reversion to criminal standards of proof. The phrase thus smacks of useful duality for legislators.

The second element of the semantics involved is that to be a nuisance at all, one must be a nuisance *to* someone – anyone. Marriages and friendships founder when each in the relationship thinks the other is or is becoming a nuisance. This is redolent of the medieval need to find someone – anyone – to denounce a woman as a witch. The close circumscription of behaviour which constitutes an offence has been a feature of English law, as reflected in the limited circumstances in which inaction is counted a crime, and in the rarity of crimes which are defined in terms of perceptions by relevant authorities (e.g. blasphemy). This circumscription sits oddly with the lack of specificity in defining nuisance and its victims.

We are thus faced with a category of offender whose behaviour is simultaneously characterised as serious (offending) and trivial (nuisance), and which flexibly defines an audience by whom the behaviour in question is defined as problematic without reference to the specifics of that information.

The more frequent conclusion by lawyers addressing this issue is that the legislation spawned by notions of nuisance offending and antisocial behaviour is unfair in failing to provide safeguards which are enjoyed by defendants in criminal justice. Our conclusion is at odds with this. We see the situation as reflecting the failure of the criminal justice system to reflect cumulative harm, and an attempt to remedy it. Thus nuisance offender legislation and action is a stopgap response to a situation where cumulative harm and distress is so great that it cannot be ignored. It is a policing style directed at chronic offenders by alternative means, but once successful, is reported again in terms which give crime rather than antisocial behaviour primacy.

In many circumstances the criminal justice system takes a process involving cumulative harm and treats it as a one-off event. Illustrations of this tendency include the following:

- the use of sample charges in contexts where a relationship involves numerous offending events (such as incest);

- the practice of taking crimes into consideration which, while pragmatically defensible, converts a lifestyle into an isolated crime;

- Home Office counting rules, which designate a principal event under which a set of related events is categorised (for example a hook and cane burglary of car keys and subsequent theft of a vehicle from the drive being subsumed under a single offence of domestic burglary, or the use of separate cheques in different departments of the same store being treated as a single event);

- an offender convicted of a variety of offences flowing from a single criminal adventure, e.g. a man going equipped to steal with a screwdriver which he used to unlawfully take a car and before abandoning the vehicle he relieves it of its radio – where imprisonment is imposed, almost inevitably the terms will be concurrent rather than consecutive;

- the limited circumstances in which prior convictions, even against the same crime victim, are admissible;

- the de facto inclusion of individually trivial events (albeit in a protracted series) in 'interests of justice' discontinuances by the Crown Prosecution Service;

- all legislative attempts to punish persistence (preventive detention, corrective training and extended sentences) have fallen into disuse.

In short, systemic pressures convert series into one-off events for criminal justice purposes. Compounding this tendency is the relevant psychology of policing. Fully recording events which do not in themselves justify official processing likely to result in serious consequences for an offender is not intrinsically rewarding. Documenting actions which constitute the first brick of the hundred which will be needed to justify the imposition of an Anti-Social Behaviour Order is not enthralling. Older officers will recall being chewed up and spat out by sergeants who believe that bringing in people for individually trivial events reflects the officer's lack of perspective and competence. The obstacles are particularly great when a juvenile is concerned. The procedural safeguards in such a case mean that the officer is removed from the street perhaps for several hours. When the end result is, to quote the song lyrics, 'just another brick in the wall', the lack of police enthusiasm is scarcely surprising.

Criminal justice and the dripping tap

The cumulative impact of individually trivial events upon crime victims is well established, with Shaw (2002) making an analogy with the stages following bereavement, exacerbated because it constitutes an interrupted process where the stages can never be completed because another victimisation event precludes emotional closure. It could be argued that the political drive for action against 'nuisance offenders' from 1997 stemmed from an implicit recognition of the mismatch between accumulating distress for victims and non-accumulating impact upon offenders because of the way in which the criminal justice system segments the criminal career, with limiting retributive principles holding sway. The day before writing this, one of the writers was at the scene of a nightly disturbance involving lighting fires in parkland, stoning buses and abusing residents. Police action had provided temporary respite and one of the householders, seeing a police car, came out and gave effusive thanks, saying 'That was the first time this year I could sit in my conservatory without worrying what was going to happen'. In short, the contrast is stark between the dripping tap of trouble for those whose community is blighted by it and the systemic and psychological pressures which lead criminal justice to conflate chronic conditions into single events for the purpose of efficient processing. A serious one-off event like the Great Train Robbery for all its gravity does not eat at the fabric of a community like sequences of often minor criminal and nuisance events.

The poor fit between traditional criminal justice process and life as lived in the areas most affected is best illustrated by an example which gained national publicity. This will be followed by a more detailed consideration of an anonymised case, and thereafter by an analysis of the issues and suggestions about how they might best be addressed.

'Bath Boy'

In early 2002, the Bath and North East Somerset (Banes) policing district of the Avon and Somerset Constabulary experienced a chronic problem. The frustrations of the police and the community, which led to nationwide publicity, centred upon a small group of young people engaged in both crime and antisocial behaviour with apparent impunity. Intelligence received by the police about their activities, police operations mounted to counter these activities and community sanctions that were imposed almost weekly by the courts, all seemed to have no effect on their predation. By way of example, we may use one 15-year-old boy who earned the soubriquet 'Bath Boy' in the media coverage of the events reported here. He will here be referred to as BB for the sake of brevity. BB was disqualified from driving until 2003. His offences included at least two against people, 13 against property, two of public disorder, one firearms offence and one other. For these, he accumulated six convictions, one caution and one warning. Between 4 March and 26 April 2002 he was the subject of a number of police intelligence reports indicating:

- that he was seen by a police officer driving a vehicle stolen following a burglary the previous week;

- that he was seen by a detective driving a stolen vehicle, the vehicle having been stolen during a burglary just prior to the sighting;

- that while police were searching his home address as part of one investigation, the boy's mother was caught hiding money stolen during burglaries behind a radiator. She stated that it was her son's money for purchasing heroin.

The local police were expending a disproportionate amount of energy dealing with this and other individuals, putting them before the courts to find them released back into the community the following day. The courts seemed powerless to order secure remands for any but the most serious offences, which BB's were not deemed to be. What made BB hard to target was the fact that he slept overnight in a variety of friends' addresses and stayed on the move. This protracted police operations as the first task was to locate him. Each time he was released by the court the process had to start all over again. At times it was taking two weeks to gather sufficient evidence to put him before the court again. Officers from the same station found themselves investigating someone their colleagues on another shift had arrested for significant offences the day before. House burglaries, stolen vehicles, drive-offs from garage fore-courts and episodes of dangerous driving were commonplace and could be ascribed to BB and his friends. Conditions applied as part of his sentences, which included appointments with the Youth Offending Team, were being ignored or missed. In some desperation the police sought support from the local authority to apply for an anti-social behaviour order (ASBO, see discussion below) and a condition being considered as part of the application included a restriction on the individual entering certain parts of the city. There was reluctance on the part of the authority to take out such an order.

Eventually this boy was sentenced to secure accommodation for a significant period of time but a heavy price was paid by the community. What seemed to add insult to injury was that the individual knew that at some stage he would be imprisoned so took full advantage of his freedom to commit crime in the meantime. Our interpretation of the situation is that the BB saga was possible only because of the failure of the criminal courts to take account of the cumulative impact on a community of actions which, taken individually, may arguably not merit a custodial sentence. That failure is attributable in part to the conflation of events into a single one for criminal justice purposes, and in part to the limited relevance of tariff sentencing for juveniles. The ASBO is the provision which comes closest to recognising cumulative impact and experience with it will be discussed next.

Anti-Social Behaviour Orders

ASBOs were introduced by section 1 of the Crime and Disorder Act 1998 and first used in 1999. They are the flagship disposal for the chronic nuisance offender. Between April 1999 and March 2002, a total of 583 ASBOs were granted, of which 36 per cent were breached within nine months (see Armitage 2002). Just over half of those breached had custodial sentences imposed. This extremely meagre level of use (fewer than two ASBOs per Crime and Disorder Reduction Partnership) led to changes in the Police Reform Act 2002, specifically the following:

- Courts may decide that an ASBO will be valid throughout the country.
- It will be possible to apply for interim ASBOs.
- Registered social landlords and the British Transport Police will be able to apply for ASBOs.
- It will be possible for a court to impose an order at the same time as passing sentence for a criminal conviction.
- County courts will be empowered to impose orders under certain circumstances.

The novel feature of ASBOs is that, at their imposition, the balance of probabilities criterion of civil law applies, but their *breach* is a crime, punishable by a custodial sentence of up to five years. Local authorities and chief officers of police in consultation apply to a court for an Order against an individual or individuals who cause harassment, alarm or distress to 'others not in the same household as themselves'. An order prohibits its subject from doing anything specified in it.

The natural history of an ASBO case

Because Bath Boy gained national notoriety, he may be thought an atypical case. Thus one case, selected as typical in a city many miles from Bath, will be analysed in more depth. Details will be changed further to guarantee anonymity. Table 4.1 sets out the events which were logged in support of an ASBO application for a 15-year-old white boy. The table includes dates, the behaviour at issue and outcome.

What fails to emerge from this summary is the shrewd awareness of the system which informs the actions of the child concerned. One of the 'threatening behaviour' incidents was much more serious than the label implies, including the attempt to prevent one officer getting out of the patrol vehicle, accompanied by the welcoming remark 'F*** off out of

Table 4.1 Events documented in support of ASBO

Date	Behaviour	Outcome
7 July 1999	Public Order Act, s. 5	Caution
15 September 1999	Racially aggravated assault	1-year supervision order
9 January 2000	Theft from motor vehicle	Not proceeded with
17 March 2000	Burglary	40 hours community service
22 April 2000	Unauthorised taking of motor vehicle	Not proceeded with
25 April 2000	Interfering with motor vehicle	Fine
27 April 2000	Commercial burglary	No record in file
17 May 2000	Comment to police officer 'You want to watch out for your wife and babies. Take that uniform off, and I'll smash your f* face in'	Logged
22 May 2000	Comment to woman PC 'I'll set my dog onto you. You'll cry like a bitch.' To friends 'It'll f* rip her'	Logged
25 May 2000	Comment to PC 'Suck my dick. You know the score, don't you, Tom'	Logged
28 May 2000	Comment to woman PC 'Suck my cock, slag'	Logged
28 May 2000	Comment to PC 'Kiss my arse'	Logged
1 June 2000	Comment to PC 'I'm a sneak thief. I'm going to burgle your house'	Logged
11 June 2000	Driving without VEL, valid licence, insurance	No record in file
12 June 2000	Driving without VEL, valid licence, insurance	No record in file
15 June 2000	Comment to PC 'I'm going to come round your house and rob you while you're asleep.' Signs comments in PC's notebook 'The Mafia'	Logged
22 June 2000	Threatening behaviour	CPS advise discontinuance
23 June 2000	Unauthorised taking of motor vehicle	No record in file
30 June 2000	Threatening behaviour	Fine £15

our Close', an attempted head-butt and an ensuing scrum on the ground during which the child commented to bystanders 'I'll get five grand out of this'. Similarly depressing was the sequence of events linked to the UTMV of 23 June 2000. The child and other occupants of the car were headed for a major pop festival. After being stopped on a motorway en route (the ill-fitting rear number-plate belonged to a different make and model), the child's interview at the police station included the following: 'Look, the car is robbed. Let's get this interview over so we can be on our way to Glastonbury.'

What does emerge with clarity from Table 1 is the profound change in what was logged after the ASBO route came to be contemplated in April 2000. Insults and foul abuse had certainly not started to be hurled at that time. They simply became salient when an organisational choice had been made. The file also leaves the impression that the ASBO route also led to the less stringent policing of putative offences. For example, one of the post-April 2000 exchanges involved questioning about ownership of a car. Asked whether he owned it, the reply came 'Yeah, me and my mates own it,' but no follow-up determination of actual ownership is recorded. This may be unfair to the police officers concerned, since it is based on documentation, none of the writers having direct involvement in the case. Nonetheless, in so far as more detailed analyses of more cases confirm, the impression gained from experience with Bath Boy and scrutiny of the case described, we have a situation in which the nuisance offender/ASBO route demands a very different policing 'head'. What had hitherto been the hurly-burly of exchanges with very disaffected youth, seldom worth reporting still less officially processing, becomes the substance of an incremental process leading to consequences which can never be achieved by one-off criminal processes.

How are ASBOs reported?

To recapitulate, refocusing attention from crime to antisocial behaviour occurs because of a failure of criminal justice to punish persistence in crime in ways commensurate with community impact. It requires a profound change in policing style. But just as diplomacy may be war conducted by other means, is the focus on nuisance offenders really about crime? From reading the press reports and press releases which follow the making of an ASBO, we provisionally conclude that it is. Some illustrations are necessary for the point to be persuasive. A press release from the Borough of Fareham of 18 December 2002 reads as follows:

On Tuesday 17 December 2002 Terence Miller, aged 20, became subject to the Borough of Fareham's first Anti-Social Behaviour Order, at a hearing held at Portsmouth Magistrates' Court.

The order has been placed on Mr Miller taking immediate effect and lasts for a minimum of two years, following a period of extensive consultation involving: Fareham Police; Fareham Borough Council; Fareham Shopping Centre; The Probation Service; and Two Saints Limited (who manage the night shelter in Fareham).

The ASBO will prevent Terence Miller from entering Fareham Town Centre, including the shopping centre, and from consuming alcohol in public open spaces within the Borough of Fareham.

The decision to apply for the ASBO was as a result of a string of offences which were concentrated in and around Fareham Town Centre, the most serious of which included unprovoked assaults on three separate people in the shopping centre.

Thus, although the outcome is an ASBO, the focal concern was 'a string of assaults'. An assault could be dealt with by the criminal courts. The serial nature of the assaults gives the hint to the inadequacy of criminal justice in dealing with such repetition.

In Lancashire in March 2002, the newsletter *Nuisance News*[2] informs us that a man with a history of over 50 convictions 'with a consistent theme of disorder' received an ASBO.

A Manchester City Council press release of 14 October 2002 reads as follows:

Convicted thief Lee Vasey, aged 19, from Heybrook Road in Baguley has been placed on a five-year anti-social behaviour order at Manchester magistrates court after admitting stealing from local shops and cars and damaging property. The court heard that Vesey had convictions for stealing from cars and for shoplifting.

He had also been cautioned for causing damage when he threw eggs at house windows in Blackcarr Road, Baguley, and for stealing magazines from a newsagents in the same road.

The order prevents Vesey from using abusive or threatening behaviour or language in public, and grouping with more than three people, unless they are family members. He is also prevented from associating with named individuals.

A Salford City Council press release of January 2003 reads as follows:

Salford's Crime and Disorder Partnership has secured what is believed to be the first anti-social behaviour order using new powers introduced last month. The ASBO was granted when a 16-year-old youth was sentenced for various criminal offences, including Public Order Act offences, possessing an offensive weapon (an eight-inch kitchen knife) and damage.

And again:

A teenager from Gorton is the first girl in Manchester to be placed on an anti-social behaviour order. According to District Judge Alan Berg at Manchester magistrates' court, 14-year-old Lorraine Ogden, of (152) Abbey Hey Lane, had carried out a 'catalogue of misbehaviour'.

He placed her on an indefinite anti-social behaviour order and banned her from an area of Abbey Hey. Ogden, one of eight children, didn't contest the order. She appeared in court accompanied by her mother. Mr Berg was shown 20 separate incidents in which Ogden was accused of offences ranging from inciting someone to make threats to kill, vandalism, harassment, throwing missiles, racist behaviour and bullying between June 2001 and January this year. One resident's car was vandalised by Ogden and her associates in full view of the neighbour and Ogden herself stripped lead from the resident's windows.

It must be borne in mind that the quotations above come from press releases. They are not media reports, hence cannot be ascribed to editorial changes to information which the police service has provided, although it is our impression that press reports emphasise criminality even more than press releases themselves. The Home Office's own crime reduction website at the time of writing offered five ASBO case studies, in all of which the crime element seems to predominate. The final such case study merits quotation at length.

In one area, anti-social behaviour was largely due to a 13-year-old boy who effectively 'ruled' the area in which he lived: a deprived area of a large metropolitan city. Commonly a number of young people were involved, but the 13-year-old was the ringleader. The behaviour consisted of smashing windows, throwing missiles and seriously damaging a neighbouring school. The five neighbours in the houses adjacent to his, including a local councillor, had been intimidated out of their homes, and the houses subsequently vandalised to such an extent that they were uninhabitable. There were also incidents of arson against property, including setting fire to neighbours' back doors and posting firebombs through their letterboxes; racial harassment; intimidation; robbery; and the petrol bombing of a car.

The impression that ASBOs are really Plan B for targeting chronic offenders rather than addressing nuisance behaviour is strengthened by a question we have taken to asking those tasked with applying for ASBOs. The question is: 'Would you contemplate applying for an ASBO where no actual criminal behaviour was entailed?' No one has yet answered 'Yes' to this question.

As noted earlier, the number of ASBOs made has fallen below government expectations, but there is a diversity of experience across police force areas. Table 4.2 shows some of the forces which illustrate differences in two respects: the number of orders made and the proportion of applications for orders which have been refused.

Looking at all police force areas shows that the number of orders imposed does not bear a simple relationship to area population or urbanisation. Neither is it the case that refusals are a product of inexperience (in which case areas with few orders would have a higher proportion of refusals) or conversely a product of high rates of application (in which case areas with many orders would also have many refusals). Any explanation of different rates has to be speculative at this stage. Our speculation is predictable in the light of the argument advanced to this point – namely that different areas have different levels of willingness to give up on criminal justice remedies and adopt Plan B for offender incapacitation, namely the ASBO.

Table 4.2 ASBOs granted and refused between 1 April 1999 and 30 September 2002

Force area	Number imposed	Proportion of applications refused
Avon and Somerset	32	0
Hampshire	12	18
Greater Manchester	55	2
Merseyside	19	25
Suffolk	7	12
West Midlands	96	1

Offenders found committing offences enter a system that considers incremental punishment ranging from a reprimand, a final warning and an adult caution for 18 years old and above, then on to the normal punishments available to a court of law, with a lengthy tariff ladder and an informing spirit of limiting retribution whereby punishment must not exceed that appropriate for the event immediately precipitating the court appearance. Most areas, we believe, see the ASBO as a tool which might succeed in offering a community relief from chronic predation by crime as a result of the coincidence of crime and antisocial behaviour in the same individuals. Other local authorities seem to take a different approach. They view the inception of an ASBO as an instrument that fills a gap to deal with those who are on the fringes of committing crime. It is adherence to this philosophy, we speculate, which makes some local authorities reluctant, in the face of a contrary police view, to make ASBO applications on people found to be committing crime.

It is not in doubt that all the agencies operating under the greater criminal justice umbrella make it their daily business to improve the safety of their communities but do differing performance indicators lead to potential clashes between these agencies? The Youth Offending Team (YOT) has a Best Value Performance Indicator that rewards measures to keep young people out of prison.

Police and YOT consider different material. The YOT only considers convictions and will not consider pending cases or police intelligence. Take, for instance, the intelligence referred to above in the Bath City case. BB's mother tells the police that she hides his drug money stolen from recent burglaries. Is this something which merits action? What about witnesses too afraid to give statements about unlawful activity for fear of retribution? Would a face-to-face interview between YOT and these victims/witnesses be sufficient to influence the decision-making process about rehabilitation or incarceration?

The situation could arise whereby someone subject to an order working with YOT and tagged could commit offences and be charged for breach of the order yet still not have such detail considered until conviction. Tagging can be applied to an offender while they are on bail. Any significant breaches, provided they are notified to the police by the monitoring company, will be enforced immediately. Tagging, however, can also be used as part of a sentence where YOT and the probation service have responsibility for enforcing breaches. We suspect that they are considerably more lenient than the police approach! Even if breaches are accepted as reasonable by the responsible authority, the police should be notified of the breaches for intelligence purposes. They will at least know that a potential prolific offender is out and about when they weren't supposed to be. They may even fit the description of an offender seen at the scene of crime and not be inadvertently ruled out by the investigators on the supposition that it could not have been them as they were tagged and at home at the time.

In an earlier paragraph concerning 'Bath Boy' we referred to the apparently helpless situation the courts found themselves in when ordering secure remands for young offenders. Courts can now order secure remands for young people with a recent history of repeatedly committing imprisonable offences while on bail. However, the limited availability of these places makes it difficult for the courts and only the more serious offenders are likely to be considered for such places.

Although the legislation requires consultation, not agreement, between partner agencies in the making of ASBOs, clearly division makes a case less persuasive to a court. In the Home Office review of ASBO processing, it was partner relationships which underpinned most of the dissatisfactions, together with a court process which lasted for an average of 66 days. Before the introduction of interim ASBOs, this period left communities unprotected and witnesses often frightened (Campbell 2002).

Implications and conclusions

The central issue in dealing with chronic predators is how the individual elements of the predation accumulate their impact to diminish the quality of life in the hard-pressed communities in which they live, and how this accumulation is translated into commensurate sanctions. Criminal justice is better at establishing facts in respect of individual events. It uses a number of devices to ensure that the extent of retribution is limited, and that the accumulation of individual offences does not yield an oppressive total punishment. This is in tension with life as lived by those who suffer from crime and disorder. In short, the impact of a series of events, not individually serious, is not allowed to accumulate in sentencing, but does accumulate in victims' quality of life. This is the central mismatch, the point at which retributive justice and distributive justice contend. *Justice for All* in its own words sets out a long-term strategy to modernise the criminal justice system from end to end – from detection to rehabilitation of offenders – with a clear focus on fighting and reducing crime. Its aim in its foreword is 'to rebalance the system in favour of victims, witnesses and communities and to deliver justice for all, by building greater trust and credibility'. This central tension is played out in many ways, these having been illustrated in the body of this chapter. It is played out in consultations between partner agencies leading to the joint (or failing that, post-consultation) application for an Anti-Social Behaviour Order, and in the acceptance or rejection of such applications. It is played out in policing style, where the script is to make out a case against an individual in respect of an individual crime, with its consequences limited by retributive principles, or a series of events on the margins of criminality which must be accumulated in a totally different policing style. Much of the evidence presented to the court bespeaks criminality, and hence could have been processed through criminal courts. Once processed, the crime elements are emphasised in the presentation of the ASBO to the world, reinforcing the belief that protracted criminality was always the primary target.

The tension between single offences and cumulative victimisation also emerges at the stage of breach of orders. While the evidence for the order is cumulative, the evidence for breach reverts to a single event, with all the shortcomings of the original criminal process from which the ASBO affords an escape. We admit to amazement that, having worked so hard to get an ASBO, an offender escapes custody in almost half the cases where the order is breached, presumably because the focus of the court reverts to evidence on a single event which may of itself not be serious and the principle of limiting retribution resumes its place. The process is reminiscent of the injustices which flowed from court orders being imposed as an alternative to custody, with revocation being confused as to the reason for the original order being made (see, for example, Pease 1980). The central tension between retributive and distributive justice, between the cumulative impact of victimisation and the event-specific impact for the offender, will not be resolved any time soon, but this is where we are sure the problem lies. Until it is resolved, remedies like the ASBO will serve to provide some sort of temporary remedy, limited by the extent to which the partners in the application have the same perspective, the extent to which the police change their style to record and process events that they would hitherto have regarded as an unpleasant part of the officer's lot, and the extent to which the courts concur and reflect the seriousness of the accumulation of crime and nuisance which led to an order's imposition rather than the single event which led to its breach. That's a lot of qualifiers.

Note

1. We are grateful to Chief Superintendent Bill Hughes for comments on an earlier draft of this chapter.
2. *Nuisance News* is the quarterly newsletter of the Social Landlords Crime & Nuisance Group, c/o Whitefriars South, 42b New Union Street, Coventry CV1 2HN (Tel: 024 7683 2699).

References

Armitage, R. (2002) *Tackling Anti-Social Behaviour: What Really Works*. London: NACRO.

Campbell, S. (2002) *A Review of Anti-Social Behaviour Orders*. Home Office Research Study No. 236. London: Home Office.

Pease, K. (1985) 'Community Service Orders', in Tonry, M. and Morris, N. (eds), *Crime and Justice: A Review of Research*, Vol. 6. Chicago: University of Chicago Press.

Shaw, M. (2002) 'Time Heals All Wounds?', in Farrell, G. and Pease, K. (eds), *Repeat Victimization*. Monsey, NY: Criminal Justice Press.

Chapter 5

Procedural and evidential protections in the English courts

Nicola Padfield and Richard Crowley

> Our reforms are intended to secure that there is a fair balance between the defence and the prosecution and to ensure that the needs and rights of victims and witnesses are considered at every stage.
>
> (Home Office 2002a)

This quotation is typical of the White Paper *Justice for All* and sums up our concerns: the statement fails to explore in details the generalities it espouses. In this chapter we describe in some detail the changes the government proposes to make to the procedural and evidential protections available in the English criminal courts, questioning whether the changes will indeed secure a fair balance. We also seek to dig a little deeper, teasing all the while at a number of questions: How does one decide in theory what will provide a fair balance? How does one decide in practice whether these proposals provide a fair balance? Are the assumptions about what victims and witnesses 'need' justified? Are the proposals in reality reforms, or merely tinkering?

I. Measuring the criminal justice system in theory

The government's aim is clearly articulated in their latest business plan (Home Office 2002b). We may all agree with the aim:

> To reduce crime and the fear of crime and their social and economic costs; and to dispense justice fairly and efficiently and to promote confidence in the rule of law.

But the government may be failing to ask itself the preliminary question, whether the criminal justice system itself is actually capable of delivering all that the aim espouses. Put another way, the criminal justice system is a blunt instrument by which to seek to effect social change and regulation.

In order to make our own evaluation, we could adopt a number of traditional approaches. First, we could compare the current system with the theoretical 'models' which have been offered over the years. Packer's (1968) due process and crime control models still allow us to recognise the value choices that underlie the details of the criminal process. As long ago as 1981, McConville and Baldwin suggested that the English system conformed to the crime control model, pointing out, for example, the lack of due process safeguards in a system where 90 per cent of all defendants plead guilty, and trial by jury was so rarely used. Changes since then have tipped the balance yet further in the crime control direction. Perhaps this is the price that is being paid in order to address public fear of crime? The White Paper does not seek to address the problem that, despite the evidence, the public perception is that crime is rising.

More recently, those who have sought to evaluate the criminal justice system have sought not to measure it against 'models' but to identify fundamental values and principles. Thus Ashworth's human rights approach (1998: chapter 2) singles out, for example, the right of an innocent person not to be convicted and the right to consistent treatment within declared policies, the principle of equality before the law, the integrity principle. Ashworth's approach may not have all the answers (it still leaves us 'balancing' conflicting rights and principles[1]), but his insistence on a principled approach is particularly important at a time when government puts ever increasing emphasis on 'efficiency'.

Perhaps it is not surprising that the government avoids such evaluative tools. The packaging of the White Paper is typical of New Labour. Much of the trumpeted reforms and changes are already under way in one form or another. This is not a White Paper of a radical 'reform agenda' government, driven by a coherent principled constitutional restructuring of the criminal justice system. Rather this is a repackaging/relaunching of old ideas in new clothes designed to create the image of radical reform. We are also concerned that the absence of evaluation may reflect not only a desire to secure short-term political gains but something more worrying: a recognition that the service currently offered is deeply inadequate, something which no government could dare to point out. Recent government documents (Home Office 2001a, 2001b, 2002b) are depressingly lacking in reflection, not least this White Paper. An approach based on 'what works' and output-oriented management should also be based on sound principles.

II. The White Paper, *Justice for All*

The first startling message for us appears in Chapter 1, 'The need for reform'. The government boldly identifies the 'justice gap' as the gap between the number of crimes recorded by the police and the number where an offender is brought to justice. Is this the real 'justice gap'? The White Paper is short on detail. Not only are the statistical and definitional details missing, but there is no recognition that the statistics (for example, on recorded crime) mask as much as they reveal. The failure to define 'justice' when it is being set up as the model for the whole White Paper is deeply depressing. If 'justice' is the new political football, we should at least understand the rules of the game.

Chapter 2, 'A better deal for victims and witnesses', promises more measures for vulnerable and intimidated witnesses, e.g. pre-recorded video evidence and screens around the witness box.[2] However, this is before, as far as we know, any attempt to evaluate the changes already introduced by the Youth Justice and Criminal Evidence Act 1999. These special measures include screens (section 23), TV links (section 24), clearing the public gallery (section 25), removal of wigs and gowns (section 26), the use of intermediaries to help a witness communicate with legal representatives and the court (section 29) and aids to communication (section 30) (see Hoyano 2001). It took until July 2002 to introduce many of these measures,[3] and the most protective, complicated and expensive (Wurtzel 2002) (for example, evidence which is entirely on video and the use of intermediaries) have still not been brought into force. Everything is, and will remain, 'subject to availability': no matter that a court is satisfied that a special measures direction is appropriate, it cannot assume that it is available unless the Secretary of State has notified the court that the relevant arrangements may be made available in the area and that notice has not been withdrawn (section 18(2)). Further, the Secretary of State may, by order, amend the Act by modifying, adding or removing the special measures available to an eligible witness (section 18(5))! The reality of the service offered to defendants, victims and witnesses is not improved by simply passing yet more legislation. Indeed, the gap between the theoretical protections offered by statute and the reality to be seen in practice seems in danger of growing ever wider.

Even where these 'special measures' are available, they are rarely used. Even before July 2002, courts could be flexible. Thus in *R v D (Video Testimony)* [2002] EWCA Crim 990, [2002] 2 Cr App R 601, the accused was charged with the rape and indecent assault of a woman of 81, recently diagnosed as suffering from early Alzheimer's disease. There was a video interview available. The judge held that she was incompetent to be examined further and admitted the video under section 53(3) of the 1999 Act which had not then been brought into force. The Court of Appeal approved, saying that there was no absolute right that witnesses should be available for cross-examination and that the essential question was whether the trial process was fair. The judge had acted correctly in applying the test in the Act notwithstanding the fact that the Act was not in force at the relevant time. There was no breach of Article 6.3(d) of the ECHR.

Another power rarely used is the power to admit into evidence the statement of a witness who cannot be cross examined (section 23 of the Criminal Justice Act 1988), either because he is dead, unfit, abroad, cannot be found or does not give oral evidence through fear or because he is kept out of the way. The judicial discretion is largely unfettered. While such a flexible approach is to be welcomed, it leaves many tensions to be explored further. For example, the rules expect applications to be made in advance of the trial, and the judge's directions are binding. There are dangers in this, as the Court of Appeal recognised in *R v Littlechild* [2002] EWCA Crim 1784 (12 June 2002). Littlechild contended that the trial judge had been wrong to allow witness statements to be read to the court pursuant to an order made under section 23, because the order, made three months after the offence, could not have been made properly at that time. The appellant contended that the evidence on which the order had been based was dated no later than approximately six weeks after the offence. Therefore by the time the evidence was admitted at trial, it was impossible to determine whether the requirements of section 23, in terms of establishing the necessary fear of the witnesses, had been satisfied. His appeal was allowed. The appropriate time for the court to determine under section 23 that a witness was not going to attend to give evidence as a result of fear was at the date when the witness would be required to give evidence. There might be circumstances where a ruling under section 23 given immediately before a trial would be appropriate, but a ruling made months before was not appropriate. Furthermore, it was inappropriate to make a ruling under section 40 of the Criminal Procedure and Investigations Act 1996 for these purposes in advance of trial because it was impossible to assess what would happen in the intervening period. In the instant case, following the order, there had been no attempt to secure witnesses' attendance or to confirm that the evidence as to their fear was still correct at the time of the trial. Therefore the witness statements had been wrongly admitted. (A retrial was ordered.)

Until the law of evidence is codified in some way, there will be little guidance as to what should be done when a witness is not willing to come to court from fear but is, say, willing to be examined and cross examined by live link. Should the court grant an application to have his statement read? For a government which is busy promoting the merits of 'joined up justice', the law of evidence remains an unjoined-up state of affairs.

Other criticisms of the existing measures have been made. For example, the Bar Council's response to the White Paper[4] deplores the exclusion of defendants from the 'special measures' as illogical and unjustified. Instead of seizing the opportunity for wholesale reform, the White Paper simply promised a new strategy document, a new Victims' Code of Practice, a new Victims' Commissioner, a new National Victims' Advisory Panel and new Victim Liaison Officers on YOTs. Victims have votes, but the proliferation of pseudo-democratic palliatives is no substitute for a logical and coherent body of criminal procedure and evidence.

We would have expected to find in Chapter 3, 'Getting the process right at the start', a clear analysis of the changes that the government proposes. But apart from the old mantra of 'better case preparation and effective case management', there is little that is new.[5] We are told that O'Dowd's Task Force is looking into reducing the bureaucratic burden on the police and a review of PACE and its Codes of Practice. This Task Force, we are told, is asking big questions:

- Do all arrested people need to be taken to a police station for questioning?
- Are the detailed requirements of PACE necessary?
- Are the current time limits realistic and sufficiently flexible?
- Does the 'sheer detail' of PACE and the Codes create too much potential for the police to be tied in legal and procedural knots?

These questions certainly need answering, but not only by a police-led Task Force. The White Paper could have done it, but all it offers us is the suggestion that a judge or magistrate should be in control of pre-trial management once a charge is made 'putting incentives and measures in place which encourage and allow all parties to prepare cases adequately for an effective trial, on the day it is scheduled'. These ideas may sound politically attractive, but to us they are simply naive.[6] Criminal justice is not something to be neatly negotiated between the parties: the duty is on the prosecution to present a case. We are told that early discontinuance is to be welcomed, as is improved disclosure procedures. Here's the rub: in theory, disclosure may be a good way to improve the 'process' – prosecution disclosure as a safeguard against injustice, and defence disclosure as a safeguard against waste? But the practical reality is not so neat. Note that Chapter 4 says the previous chapter explained the proposed reforms for proper disclosure of evidence *by the defence*, which perhaps gives the game away: the rules are going to be changed to curtail supposed defence abuse of the rules of the game.

At the same time the police will be given powers to impose bail conditions before charge, subject to judicial safeguards, if they think it necessary to protect victims and witnesses and to prevent offending.[7] What is the likely effect of this to be in practice? The relationship between the CPS and the police remains unclear. We would suggest that the position of the CPS needs to be clarified: an independent CPS was introduced in 1985 as a protective mechanism, as a counter-balance to increased police powers. The involvement of the CPS in the charging process is to be welcomed, but they must maintain their independence. Is the proposed police power to grant bail conditions before charge simply a practical reflection of the pragmatism needed to make charging by the CPS effective, or an undermining of the independence of the CPS? Common sense tells us that this proposed power is a reaction to the changing face of the criminal justice system rather than a response to any perceived or actual failing of the Bail Act which has stood the test of the last quarter century reasonably well.

The Law Commission undertook an audit of the Bail Act 1976 at the time of the coming into force of the Human Rights Act 1998. Essentially the exercise was to ensure that the primary legislation governing the granting of bail in England and Wales was human rights compliant. This 'Euro proofing' was a reaction to concerns that suggested the existing state of English law may infringe the Article 5 rights of persons suspected of criminal offences. The proposal to permit police officers to grant conditional bail prior to a decision to charge (or refuse charge) seems to be a departure from the spirit of Article 5, which focuses essentially on the speedy disposal of allegations and the right of release from unlawful detention. Clearly granting the police the right to impose conditional bail disturbs the balance between the rights of the individual and the necessary and proportionate aims of the police.

Article 5 recognises the importance of the right to liberty. Article 5(3) provides that a person detained under 1(c) (suspected of offence) should be brought promptly before a judge or other officer authorised by law to exercise judicial power and should be entitled to release pending trial. Release may be conditioned by guarantees to appear for trial. The power to arrest to prevent further offences under Article 5(1)(c) is not matched by a proviso entitling anyone authorised by law to release on conditional bail in circumstances other than to secure attendance at court, i.e. surety. What basis of legitimate authority will underpin the new power to grant conditional bail, who will exercise it and in what circumstances?

If the condition sought to be imposed is a surety to guarantee the surrender of the suspect back to the police station or to surrender a passport to prevent escape from the jurisdiction then arguably the conditions could be within the spirit of the Article 5(3) provisions. However, in reality the greater use of conditional bail will be to prevent further offending. Article 5(3) does not envisage the use of conditional bail in such circumstances.

It is possible to mount a not entirely convincing argument that the proposal strengthens the rights of an individual against the state. Thus in a case of domestic violence, for a first-time offender the opportunity to be released on condition not to return to the matrimonial home will avoid the stigma of charge and due process, at least until the investigators and prosecutors have resolved if there is any reliable evidence and whether the case should proceed. The ability of the police to impose conditional bail attractively meets the state's obligation to protect victims of violence without the effective but unwieldy and costly entry into the justice system being implemented. One can see the practical merits if not the principles of justice which underpin this argument but whatever happened to 'equality of arms'?

Care will also need to be taken in the creation of administrative and procedural safeguards to avoid abuse of this new power. As now the promise of police bail without charge might be a powerful inducement available to a few unscrupulous police officers to elicit confessions, recruit informers and obtain intelligence – more so if it is masked by the imposition of conditions. Any change deliberately encouraging greater use of pre-charge bail needs scrutiny of its ethical operation. Will the government tell us how it intends to monitor these powers?

Equality of arms requires competent defence lawyers. Let us hope that the government means what it suggests at the end of the chapter: the need to review remuneration schemes to improve legal standards and incentives – while we welcome a strengthened public prosecution service, the necessary corollary is a properly funded legal defence service. But the new graduated fee system has given the Bar some unhealthy interest in the outcome of cases (Cook 2002). There can be wide differences in what is paid according to the outcome of a hearing, with the advocate who appears on the day the winner and not he or she who may have done the preparation.

Chapter 4 of the White Paper, 'Delivering justice – fairer more effective trials', is no more helpful in detailing the changes which the government has in mind. We welcome the government's commitment to a criminal evidence code and a criminal procedure code, as well as to a code of substantive criminal law. Codification of the criminal law on procedure must be seen as a significant strengthening of the rights of all individuals. Accessibility to justice is more than just availability of legal aid or affordable legal procedures. It is also about making available to the citizens of a country, in a clear and easily understood format, a body of information that comprises (some at least) of the laws of that society. The removal of the elasticity of the common law and the move to a statute-based corpus widely available through new technology must be a welcome step in a civilised society.

The issues around admissibility of evidence raise different problems. Of course relevant evidence should be admissible unless there are good reasons to the contrary. But again there is little acknowledgment of the difficulties. The Law Commission has produced a wealth of detailed reports in recent years which have not been adopted. We highlight the Law Commission's *Report on Evidence of Bad Character in Criminal Proceedings* (Law Commission 2001). It would be difficult to disagree with the Law Commission's call for a code setting out the circumstances in which previous misconduct of any victim, witness or defendant is admissible. The bad character of witnesses should be admissible if genuinely of relevance. As McEwan comments, 'the Law Commission has shown considerable courage and imagination in tackling the problem of protecting witnesses from illegitimate attacks on their character. These proposals, in combination with the new system to shield the defendant from evidence of his bad character, would produce an almost symmetrical scheme' (McEwan 2002).

It is time for legislation, and the Law Commission offered a Bill.[8] The White Paper offers no comment on the details of the Law Commission's report. But it does reject the routine introduction of all previous convictions as evidence in a case, preferring an approach

> that entrusts relevant information to those determining the case as far as possible. It should be for the judge to decide whether previous convictions are sufficiently relevant to the case, bearing in mind the prejudicial effect, to be heard by the jury and for the jury to decide what weight should be given to that information in all the circumstance of the case.
>
> (para. 4.56)

If the judge is to have a wide discretion to include details of previous convictions against such a loose test, is the only procedural protection against the misuse of such discretion to be an appeal against conviction on the grounds that the conviction is 'unsafe'? A more detailed framework is necessary.

The White Paper suggests that the hearsay rule will be relaxed but is depressingly short on detail. The Law Commission has explored the subject in great length. Their Consultation Paper published in 1995 was considered by many academics as 'unduly timid' (see Spencer 1996). Zuckerman argued that all that is required is to subject all evidence, especially hearsay evidence, to a test of quality at a pre-trial review (Zuckerman 1996; Ashworth and Pattenden 1986). The Commission's Report (1997) on *Evidence in Criminal Proceedings: Hearsay and Related Topics* was widely welcomed, with the hope that it would be enacted as soon as possible (Tapper 1997). Nothing has happened.[9]

The proposals to amend the double jeopardy rule to abrogate the rule that a defendant may not be tried for the same offence twice smacks of vague popularism and a further erosion of the rights of the individual. This topic too has been the subject of a Law Commission Report (2000), though this received little welcome from the academic community, condemned as more a reaction to the Macpherson Report (Macpherson 1999) than a real priority for the law reformer. The White Paper accepts the proposal that the Director of Public Prosecutions (DPP) should be able to give his 'personal consent' for an acquitted defendant to be reinvestigated where fresh evidence appears that strongly suggests that a previously acquitted defendant was in fact guilty. The Court of Appeal would have the power to quash an acquittal on the application of the DPP.

The background of the proposed legislative change reaches back to the outcome of the failed private prosecution of the 'Acourt gang' for the murder of Stephen Lawrence and the subsequent recommendations of Macpherson and the Law Commission. It is worthy of note that the Law Commission recommended altering the rule in respect of murder only. The government has gone one step further proposing the change to 'serious offences'.[10] A whole range of issues arise. What amount, quality and type of 'new and compelling evidence'[11] will be sufficient to justify the DPP's consent? Will it depend on whether the evidence was undiscovered/unknown at the time of the original enquiry/prosecution or could have/should have been discovered in a diligent police enquiry? Will it be restricted to new evidence that was incapable of being put before a court at the time of the original prosecution? Will it require the DPP to consider the entire evidence of the original trial to evaluate the significance, value and relevance of the new evidence in order to grant consent? If so, this has implications for the amount of money and time (and therefore the number of cases) per year that might be devoted to this activity.

Nowhere is it indicated whether the relaxation of the double jeopardy rule will open a floodgate of reinvestigated and relitigated cases. We simply do not know the nature and extent of the problem being created. The small number of murder acquittals considered by the Law Commission may have been a manageable caseload for the Director and the Court of Appeal but in the absence of any clear definition of the case population likely to be affected by these changes it is impossible to say whether the so-called safeguards will operate satisfactorily, or at all, or, if they do, whether they will be sitting upon such a small caseload as to have a negligible impact on the 'fair balance' sought by the government. Is this proposal anything other than a reaction to the Macpherson Report which, in reality, will have no or little impact on the daily practice of law in the criminal courts?

Even if this change will have little impact in practice, we are concerned that, as the Bar Council put it, verdicts should not be provisional. They argue that the inevitable media hounding that would follow any erosion of the rule is not acceptable, and that the reasons for retaining the rule without any qualification are compelling. Again we ask whether the proposals undermine a system based on recognised principles of justice and fairness.

The White Paper argues for the 'right court for the most effective trial', specifically consulting on the question whether the court should have the power to direct trial by judge alone for complex and lengthy trials and where a jury is at risk of bribery and intimidation.[12] Those of us who have grave concerns about the merits of trial by jury cannot but welcome this proposal. It is arguable that the option of trial by judge alone should be extended also to cases where the defence can satisfy the judge (or a judge so determines on his own motion) that a fair trial by jury cannot occur due to pre-trial publicity. But there is a real need for much more serious research into different modes of trial: otherwise we continue to 'believe' in different alternatives for no valid reason. Why is the government set against amending section 8 of the Contempt of Court Act 1981 so that we can have some serious understanding of how juries in fact function?

The government also asks whether the Crown Court should retain the discretion to try 16- and 17-year-olds when there are adult co-defendants. The presumption should surely be that youth should be tried before youth courts. Can there ever be justification for reversing this position? The Bar Council does so argue, suggesting that there are sound reasons why juveniles tried for the most serious crimes should be tried in the Crown Court, and why juveniles charged with adults should be tried together in the Crown Court. While this response may smack of naked self-interest, these proposals certainly demand greater discussion.

The White Paper goes on to argue for a 'clearer tariff of sentence discount' or advance indication of sentence. The proposals to permit an indication to be given of likely sentence in the event of a guilty plea must surely be an improved protection to the defendant. The present uncertainty around plea and sentence ultimately reflect to the detriment of both the 'system' (and thus the state) as well as the individual. While many a defendant might welcome a form of sentence canvas, it is not clear that the judge should be involved in such early negotiations. But currently the CPS has no role in sentencing: plea bargains with the prosecution are ostensibly not about sentence. Ultimately nobody but a fool enters negotiations without knowing the 'purchase price' or the cost of the deal. An uninformed or ill-informed negotiation may be no negotiation at all. Is there injustice in allowing a defendant to look down the line, and to be in a position to make an *informed* choice about his or her plea in the knowledge of the outcome that will follow his or her decision on plea? Many legal practitioners would welcome the development as an opportunity to be able to give better and more complete legal advice to defendants. The danger that a defendant will opt for a quick but convenient guilty plea in the knowledge that a non-custodial sentence will follow may alarm those who advocate the principled approach to justice. However, it is a regular occurrence in courts all over the country that an unrepresented defendant tries to enter a guilty plea by saying 'I did not do it but will plead to get it over with today'. The magistrates' courts have long had to be vigilant against convenience pleas of this sort and the new proposals will require equal vigilance in Crown and magistrates' courts. A 'system in which it is clear the guilty have nothing to gain by delaying their plea' assumes the guilty all know they are guilty. Any lawyer knows that the vagueness of current definitions, whether of key terms such as 'dishonestly' or the parameters of many a defence (such as provocation or self-defence) leaves this proposal deeply problematic. Both prosecution and defence advocates should be instructed in their professional conduct codes to offer a further safeguard against improper pressure on a defendant. Is this 'simply' a cost-cutting measure?

The need for procedural safeguards is no less important at the sentencing stage, and Chapter 5, 'Putting the sense back into sentencing', offers us little by way of encouragement. We wonder whether the CPS should be given a role in sentencing: presenting a clearly researched view to the court on an appropriate sentence. Pre-sentence reports now have an ambivalent status; an articulate proposal from the public prosecutor might help, for example, promote the use of well-planned community sentences and serve as the basis for the sentence plan. The defence would be able to challenge it. This proposal needs careful evaluation: on the one hand, it will undoubtedly increase the cost of pre trial preparation and presentation and a prosecution involvement in sentencing might be seen as likely to increase sentences. Conversely, as we have said, a properly funded legal defence service is a prerequisite of a strengthened CPS. But it might well result in more reasoned (and reasonable?) sentencing decisions. We are concerned at the absence of procedural safeguards at the sentencing stage (e.g. real legal debate is needed before the imposition of extended sentences or life sentences for sexual and violent offenders) and at the sentence enforcement stage (e.g. fines which increase if the offender fails to pay). The National Audit Office report on the collection of fines and other financial penalties in the criminal justice system (HC672, Session 2001–2, published 15 March 2002) suggests that only 63 per cent of the £385 million penalties imposed in 2000–1 have been collected. It concluded that the Lord Chancellor's Department and the Home Office 'should, when reviewing the sentencing options available to the courts, consider whether the range of sentencing options is wide enough to minimise the imposition of uncollectable fines'. One suggestion would be an increased use of money payment supervision orders.

Chapter 8, 'Focusing the CJS on fighting and reducing crime and delivering justice', returns to some of the government's favourite themes. We question whether the government has blurred the line between criminal behaviour and antisocial behaviour, putting too great a political emphasis on the merely antisocial. Perhaps rightly, the White Paper singles out domestic violence and tackling drugs, but we question the overemphasis on street crime and antisocial behaviour: what about serious fraud? organised crime? The Paper seeks public consultation on their proposals on domestic violence, yet it is not obvious to us why any new 'measures' are needed to tackle domestic violence. What is needed is less law and more action; perhaps the police need to divert resources towards better training of officers in this area, but more powers are not necessary. By, once again, seeking to blur the boundaries between civil and criminal law, the government is again in danger of missing the point: no one should be convicted of criminal offences without ap-propriate human rights safeguards. Much more could be done in the social, educational and economic spheres to reduce domestic violence:

more criminal law is not the answer. There are, of course, arguments for providing anonymity to all suspects, victims and witnesses in all criminal cases, but it is not obvious why victims of domestic violence should be singled out.

There are a number of other procedural matters which we could comment upon: we welcome measures to prevent 'middle-class opt-out of jury service' (though avoid commenting on whether trial by judge alone might not be preferable in many cases).

Finally, Chapter 9, 'Joining up the CJS', confirms the disappointment of the rest of the Paper. It fails to highlight the practical and theoretical risks of a joined-up criminal justice system (the need for systems of accountability, of individual rights to redress the balance against an ever more powerful centre).

III. Measuring these proposals in practice

Our task was to explore the weakening of procedural and evidential protections which the White Paper proposes. But the task is not easy without a much more detailed analysis. The government suggests that the proportion of offences for which offenders are brought to justice is 'unacceptably low' (4.5). But where is the careful analysis of existing statistics? The government 'believes we have got the proposals right'. Where is the careful evaluation of what these proposals may mean in theory and in practice? The devil is in the detail (and the funding): neither is articulated in this White Paper. One measure of whether the system is working well is whether there is evidence of bias. Much greater scrutiny of the statistics gathered under section 95 of the Criminal Justice Act 1991 is required (Matravers and Tonry, this volume).

Returning to our measures mentioned at the beginning of this paper, it is clear that the message of this White Paper is more 'crime control' than 'due process'. Human rights are barely mentioned, whether these are the rights of the suspect, or of the victim/witness who the White Paper seemingly champions. A principled approach is not in evidence, nor is the 'balance' clear. Perhaps there are some proposals in the White Paper which strengthen the procedural protections of the individual against state power. The proposal to remove the decision to charge from the police to the CPS might at first instance appear an unlikely candidate but it is undeniable that the move could represent a significant step up the ladder of sufficiency of evidence. An officer can arrest on reasonable suspicion that a suspect has committed an arrestable offence. The police can charge when satisfied they have sufficient evidence (whatever that means), but a prosecutor applying the test under the Code for Crown Prosecutors has to be satisfied there is a realistic prospect of conviction. This is somewhere between *R v Galbraith* [1981] 1 WLR 1039 *'prima facie* case' and a tribunal's 'beyond reasonable doubt'. Evidence from the charging pilots suggests that a higher proportion of guilty pleas are being entered earlier in the process at sites where the charging initiative is in force than before. One explanation may be the defence belief that the CPS has got the charge right, and that room for manoeuvre or plea negotiation is thus limited. The dramatic fall in the CPS rate of discontinuance supports the proposition (CPS Report 2001–2). Does creating a justice system whereby more defendants plead guilty earlier to a correct charge represent a weakening of procedural protections or indicate a strengthening of the protections at an earlier point in the process? These questions need to be explored further.

The government clearly believes it has public opinion on its side – but it may be wrong. The public may be ignorant of criminal justice details but the research suggests that when people are well informed they are less punitive than the government assumes (see Russell and Morgan 2001; Chapman *et al* 2002). They forget too that victims are also offenders and suspects. It may be true that too few criminals are caught or convicted, but the weakening of procedural protections is not the answer.

Reading this White Paper we are left profoundly disappointed. The government sees a need for redefining the rules without explaining in any serious form why the changes are necessary, or indeed what the changes will really be. The goalposts are shrouded in mist: are we looking at the whole process – pre-arrest to post-sentence rehabilitation – or simply pre-trial to post-sentence? How does the government believe the vague generalisations of the White Paper will help to reduce crime and the fear of crime and their social and economic costs, and to dispense justice fairly and efficiently and to promote confidence in the rule of law? There is no reason to hope for a halt in the government's frantic scratching at the criminal justice process. What we urge is a more principled approach. We suggest three pointers for the next stage of reform:

- a *simplification by way of codification* of the criminal law, procedural, evidential and substantive: less tinkering and real reform;
- significant *research* into the 'needs and rights' of victims and witnesses;
- better *resourcing* of criminal justice agencies, with fewer key agencies not more.

Notes

1. Sanders and Young therefore suggest the need for an 'overriding principle', which they identify as promoting freedom (see Sanders and Young (2000). This alternative framework, the enhancement of freedom, derives from their recognition that all applications of state power reduce freedom; that victims and offenders are not separate categories; that most applications of state power fail to enhance freedom; that victims, suspects and offenders must all respect the criminal justice system.
2. Part 8 of the Criminal Justice Bill, published in November 2002, will allow the court to hear evidence from any witness by live video link from outside the court building 'where it is in the interests of the efficient or effective administration of justice' to do so (see clause 43).
3. The Crown Court (Special Measures Directions and Directions Prohibiting Cross-Examination) Rules 2002 and the Magistrates' Courts (Special Measures Directions) Rules 2002 (see SI No. 2002/1687 and SI No. 2002/1688).
4. Approved by the Bar Council on 12 October 2002 and available on their website <http://www.barcouncil.org.uk/>.
5. As simplistic is the comment in the Notes on Clauses accompanying the Criminal Justice Bill 2002 that 'The Government believes that the management of cases through the courts will be improved by involving the CPS in charging decisions'.
6. O'Dowd appears to have reported in September and the Bill contains many worrying fundamental amendments to PACE, presumably based upon this report. Not only have these not been publicly discussed but the Bill will reduce yet further the requirement for public consultation in future. When it comes to future revisions of PACE Codes, in the words of the Notes on Clauses, 'the amendments provide for a more limited consultation process and a simple requirement to lay a new code or revised code before Parliament'.
7. In fact, the Bill goes so far as to authorise a police constable to release someone on bail even before he has been taken to the police station.
8. This Bill is the basis of the clauses in the new Criminal Justice Bill, but there are important differences, particularly on the question of leave. Evidence of bad character is defined, and the common law rules governing the admissibility of evidence of bad character in criminal proceedings will be abolished. The Law Commission admitted that it would be difficult to predict with confidence whether their approach would increase the number of occasions when fact-finders would be told about a defendant's previous convictions. But they start from a different perspective: first, all parties to the trial should feel free to present their case on the central facts in issue free from the fear that this will automatically result in previous misconduct being exposed. Secondly, in so far as the context permits, defendants and non-defendants should be equally protected from having

their previous misconduct revealed for no good reason. Whether the clauses in the new Bill satisfy these principles remains to be seen.

9. Now at last we have it: see clauses 98–120 of the new Bill.
10. Now defined in Schedule 4 of the Criminal Justice Bill.
11. See clause 65 of the Bill.
12. The consultation was clearly swift, with little time for digestion: Part 7 of the Criminal Justice Bill legislates for trials on indictment without a jury.

References

Ashworth, A. (1998) *The Criminal Process: An Evaluative Study*, 2nd edn. Oxford: Clarendon, chapter 2.

Ashworth, A. and Pattenden, R. (1986) 'Reliability, Hearsay Evidence and the English Criminal Trial', *Law Quarterly Review*, 102, 292–331.

Chapman, B. Mirrlees-Black, C. and Brawn, C. (2002) *Improving Public Attitudes to the Criminal Justice System: The Impact of Information*, Home Office Research Study 245. London: Home Office.

Cook, G. (2002) 'On Guaranteed Fees', *Archbold News*, 10, 4–5.

Crown Prosecution Service (2002) *Annual Report 2001–2*. London: TSO.

Dennis, I.H. (2000) 'Rethinking Double Jeopardy: Justice and Finality in Criminal Process', *Criminal Law Review*, 933–51.

Home Office (2001a) *Criminal Justice: The Way Forward*, CM 7074. London: TSO.

Home Office (2001b) *Making Punishments Work*. London: Home Office Communication Directorate.

Home Office (2002a) *Justice for All*, CM 5563. London: TSO.

Home Office (2002b) *Business Plan 2002–2003*. London: TSO.

Home Office (2002c) *Charging Suspects: Early Involvement by CPS: A Pilot Report*. London: Home Office.

House of Commons Report No. 672, Session 2001–2, published 15 March 2002.

Hoyano, L.C.H. (2001) 'Striking a Balance Between the Rights of Defendants and Vulnerable Witnesses', *Criminal Law Review*, 948–69.

Law Commission (1997) *Evidence in Criminal Proceedings: Hearsay and Related Topics*, No 245. London: TSO.

Law Commission (2000) *Double Jeopardy and Prosecution Appeals*. No. 267, CM 5048. London: TSO.

Law Commission (2001) *Evidence of Bad Character in Criminal Proceedings*, No. 273, CM 5257. London: TSO.

McConville, M. and Baldwin, J. (1981) *Courts, Prosecution and Conviction*. Oxford: Oxford University Press.

McEwan, J. (2002) 'Previous Misconduct at the Crossroads: Which "Way Ahead"?, *Criminal Law Review*, 180–91.

Macpherson, W. (1999) *The Stephen Lawrence Inquiry*. Cm 4262–1. London: TSO.

Packer, H. (1968) *The Limits of the Criminal Sanction*. Oxford: Oxford University Press.

Russell, N. and Morgan, R. (2001) *Sentencing of Domestic Burglary*. London: Sentencing Advisory Panel.

Sanders, A. and Young, R. (2000) *Criminal Justice*, 2nd edn. London: Butterworths.

Spencer, J.R. (1996) 'Hearsay Reform: A Bridge not Far Enough?', *Criminal Law Review*, 29–33.

Tapper, C. (1997) 'Hearsay in Criminal Cases: An Overview of Law Commission Report No. 245', *Criminal Law Review*, 771–84.

Wurtzel, D. (2002) 'Special Measures Directions', *Archbold News*, 8, 5–8.

Zuckerman, A.A. (1996) 'Law Commission Consultation Paper No. 138 on Hearsay: The Future of Hearsay', *Criminal Law Review*, 4–15.

Chapter 6

Sentencing guidelines

Neil Hutton

Introduction

In 2001, the Halliday Report outlined an ambitious review of the sentencing framework for England and Wales (henceforth, with apologies to the Welsh, England). The report presented the most radical and far reaching proposals for the reform of sentencing for many years. The government's response to Halliday's proposals are contained in Chapter 5 of the White Paper, *Justice for All* (Home Office 2002) entitled 'Putting the sense back into sentencing'. The final part of the government's proposals for sentencing reform can be found in Part 12 of the Criminal Justice Bill published in November 2002, which at the time of writing is before Parliament (<http://www.publications.parliament.uk/pa/cm200203/cmbills/008/2003008.pdf>).

This essay does not provide a detailed analysis of the differences and similarities between the Halliday Report, the White Paper and the Bill although this would provide the material for an interesting essay. The documents were produced by very different mechanisms. They were intended to achieve different ends and to reach different audiences. The Halliday Report was produced as an independent review (albeit, as Tonry in this volume points out, with a politically established remit) by a senior civil servant and was intended for a well informed audience primarily of stakeholders. The White Paper was written as the government's response to Halliday and was concerned with making statements about government policy on sentencing for consumption by wider public audiences, including the media. The Criminal Justice Bill is the proposed legislation which will bring some of the White Paper's proposals into practical effect in the courts. It will be scrutinised by practitioners and academics but it is unlikely to be read by a non-specialist audience.

Despite these differences, the three documents deal with the same major issues. For the first time, there is a legislative statement which specifies the aims and purposes of sentencing. There is a new framework of sanctions through which these aims are to be achieved. Greater consistency in sentencing is to be secured by the introduction of a new judicial institution, the Sentencing Guidelines Council, which has the task of formulating and publishing sentencing guidelines. All of this is intended to increase public confidence in the criminal justice system.

The aim of this essay is to examine the extent to which the government's proposals will make a significant difference to sentencing. Section I of this essay sketches the main issues and public policy problems raised by sentencing and outlines the main elements of what this author takes to be a rational approach to sentencing. Section II summarises the proposals for sentencing reform in the White Paper and the Criminal Justice Bill. Section III presents an assessment of the extent to which the government's proposals can be described as making sentencing more rational.

The essay concludes that the proposed legislation is unlikely to make sentencing much more rational. Sentencers will continue to exercise considerable discretion, although there will be a considerable effort involved in learning the procedural niceties of the new legislation. It will be difficult to know whether the legislation will bring any improvements in consistency because there are no procedures for monitoring the extent to which judges adhere to any new guidelines formulated by the Sentencing Guidelines Council. Finally it seems highly unlikely that the proposals will increase public confidence in sentencing, even if we had reliable means for measuring this.

I. Issues and policy problems

The issues addressed by the White Paper are fundamental to the criminal justice process and they are addressed quite explicitly. They can be expressed as a list of questions. What are the aims of sentencing? How can these aims be achieved? How can excessive variation in sentencing be reduced? How can public confidence in sentencing be improved?

What are sentencing and punishment supposed to achieve?
What is the purpose of sentencing?

These are, of course, the questions which have occupied philosophers of punishment for hundreds of years and which remain unresolved (irresolvable?) and contentious. Liberal societies have traditionally justified punishment on the grounds of retribution, deterrence, re-habilitation, protection of the public and reparation. The 1991 Criminal Justice Act established proportionality as the primary rationale for sentencing in England. This attempted to implement the retributive or desert-based approach to punishment which argues that justice in punishment is best secured by ensuring that punishment is com-mensurate with the seriousness of the offence. However, the 1993 Criminal Justice Act and the judicial interpretation of proportionality in Cunningham (1993) 14 Crim. App R(s) 444 effectively destroyed the primacy of proportionality. Proportionality remains an important principle in the government's current proposals, but its significance is diminished by a return to the utilitarian aims of crime reduction and public protection and, perhaps more seriously, by the aggravating effect on sentence of previous convictions.

The key issue concerns what the proposals have to say about the relationship between these aims/justifications. Frase (2001) has argued that comparative study of Western jurisdictions suggests that there is a broad consensus on some basic principles of an approach to punish-ment. Most jurisdictions accept that the overall aim of criminal justice is to reduce/control/prevent crime. There is broad agreement on the relative seriousness of different sorts of offending as well as on the most important factors which mitigate and aggravate a typical case. Most jurisdictions place a high value on proportionality and on parsimony. The Criminal Justice Bill, for example, states that the seriousness of an offence comprises the harm caused and the culpability of the offender (clause 127) although, as noted above, recent and relevant previous convictions are to be seen as aggravating. The Bill also states that custodial and community sentences should only be used where the offence is sufficiently serious and that any custodial sentence should always be the lowest necessary to mark the seriousness of the offence.

However, beyond this consensus lie a series of tensions which require some sort of principled reconciliation if there is to be anything resembling a rational approach to sentencing. The principle of desert requires that punishment is proportionate to the seriousness of the offence. The desert-based sentence may be quite different from a sentence chosen in order to protect the public, or to offer the best chance of reducing the offending behaviour of the offender or to provide what the judge considers an effective deterrent to other potential offenders. How should we reconcile desert with crime control-based aims? How should we reconcile factors concerned with the seriousness of the offence with factors concerned with the culpability of the offender? How can we balance the desire to take into account all the relevant factors in an individual case with the desire to ensure a broad degree of uniformity in sentencing? These are questions which can only be answered if there is a rationale for sentencing which describes in a principled way how these difficult practical questions should be addressed.

The implementation of the rationale

Once a broad rationale for sentencing has been agreed and accepted by the relevant 'stakeholders', the next problem is to find a means of putting this into practice. Traditionally, sentencers in England have enjoyed a very wide discretion. Ashworth (2001) has argued that sentencing is 'lawless' in the sense that there are virtually no rules which specify how the nature and amount of sentence should be selected for a given case. Under these circumstances, it would be very unlikely that judges would voluntarily change their practice to fit the new rationale. Even if there was judicial goodwill, a rationale alone would not be able to guarantee consistent practice. Judges would need some sort of guidance which defined and elaborated the rationale and which indicated how types and amounts of penalty should be related to different types of case.

The most common means of achieving this has been by the use of sentencing guidelines. There are two sorts of guidelines currently operating in England. The Magistrates' Association have for some time issued voluntary sentencing guidelines for magistrates' courts. The Court of Appeal has issued, latterly with the advice of the Sentencing Advisory Panel, a series of guideline judgments. The magistrates' guidelines are comprehensive but they are neither detailed nor prescriptive and, as the White Paper recognises, do not prevent apparently considerable variation in sentencing across different court areas. The Court of Appeal guidelines are not comprehensive and have so far been issued only for a small number of more serious offences. There has been no evaluation of their impact on consistency in sentencing. In the United States, many jurisdictions have developed various forms of sentencing grid which provide a comprehensive and detailed means of relating case seriousness to level of sanction (Reitz 2001).

There are many issues which have to be considered in designing sentencing guidelines to implement a broad rationale. It is perhaps worth drawing attention to two of the most important (see Tonry (2001) for a discussion of commissions and guidelines).

- Systematic and comprehensive guidelines of the US variety are inimical to the English tradition of individualised sentencing and are likely to be deeply unpopular with judges. In the USA, most guideline systems operate with the support of the judiciary but in some highly publicised cases, most notably the Federal Sentencing guidelines produced by the US Sentencing Commission, many judges have been critical of the guidelines and have found 'creative' ways to circumvent them where they have produced a substantively unjust result (Stith and Cabranes 1998). There is a need to 'sell' the idea of guidelines to judges in England.

- The design and implementation of guidelines is a complex task which requires a wide range of skills and which needs to be adequately resourced. Most US jurisdictions have used an independent agency, usually designated as a Sentencing Commission, for this purpose. Some of these commissions have failed to produce guidelines because they felt the task was too difficult (Tonry 2001). What sort of body would be best able to produce sentencing guidelines in England which would both command the confidence of stakeholders and have the necessary skills and expertise? Thus far in England, sentencing guidelines have been produced by the Court of Appeal and the Sentencing Advisory Panel. The proposals for a Sentencing Guidelines Council are unlikely to make a significant change to the English way of developing guidelines.

What can be done to reduce the excessive variation in sentencing?

This issue is explicitly addressed in the White Paper referring to data which purports to demonstrate excessive variation in levels of sentencing in different magistrates' courts areas. As the data does not take into account differences in the seriousness of caseloads between each area, one should perhaps not place too much faith in their accuracy. Having said that, evidence from research in other jurisdictions can be extrapolated to England to suggest that the extent of discretion enjoyed by judges is very likely to produce considerable variation in sentencing, not just in magistrates' courts. A system of sentencing guidelines as outlined above would be an obvious way of trying to reduce this level of variation. Carefully drafted guidelines implemented across the country and monitored to measure judicial adherence would provide an effective means of improving consistency in sentencing practice across the country.

What can be done to reduce the prison population?

Many Western jurisdictions are confronting similar concerns about rising carceral populations (Tonry 2001). Prison populations are rising even in European jurisdictions such as the Netherlands which had managed to sustain relatively low rates of incarceration in the later half of the last century and even where crime rates are falling or stable. The high costs of imprisonment are beginning to require politicians to consider whether prison offers good value for money. The effectiveness of prison as a means of reducing offending behaviour has been challenged at the same time as the 'what works' agenda has demonstrated that non-custodial sanctions can be at least as effective (Home Office 2001: 1.49; Vennard, Sugg and Hedderman 1997).

Halliday was concerned with the effect of sentencing policy on the prison population and the White Paper reflects these concerns and reiterates the 'bifurcation' approach which reserves the use of custody for serious, dangerous and seriously persistent offenders while suggesting that other sorts of offenders do not need to be incarcerated. Not surprisingly, the Criminal Justice Bill contains no explicit clauses concerned with reducing the prison population. However, the Bill does reflect a concern for the principle of parsimony in sentencing. Courts are instructed not to use either community orders or custodial orders unless they are justified by the seriousness of the offence (including the criminal record of the offender) and where custody is chosen courts are instructed to use 'the shortest term' that would be commensurate with the seriousness of the case (136.2). This is perhaps a more explicit gesture towards reducing prison use than is normally found in legislation; however, there is no attempt in the Bill to describe any more detailed criteria for the custody threshold. This is left to judicial discretion as before.

How, if at all, can sentencing be regulated to ensure that only certain kinds of offender or certain kinds of cases receive custodial sanctions? How can the custody threshold be represented? Although English sentencers have for some time had available to them a wide range of community sanctions, and although the use of these sanctions has increased over the last ten years, the prison population has also risen steadily. If the government wishes to reduce or even limit the rise of the prison population, there needs to be careful thought given to how sentencers might be persuaded to reduce their resort to custodial sentences.

Increasing public confidence in sentencing and criminal justice

The term populist punitiveness, coined by Tony Bottoms at a conference in 1993 (Bottoms 1995), refers to the ways in which politicians propose harsher punishments for one or more of three main reasons: because they think this will reduce crime, strengthen a moral consensus against particular offending and enhance their popularity among the electorate. This might be described as a populist narrative of crime and punishment. Crime is a (rising) problem to which harsher punishment is the solution. In an important sense, the belief in the story is more important than its veracity. There is considerable research evidence which shows that punishment has very little impact on crime rates, whether by deterrence or incapacitation (Home Office 2001: 1.62–1.68 and Appendix 6). There is also growing evidence that the public are not as punitive as some of the general abstract survey evidence suggests (Roberts and Hough 2002). Despite these 'facts', the populist narrative which says that harsher punishment is necessary to control crime persists and is used by politicians to their own advantage.

David Garland (2002) has argued that this 'criminology of the other' is only part of the picture. Alongside the pursuit of punitive policies which cast the offender as a dangerous outsider who needs to be severely punished, governments have also pursued more rational crime management policies which treat offenders as rational actors who need to be managed by agencies working in partnership with communities. This is a version of 'bifurcation' which Bottoms (1995) calls a 'classic modern strategy' of being tough on offenders perceived as dangerous and more moderate on offenders perceived as posing a less serious risk. There is clear evidence of this in the White Paper.

What is less clear is the precise nature of the balance between the punitive and managerialist threads of the White Paper. Does the White Paper offer a realistic opportunity for sentencing to reduce the use of custody? Are the punitive aspects of the White Paper merely rhetorical, or are they likely to result in greater use of custody?

The White Paper frequently notes the need to improve public confidence in sentencing. This is perhaps most clearly seen in the title of the chapter, 'Putting the sense back into sentencing', based on a perception that the public are 'sick and tired' of the system (5.2). There are also calls for greater clarity in sentencing and for a clearer framework of penalties. However, there is nothing in the White Paper which is specifically aimed at providing the public with better or more accurate information about sentencing. The Criminal Justice Bill provides for an amendment to the Criminal Justice Act 1991 requiring information to be published to enable assessment of the effectiveness of sentencing in reducing offending and promoting public confidence in the criminal justice system (clause 158). However, in the absence of more specific proposals, it must be assumed that the broad changes proposed in the White Paper and the Bill are intended to have the effect of improving public confidence.

Whatever the final form of the legislation which emerges from this White Paper, and whether or not a public rationale for sentencing is articulated, the result of the implementation of the legislation will, de facto, express a sentencing policy. Sentencing guidelines can never be simply a technical procedure for injecting greater rationality into sentencing; they are unavoidably political and express, both in theory and in practice, a series of choices between competing values.

To return to the beginning of this section, most commentators argue that the values underpinning an approach to sentencing and punishment ought to be explicit. Both Ashworth (2001) and Frase (2001), writing in the same volume, argue that sentencing needs a rationale. Ashworth calls for a primary rationale and a set of justifications for departures from this. Frase describes a limiting retributivist approach to which he subscribes and which he argues provides a principled basis for seeking greater rationality in sentencing. It is arguably impossible to balance all of the competing values in any approach to sentencing and punishment without first setting out a rationale of what it is the approach wants to achieve.

The components of a rational approach to sentencing

In this section I want to sketch the main features of what I take to be a rational approach to sentencing. The title of Chapter 5 of the White Paper, 'Putting the sense back into sentencing', can be read as a response to perceived public impatience with criminal justice. The 'sense' that is being put back in is presumably the 'common sense' that has been removed by 'out of touch' judges. We can all agree that sentencing should be sensible. On another interpretation, the title of the chapter could be read by liberal penal reformers as a call for greater rationality and legality in sentencing. This may be taking the title too seriously – it may be no more than a cute alliterative title. However, writing as someone who thinks that sentencing should be rationalised, I am inclined to take the title seriously. What follows outlines a personal view of what a rational approach to sentencing should look like.

A principled rationale of what sentencing is supposed to achieve
This should be some form of limiting retributivism in which desert or proportionality fixes the boundaries of punishment. Within these boundaries other aims of punishment can be pursued. There should be guidelines which specify the kinds of conditions under which different approaches (rehabilitation, incapacitation, etc.) might be appropriate. This recognises the evidence of the limited effects that sentencing and punishment can be expected to have on crime and asserts the importance of ensuring that the allocation of punishment should be based on the principle of proportionality.

A comprehensive (both within offence categories and across categories) set of sentencing guidelines
There are a number of features required for a fair and effective system of sentencing guidelines:

- A classification of all offences ranked in order of severity. Sentencing is essentially a comparative exercise. If guidelines are not comprehensive, the risk is that sentencing practice for those offences outside the guidelines will be out of step with guideline sentencing. Only comprehensive guidelines allow a sentencing commission to analyse the projected impact of guidelines on prison populations and adjust the guidelines to meet target levels of incarceration.

- A range of sanctions also ranked in severity of penal value which provides a presumptive range of sanction for each offence classification. (Where relevant this should include custodial and community penalties.) Judges will be able to exercise their discretion within this range. They may select a sanction from within the range and this can be used to achieve any of the penal aims specified in the rationale.

- There should be guidance for judges as to what constitutes a typical offence in the classification and what constitute more or less serious variations from the typical case.

- Judges should be required to give reasons for departure from the guideline range.

- There should be clear specification of how criminal record will affect the level of sanction.

- There should be a clear attempt in the guidelines to describe the custody threshold and distinguish those types of case for which a custodial sentence is normally appropriate.

The use of an independent commission to draw up the guidelines
The commission should not be composed exclusively of judges, but should be chaired by an enthusiast who will ideally be a judge with the respect of his peers. The commission will be adequately staffed and resourced.

The commission should collect data on past sentencing practice, examine the projected impact of proposed guidelines on prison populations and monitor compliance with guidelines. All of this information should be published.

In simple terms what is required is a rationale, a set of procedures for putting this rationale into practice and an institution to develop, implement and sustain these procedures. At this level of simplicity, this may be stating the obvious and there is no space here to elaborate on the framework or to discuss any of the complexities involved in making something like this happen. This is really intended as a template against which to evaluate the government's recent proposals. To what extent does the White Paper meet these basic requirements for a rational approach to sentencing?

II. The proposals in the White Paper and the Criminal Justice Bill

Aims and purposes of sentencing

The White Paper is quite explicit about setting out the aims and purposes of sentencing (paragraphs 5.4 and 5.8.) Paragraph 5.4 contains a general exhortation that sentencers should consider the best way of preventing crime based on 'what works'. Consistent with this, the paramount aim of sentencing (5.8) is the protection of the public. The argument could be made that the most effective protection for the public is to be had by reducing crime but this is not made explicitly in the White Paper and no evidence is produced to support this argument. The other aims of sentencing in paragraph 5.8 are: punishment which fits the crime (desert), crime reduction, general and specific deterrence, incapacitation, reform and rehabilitation, and reparation. Sentencers are required to consider all of these and to select a sentence which achieves the 'right balance'. No further guidance is given as to the characteristics of this balance.

Paragraph 126 of the Criminal Justice Bill sets out the purposes of sentencing, and the Home Secretary makes much of the fact that this is the first time that the aims of sentencing have been set out in legislation (BBC Radio Four *Today* programme 13 January 2003). The purposes of sentencing are: the punishment of offenders, the reduction of crime (which includes reduction by deterrence and by the reform and rehabilitation of offenders), the protection of the public and the making of reparation. No one aim has priority over any other aim and the requirement set out in the White Paper for sentencers to consider effectiveness does not appear in this part of the Bill.

Restriction on the use of custody

The government's proposals retain a concern for the principle of parsimony in sentencing as noted above. Paragraph 5.6 of the White Paper states that custody should be reserved for dangerous, serious and seriously persistent offenders and those who have consistently breached community sanctions. It has long been a rhetorical claim of sentencing in England that custody should be a sanction of last resort which should be restricted to serious offenders and to those from whom the community needs to be protected. The White Paper adds, explicitly, two further types of offender to this. 'Seriously persistent' offenders and those who have 'consistently' breached community sanctions. The attention to 'seriously persistent' offenders is a response to the reaction to the 1991 Act which was perceived by the judiciary as improperly restricting their ability to take criminal record into account when choosing sentence. It might also be read as a political response to apparent perceptions that a small number of 'career criminals' are responsible for a disproportionate amount of offending.

The term 'seriously persistent offender' does not appear in the Bill. The only reference to the impact of criminal record on sentencing can be found in paragraph 127(2). This states that the court must treat each previous conviction as an aggravating factor if it is reasonable to do so having regard in particular to the relevance of the previous convictions to the current offence and to the time that has elapsed since the conviction. The only reference to persistent offenders is in clause 134 which allows the court to pass a community order for an offence which would not ordinarily be sufficiently serious to justify such a penalty where the offender has received a fine on three or more previous occasions.

The sentencing framework

According to the White Paper, the new sentencing framework is designed to enable the sentencer to 'tailor' the sentence to the offender and the offence (5.19) although no pattern is provided for this tailoring. The 'new' framework set out in the Criminal Justice Bill is much the same as that proposed in both Halliday and the White Paper.

Community order

The community order will now be a single order in place of the previous practice of combining orders. Sentencers may select from a menu of requirements: unpaid work activity, accredited programmes, prohibited activity, curfew, exclusion, residence, mental health treatment, drug rehabilitation, alcohol treatment, supervision, attendance centre, electronic monitoring. Clause 131 states that the requirements selected for an order must be suitable for the offender and where the requirements involve the restriction of liberty, they should be commensurate with the seriousness of the offence.

Custody plus order

Halliday recognised the ineffectiveness of short prison sentences. The White Paper proposed a new framework for custodial sentences of less than 12 months. All of these sentences were to consist of a period of custody followed by a period of community supervision. The Bill provides for a custody plus order which is for a period of between 28 and 51 weeks. The custodial period must be specified and can be from 2–13 weeks. The minimum licence period is 26 weeks. The licence period can have requirements attached. The requirements for a custody plus order are the same as those listed above for a community order with the exceptions of drug rehabilitation, alcohol treatment, mental health treatment or residence.

Where two custody plus orders are to run consecutively the maximum period is 65 weeks with a maximum custodial period of 26 weeks.

Suspended sentence order

The term 'custody minus' has been dropped from the White Paper. This is a suspended sentence of imprisonment subject to requirements drawn from the same menu as for the community order. Failure to comply with the conditions may result in an immediate custodial sentence.

Intermittent custody order

The White Paper proposed this option of 'weekend prison' for offenders who are not dangerous and do not have to be held in secure accommodation to protect the public. It was intended to be especially appropriate for offenders with care responsibilities including some women offenders. The Bill provides for sentences of 28–51 weeks with the number of custodial days between 14 and 90. This order may have requirements attached but only unpaid work, activity, programme or prohibited activity requirements.

Custody of twelve months or over
Those sentenced to a custodial sentence will serve half of the sentence in prison and all of the remainder under supervision in the community subject to the same menu of conditions as for the customised community sentence.

Sentencing guidelines

The stated aim of the proposals for sentencing guidelines in the White Paper is to reduce the excessive variation in sentencing. The evidence for this comes from regional variations in sentencing in magistrates' courts (5.11). These variations make it 'difficult to plan for necessary custodial facilities' for remand and sentenced prisoners (5.12). (This is the only mention in the White Paper about the need to take into account penal resources when discussing sentencing policy.)

The Criminal Justice Bill, paragraph 151 provides for the establishment of a Sentencing Guidelines Council. This judicial institution is to be chaired by the Lord Chief Justice and composed of judges from all levels of court. The Council will produce draft guidelines which will be 'considered and scrutinised' by Parliament but which will not become legislation. The Bill does not specify the aims of the SGC but at paragraph 153(5) there is a list of the 'matters to which the Council must have regard' when framing or revising sentencing guidelines: the need to promote consistency in sentencing, the sentences imposed by courts in England and Wales for offences to which the guidelines relate, the cost of different sentences and their relative effectiveness in preventing reoffending, the need to promote public confidence in the criminal justice system and the views communicated to the Council by the Sentencing Advisory Panel. These are the same as those governing the Sentencing Advisory Panel set out in section 80(3)(d) of the Crime and Disorder Act 1998.

The Council can make its own decisions about the need for guidelines, but must consider the need for guidelines when requested to do so by either the Secretary of State or the Sentencing Advisory Panel. Guidelines must include criteria for determining the seriousness of the offence or offences including (where appropriate) criteria for determining the weight to be given to any previous convictions of offenders (paragraph 153(7)). The Council will publish draft guidelines and, after consultation with the Secretary of State and any other persons whom the Secretary of State and the Council think appropriate and having made any amendments which the Council thinks appropriate, publish the guidelines as definitive guidelines. In the White Paper there was the suggestion that Parliament might have the opportunity to scrutinise draft guidelines. This does not appear in the Bill, but paragraph 153(8) leaves some such possibility open.

Courts are obliged to have regard to relevant guidelines (paragraph 155) and, as a part of the general obligation of the courts to give reasons for and explain the effect of the sentence, the courts are required to explicitly refer to the guidelines when passing sentence. Courts must also explain why a community order or a custodial sentence is justified, the effect of the sentence, the effects on the offender of failure to comply with any order of the court and any power of the court to review or vary the order, and state any reduction for an early plea of guilty and mention any aggravating or mitigating factor which the court has regarded as being of particular importance. The courts are thus required to provide a fairly detailed explanation for the sentence with regard to guidelines where these exist. There is no mention in the Bill of any procedures for monitoring the response of the courts to the guidelines. It must be assumed that monitoring will be achieved through the usual procedures of appeal where either the Crown or the defence feel that guidelines have not been properly taken into account. This approach to sentencing guidelines is essentially voluntary. The courts are not required to adhere to the guidelines. The courts are required to provide an adequate justification for the sentence which has regard to the guidelines.

III. An evaluation of the sentencing reform proposals: business as usual?

On the face of it the White Paper contains the basic ingredients of a more rational approach to sentencing. It directly addresses the aims and purposes of sentencing. It contains proposals for a set of sentencing guidelines and for an institution to develop and promulgate these guidelines. However, when one looks at the details of the proposals, my conclusion is that not only will they fail to provide a rational approach to sentencing, but that they may have only a very limited impact on sentencing practice.

I will substantiate this argument by taking in turn the aims and purposes of sentencing and punishment, sentencing guidelines, and the Sentencing Guidelines Council and the new Sentencing Framework.

Aims and purposes of sentencing

The White Paper and the Criminal Justice Bill merely reiterate the familiar aims of punishment: protection of the public, deterrence, rehabilitation, reparation and retribution. The White Paper elevates protection of the public to the pole position but provides no further guidance as to exactly how this should be prioritised beyond ensuring that dangerous, serious and seriously persistent offenders should receive a custodial sentence (as indeed they already do). There is no mention of this in the Bill and all the aims of punishment have equal status, the punishment of offenders, the reduction of crime (which includes reduction by deterrence and by the reform and rehabilitation of offenders), the protection of the public and the making of reparation. There is no rationale to guide judges towards a consistent approach to these aims.

As Tonry (2001) has remarked, agreeing the aims of punishment is not difficult but agreeing a rationale is harder. Halliday adopted a weak version of limiting retributivism in his report and tried to describe a principled approach to the use of short custodial sentences (see below). None of this has found its way into the White Paper or the Bill. The Bill may specify the aims of punishment in legislation for the first time, but it is hard to see how this can have much impact on introducing a more rational, more consistent and more principled approach to sentencing. In effect, sentencers can select from the traditional justifications for punishment much as they have always been able to do. This legislative statement of aims is unlikely to do anything to bring about greater consistency in sentencing or therefore to promote greater public confidence in criminal justice.

The advantage of a limiting retributivist rationale for punishment is that it sets boundaries based on proportionality which are clear and understandable by all stakeholders. Under this broad rationale, probation officers can write reports recommending requirements for community orders on the basis of a clear understanding of the punishment boundaries that the case is likely to fall within. The rationale can bring greater consistency across courts and between judges as it provides a broad basis for just sentencing within which variation can be explained and justified. Without such a rationale, the inclusion of aims of sentencing in legislation is unlikely to have any significant impact on making sentencing more rational.

Guidelines and the Sentencing Guidelines Council

The White Paper argues that guidelines are needed to reduce the excessive variation in sentencing and introduce greater consistency. The evidence produced to support this is data from the magistrates' courts which appear to show significant regional variations in the level of sentencing for common offences, so, for example, rates of custody for robbery are higher in one area than another.

The White Paper focuses on geographical variation in sentencing. However, disparities in sentencing can arise for a range of other reasons, most notably judges seeking to achieve different sentencing objectives in what appear to be similar cases. For example, retributive aims and deterrent aims might suggest different sentences. The White Paper does not address this source of disparity and thereby suggests that the problem of 'excessive variation' can be attributed to differences in local court 'cultures' and not to different approaches to sentencing adopted by individual judges. Nicola Lacey (1994) has pointed out that disparity assumes considerable political significance where a desert approach underpins sentencing. As desert returns to be one among many aims of sentencing in this Bill, the political significance of disparity diminishes. Disparity is seen as something which can be resolved by providing the courts with more guideline judgments and there is no need for a shared rationale for sentencing.

The Bill quite properly leaves the detail of proposed sentencing guidelines to the new Sentencing Guidelines Council. Halliday offered a number of options for the composition of this institution. The Bill follows the White Paper in selecting the most conservative of these options. The Council is to be a completely judicial body, chaired by the Lord Chief Justice and with representatives from the full range of judicial officers including the magistracy. On a positive view, changes to sentencing practice are most likely to occur if the changes have the support of sentencers and this is arguably more likely if the proposed changes come from within the judiciary.

Michael Tonry (2001) has argued that judges do not have all of the necessary skills to devise and implement a set of sentencing guidelines and that judges are unlikely to produce guidelines which are sufficiently ambitious to effect a change in practice. Evidence from a neighbouring jurisdiction, Scotland, suggests that judges can benefit from non-judicial support in the difficult exercise of sentencing reform. The High Court in Scotland has recently implemented a Sentencing Information System (Tata *et al* 2002). This is not a set of guidelines for sentencers, but rather a database which allows judges to look at patterns of sentencing for past cases. However, in order to allow judges to examine patterns of sentencing for 'similar' cases, a set of classifications which would 'represent' seriousness had to be developed in a similar way to the process of classifying seriousness for sentencing guidelines. The database was designed by judges supported by a team of lawyers, social scientists and IT experts. The experience of this complex project suggests that judges require considerable support from a range of disciplines to produce a workable solution.

A council composed exclusively of judges would have to employ external assistance to conduct the research and impact projections necessary for effective guidelines. The Sentencing Guidelines Council will in practice always have the assistance of the Sentencing Advisory Panel in framing guidelines. The Panel has judicial representatives but also has non-judicial members who bring different skills and expertise to bear on the development of sentencing policy. The Panel regularly conducts and commissions research, the results of which are published and referred to in the Panel's advice to the Court of Appeal.

The Sentencing Advisory Panel and the Sentencing Guidelines Council

The form of sentencing guidelines and their impact on sentencing practice will depend to a great extent on the working relationship between the SAP and the SGC. The legislative proposals leave these bodies with considerable discretion over the detailed shaping of the guidelines. How will they work together?

One can only speculate, but some hints might be gathered from an examination of the way in which the Court of Appeal has dealt with the advice of the Sentencing Advisory Panel in the recent guideline judgment on domestic burglary.[1] At the time of writing this continues to create ripples in the print media.[2]

The advice of the SAP took into account three main sources of evidence: a research study into public opinion about the sentencing of domestic burglary commissioned by the SAP in order to assist the Court of Appeal in fulfilling its statutory obligation to have regard to the need to promote confidence in the criminal justice system (Crime and Disorder Act 1998, section 80(3)(d)), the previous guidelines issued in *R v Brewster and others* [1998]1 Cr App R(s) 181 and section 111 of the Powers of Criminal Courts (Sentencing) Act 2000 which creates a presumptive minimum sentence of three years for a third conviction of domestic burglary.

The Panel divided domestic burglary into four broadly defined categories of seriousness. Seriousness was defined by a range of offence criteria and also by the criminal history of the offender. The sentences indicated are starting points for the guidance of the court. The existence of mitigating factors (which are described in some detail) or combinations of aggravating factors may be taken into account by the court when deciding the exact sentence.

(a) Low level burglaries: for first-time and some second-time offenders a starting point of a community order.

(b) Standard burglaries: 9 months' custody for first offenders, 18 months for second offenders and 36 months (the statutory minimum for third offenders).

(c) Burglaries displaying aggravating factors of 'medium relevance': 12 months for first offenders, 24 months for second offenders and 42 months for third offenders.

(d) Burglaries displaying aggravating factors of 'high relevance': 18 months for first offenders, 36 months for second offenders and 54 months for third offenders.

The Court of Appeal welcomed the advice of the SAP as useful and emphasised the importance of attention to public opinion as one important factor in framing sentencing guidelines. However, the Court also was required to have regard to the cost and effectiveness of sentences, and to the pressure on the prison system of overcrowding which has resulted in the use of executive release on home detention curfew. The judgment quotes research which shows public ignorance of such matters.

The Court of Appeal accepted the medium and high-level aggravating factors identified by the SAP and accepted the proposed guidelines in paragraphs (a) and (d) above. However, the Court of Appeal proposed that the starting points for first offenders in paragraphs (b) and (c) above should be community orders rather than nine and twelve months' custody. The Court of Appeal indicated that custodial sentences would still be necessary for repeat offenders and aggravated offences as set out in paragraphs (b), (c) and (d). The justification for this guideline is the research evidence on the ineffectiveness of short prison sentences on reducing offending, the costs of reoffending and the greater cost-effectiveness of community orders in reducing offending and thereby increasing the confidence of the public in the criminal justice system. The outcome will be better protection for the public and some reduction in the use of custody.

Thus the main difference between the Court of Appeal guideline and the SAP advice is that the Court recommends a starting point of a community order for first-time burglars where the offence is a medium serious burglary or less. The SAP recommended starting points for first offenders of standard and medium serious burglaries of nine and twelve months' custody respectively.

It is interesting to note that the SAP advice and the Court of Appeal guideline judgment satisfy most of the conditions noted above for the construction of guidelines. There is a clear indication of the criteria for ascribing seriousness, clear quantification of sanctions to each band of seriousness, an attempt to describe a typical or 'standard' offence, specification of how criminal record will affect sentencing and a clear custody threshold. All that is missing is a requirement of judges to explain any departures from the guidelines, but as these guidelines are both broad and voluntary, this is perhaps unnecessary. Obviously these guidelines are only for domestic burglary and are not comprehensive.

Another interesting observation is that the argument made by the Court of Appeal for departing from the advice of the SAP by recommending community orders as the starting point for sentencing of first-time burglars for standard or medium serious offences in place of custodial sentences of nine months and twelve months is based on broad policy arguments founded on research evidence, much of it drawn from a report published by the social exclusion unit (Social Exclusion Unit 2002). The argument of the Court of Appeal is that evidence shows that short prison sentences are ineffective in reducing crime. Recidivism is very costly. Community orders are more cost-effective in reducing offending behaviour. The public will be better protected and thus have more confidence in the criminal justice system if more use is made of community orders where they can be shown to have the best chance of achieving crime reduction, for a significant proportion of non-violent burglars.

The advice of the SAP only mentions the problem of prison over-crowding briefly in a final paragraph of the report and does not discuss costs at all. One might have expected more public policy arguments to have come from the SAP but in fact they came from the Court of Appeal. In any event this guideline judgment satisfies many of the criteria for rational sentencing guidelines. We can only speculate whether this approach will be applied in the new institutional arrangements. Perhaps the SAP will have greater regard to the costs and effectiveness information relied on by the Court of Appeal when drafting their next advice to the Court of Appeal or to the Sentencing Guidelines Council? Perhaps the SGC will adopt a similar approach to the formation of sentencing policy as was done by the Court of Appeal with respect to domestic burglary. Sentencing policy remains firmly in the hands of the judiciary.

Much of the information taken into account by the Court of Appeal is the sort that might be gathered and considered by a Sentencing Commission charged with producing guidelines. The main difference is that the Sentencing Commission would be collecting such information across all offence categories as opposed to one offence category. The Commission would also be in a position to take an overall view on important policy matters such as the impact of criminal record on levels of punishment and the impact of proposed guidelines on prison populations. It is very difficult to do this sort of work on a piecemeal basis.

However, it may be that the combination of the SGC and SAP is a peculiarly English approach to producing a more rational approach to sentencing. It leaves judges with considerable discretion but provides a means of injecting greater rationality, research evidence and general policy considerations into sentencing. This may suit English legal and administrative culture (Robertson 1998) more than the more bureaucratic US Sentencing Commission approach. While a rational idealist might prefer the Sentencing Commission route, in the political and cultural conditions which prevail in England, a pragmatist might well decide that the best hope for a significant shift toward greater rationality in sentencing policy lay with the SAP/SGC proposals. They have the merit of being more acceptable to the judiciary who will have to implement any reforms. The successful implementation of the High Court SIS in Scotland shows the importance of judicial leadership in UK sentencing reforms. It remains to be seen what the judges in both jurisdictions will make of the opportunity.

Compliance with the guidelines

There is no provision in the White Paper for monitoring compliance with guidelines and thus there is no internal mechanism for measuring any increased consistency in sentencing. It seems unlikely that the SGC will put any such monitoring into place. For one thing it will not have the staff or resources to conduct such an exercise. Thus far, the Sentencing Advisory Panel has not made any efforts to monitor the extent to which judges have observed or departed from the guideline sentences issues by the Court of Appeal based on the advice from the SAP. Indeed the nature of the guidelines makes measuring compliance very difficult.

Are comprehensive guidelines necessary?

Tonry argues that guidelines need to be comprehensive. They need to cover all categories of offence, they need to prescribe penalty ranges for all of these and they need to prescribe how criminal history affects penalty. They allow projections to be calculated of impact on prison populations and resource issues to be dealt with systematically. The proposals in the White Paper recognise the need for comprehensive guidelines but the method proposed seems unlikely to deliver what is required. The Sentencing Guidelines Council will proceed to draft guidelines, advised by the Sentencing Advisory Panel. This is likely to be on an individual offence basis as the White Paper indicates that guidelines will be released to practitioners as they become available. Thus rather than draft a single comprehensive set of guidelines, as has been the practice of US commissions, the SGC will continue the practice of the Court of Appeal, similarly advised by the SAP, and produce guidelines for individual offences in a piecemeal fashion.

While it is theoretically possible that these individual offence guidelines might at some point add up to a comprehensive set of guidelines, this seems very unlikely. If the council produces guidelines at the rate of the Court of Appeal and the SAP, it would take many years to reach a comprehensive set of guidelines by which time the early guidelines would almost certainly require revision. The SGC and SAP would require a significant increase in resources if the pace of guideline production was to be accelerated.

The SGC would need some procedure for selecting offences for which guidelines were to be drafted, whether these were the most serious, the most common or those of current 'public' concern. For a (lengthy) interim period, this will mean that there will be a long list of offences which do not have guidelines because they are too trivial, too rare or of little current concern to the public. This may not matter. There may well be some value in concentrating resources on the 'important' offences. However, this does mean that the guidelines are unlikely to be comprehensive.

Drafting guidelines for individual offences allows each offence to be dealt with comprehensively. It does not allow comprehensive treatment across offence categories. For example, it does not allow sanctions for rape to be assessed against sentences for robbery or sentences for large-scale fraud. Nor does it allow any systematic consideration of how aggravating and mitigating factors should apply across offence categories. However, it would be possible for some elements of guideline sentences to be applied more widely than the offence under consideration. For example, the information about the costs of re-offending, the effectiveness of prison and the problems caused by prison overcrowding which form part of the guideline judgment of the Court of Appeal on domestic burglary are equally applicable to a range of other offences. The same could be true for the treatment of previous convictions although not in the burglary judgment as there is a mandatory minimum penalty for third offences. However, much of what is said about the effects of previous convictions on sentencing for burglary is inevitably relevant for sentencing other offences. This does not amount to a comprehensive approach to the scaling of offences and sanctions.

Finally, it is not clear how the SGC will handle the issue of the effect of criminal history on penalty levels. The White Paper proposes that increased levels of penalty should apply to persistent offenders and in particular that seriously persistent offenders should receive custodial sentences. The Bill contains only a couple of references to the impact of previous convictions. Clause 127(2) provides that courts must treat each previous conviction as an aggravating factor if it is reasonable to do so having regard in particular to the relevance of the previous conviction to the current offence and the time elapsed since the conviction. The only use of the term 'persistent' is in clause 134 of the Bill which provides that offenders who have previously been fined three or more times may receive a community order for an offence which would not ordinarily be serious enough for such a penalty. These are the only two sections of the Bill which specify how previous convictions are to be taken into account in sentencing. Clause 127 leaves considerable discretion with the sentencing judge. The extent to which previous convictions should increase the sentence is not specified and recognition is given to the principle that a previous conviction might not be relevant to the current offence and that the passing of time may diminish the significance of a previous conviction.

It is conceivable that the SGC could produce a guideline judgment concerning the impact of criminal history on sentence. Clause 153(7) provides that the SGC, when framing or revising guidelines, must include criteria for determining the weight to be given to any previous conviction. This suggests that the impact of criminal history should be decided for each offence classification considered by the SGC. The most recent Court of Appeal guideline sentence on burglary indicates how criminal record should affect burglary sentencing by making clear distinctions between the starting point for sentencing first offenders and repeat offenders for burglaries at different levels of seriousness. There is no indication of how this approach to criminal record should be applied to any other sort of offence although the Court of Appeal recognises that previous convictions may be more relevant in domestic burglary than in other offences. Without a comprehensive set of guidelines linking offences to sanctions, it is hard to see how a systematic approach to the impact of criminal record on sentencing could be achieved with a sufficient level of detail to ensure consistency of approach. Halliday noted that without comprehensive guidelines on how criminal history should affect sentence, the new presumption of increased punishment for persistent offenders would be unpredictable and lead to disproportionately severe sentences (Home Office 2001: 0.7). Other commentators have also made this very important point (Roberts 2002; Von Hirsch 2002; Jones 2002). There is nothing in the Criminal Justice Bill which will prevent this inconsistency of approach.

The sentencing framework

The White Paper proposes a 'new' framework of sanctions. There is a community order, custody-plus order, intermittent custody order, suspended sentence order and custody of twelve months or over. Other chapters in this volume look at these in more detail and speculate about their potential impact on penal practice. Here I want to focus on the issues raised for the drafting of sentencing guidelines by this framework.

In the absence of a rationale for sentencing, the familiar tensions between punishment and welfare, crime control and desert, and offence and offender characteristics remain unresolved in the White Paper and the Bill. This leaves the SGC with a difficult task in ranking sanctions in terms of their severity. A desert-based approach allows punishments to be scaled in terms of their penal impact, i.e. extent of restriction of liberty, level of intrusiveness, etc. However, this scale does not apply when punishment is intended to deter, incapacitate, rehabilitate or repair. Take, for example, the community sentence. Some items from the menu are intended to punish or control (restriction of liberty, curfews, electronic monitoring), others are intended to rehabilitate (education, training, behavioural programmes, treatment orders) and others may be intended to offer reparation to the community or the victim (work, restorative justice options). While in any case this sanction allows judges to try to achieve multiple sentencing aims in one sanction, it is very hard to see how guidance could be provided to judges to ensure that consistency of approach is adopted. Clause 131(2) of the Bill states that the requirements of a community order must be suitable for the offender and restriction of liberty requirements must be commensurate with the seriousness of the offence. This suggests that some requirements are justified on the basis of the principle of effective rehabilitation and other requirements are based on the principle of proportionality. However, there is no principled rationale specifying how these competing principles are to be combined. Nor is there any recognition that requirements imposed for rehabilitative purposes may also have the effect of restricting liberty. Offenders convicted for a relatively minor offence could find their liberty disproportionately restricted by a series of conditions imposed for non-desert reasons.

In a similar way it is difficult to establish a penal ranking for the different sanctions. In practice a community order might be very similar to a suspended sentence order. What is the relationship between an intermittent custody order and a custody-plus order? What is the threshold for the use of custody-plus as against a community order which will form the final part of a custody-plus sentence in any case? These are the sorts of questions which the SGC will have to address when drafting guidelines and their task is not helped by the absence of a principled rationale. Robinson and McNeill (2003) in a forthcoming article argue that in England and Wales there has been a deliberate 'repositioning' of probation. Traditionally probation has been viewed as a less severe sanction, below custody in the unofficial 'tariff'. Robinson and McNeill (2003) argue that probation is now being positioned alongside prisons, citing the Prisons-Probation Review which sets out common objectives for the two services (Home Office 1999) and the 'Prisons of promise' agenda which views prisons, like probation, as sites for the delivery of accredited rehabilitative programmes (see also Nellis 1999 and, for a related shift in Scotland, Scottish Prison Service 2002). The White Paper and the Bill make the usual noises about parsimonious use of sanctions but do not set out any detail on a principled approach to how custodial and non-custodial sentences ought to be used. If anything the new sentencing framework further blurs the boundaries between these sanctions by adding community requirements to all custodial orders and by failing to provide any detail on the custody threshold.

The White Paper talks in general rhetorical terms of reserving the use of custody for dangerous, serious and seriously persistent offenders. There are remarks about the cost and relative ineffectiveness of prison. The new 'tougher' community sentence is described as a credible alternative to custody. All of this signals the familiar bifurcation approach and an apparent desire to limit the use of imprisonment.

Halliday certainly intended the community order to be an alternative to the short custodial sentences currently imposed. For these sorts of cases, Halliday proposed that judges be required to assess the risk of reoffending, the harm which would thereby result and the most effective way of reducing the risk of reoffending. The aim was to reduce offending by the most effective means, even if this meant imposing a community sanction where the seriousness of the offence might be sufficient to justify a custodial sentence. This can be read as an effort by Halliday to sketch out a guideline for the threshold use of custody.

None of this survives in the White Paper or the Bill. Halliday's framework of sanctions is adopted but his underpinning rationale for the use of these sanctions is not. Halliday's attempts to provide a consistent approach to the reduced use of short-term prison sentences do not appear. Of course this responsibility now shifts to the SGC. However, given the piecemeal approach in which the Council will operate, it is hard to see how a consistent approach to the use of the new sentencing framework can be achieved across all offence categories.

Conclusions

A sceptical evaluation of the government's new sentencing proposals suggests that the new framework will make little difference to sentencing practice. Judges can still pass community sentences and short custodial sentences. The main differences are that they have greater freedom to compile the recipes for the community parts of the sentence and every custodial sentence they now pass has a community element attached. The framework is rebranded rather than reformed. Whether it will make sentencing clearer to the public remains to be seen.

Despite the rhetoric of the White Paper, there is little reason to anticipate a reduction in the use of custody. In fact, there is more reason to anticipate a rise in the use of custody (see Roberts and Smith in this volume). The increase in the number of requirements which can potentially be breached in the community order creates the conditions for a significant increase in the use of custody for breaches of community orders. The opportunity offered by the custody-plus order to attach a short period of custody to a battery of requirements in a community order might prove irresistible to some sentencers. This might produce a decrease in the use of community orders with no custody attached producing paradoxically an increase in the use of short prison sentences. Of course there will be no resources in overcrowded prisons to begin any work with prisoners serving short sentences. Any programmes will only begin once the offender is serving the community order part of the custody-plus order.

The methodology proposed for the SGC will make it difficult, although not necessarily impossible, for guidelines to be drafted to achieve Halliday's aim of a reduction of the use of short-term prison sentences.

The SGC face a considerable challenge in drafting guidelines which help judges to take a consistent approach in matching cases to sanctions. A pessimistic liberal penal reformer might argue that there is little in the

White Paper or the Bill to offer encouragement to those who seek a more rational, evidence-based approach to penal policy. Sentencing policy remains firmly in the hands of the judiciary. Judicial discretion is relatively untouched. There are no procedures in place for monitoring judicial adherence to guideline judgments.

The SGC may develop a systematic and principled approach to sentencing which provides broad guidelines on the relationship between offence category and sanction and the impact on sentence of criminal history. It may develop guidelines which help judges to use custody parsimoniously and to use community sentences in a way which balances the demands of crime control and justice. Whether it does so or not will depend on the approach adopted by the members of the SGC rather than anything in the White Paper and the Bill.

Notes

1. <http://www.courtservice.gov.uk/judgementsfiles/j1464/mcinerney_keating_v_r.htm>
2. The guideline was released on 19 December 2002 and was not accompanied by a media release so was missed by much of the media. An e-mail explaining the guideline was sent by Lord Woolf to judges on 24 December 2002 on the grounds that the judgment had been misreported in the media. This was followed by a public defence of the judgment by the Lord Chancellor in early January after tabloid reports which were very critical of the judgment. The tabloid media response to the Lord Chancellor's defence was vigorous and accused the Lord Chief Justice and the Lord Chancellor of being out of touch with the public. The Home Secretary then defended the judgment, although he made some critical remarks about the way in which the judgment was initially communicated. On 14 January the Lord Chief Justice issued a second clarification of the initial judgment to correct media misreporting which, however, did not modify the guideline in any way. A *Times* article of 21 January, under the headline 'Colleagues behind softie judge', reported judicial support for the LCJ with some judges saying that the guideline represented existing practice in any case, as Lord Woolf himself had admitted, and would not change sentencing practice much.

References

Ashworth, A. (2001) 'The Decline of English Sentencing and Other Stories', in Tonry, M. and Frase, R. (eds), *Sentencing and Sanctions in Western Countries.* Oxford: Oxford University Press.

Bottoms, A.E. (1995) 'The Philosophy and Politics of Punishment and Sentencing', in Clarkson, C. and Morgan, R. (eds), *The Politics of Sentencing Reform*. Oxford: Clarendon Press.

Frase, R. (2001) 'Comparative Perspectives on Sentencing Policy and Research', in Tonry, M. and Frase, R. (eds) (2001), *Sentencing and Sanctions in Western Countries*. Oxford: Oxford University Press.

Garland, D. (2002) *The Culture of Control*. Oxford: Oxford University Press.

Home Office (1999) *The Correctional Policy Framework*. London: Home Office.

Home Office (2001) *Making Punishments Work: Report of a Review of the Sentencing Framework for England and Wales* (the Halliday Report). London: Home Office.

Home Office (2002) *Justice for All*, CM 5563. London: Home Office.

Jones, P. (2002) 'The Halliday Report and Persistent Offenders', in Rex, S. and Tonry, M. (eds), *Reform and Punishment: The Future of Sentencing*. Cullompton: Willan.

Lacey, N. (1994) 'Government as Manager, Citizen as Consumer: The Case of the Criminal Justice Act 1991', *Modern Law Review*, 534.

Nellis, M. (1999) 'Towards 'the Field of Corrections': Modernizing the Probation Service in the late 1990s', *Social Policy and Administration*, 33(3): 302–23.

Reitz, K. (2001) 'The Disassembly and Reassembly of US Sentencing Practices', in Tonry, M. and Frase, R. (eds), *Sentencing and Sanctions in Western Countries*. Oxford: Oxford University Press.

Roberts, J. (2002) 'Alchemy in Sentencing: An Analysis of Sentencing Reform Proposals in England and Wales', *Punishment and Society*, 4(4): 425–42.

Roberts J. and Hough M. (eds) (2002) *Changing Attitudes to Punishment: Public Opinion, Crime and Justice*. Cullompton: Willan.

Robertson, D. (1998) *Judicial Discretion in the House of Lords*. Oxford: Clarendon Press.

Robinson, G. and McNeil, F. (2003 forthcoming) 'Purposes Matter: Examining the "Ends of Probation" ', *Probation Journal*.

Scottish Prison Service (2002) *Making a Difference*. Edinburgh: Scottish Prison Service.

Sentencing Advisory Panel (2002) 'Domestic Burglary: The Panel's Advice to the Court of Appeal', <http://www.sentencing-advisory-panel.gov.uk/c_and_a/advice/dom_burglary/page1.htm>.

Social Exclusion Unit (2002) 'Reducing Re-offending by Ex-prisoners', <http://www.socialexclusionunit.gov.uk>.

Stith, K. and Cabranes, J. (1998) *Fear of Judging: Sentencing Guidelines in the Federal Courts*. Chicago: University of Chicago Press.

Tata, C., Hutton, N., Wilson, J., Paterson, A. and Hughson, I. (2002) *A Sentencing Information System for the High Court of Justiciary in Scotland: Report of the First Phase of Implementation and Enhancement*. Glasgow: University of Strathclyde, Centre for Sentencing Research.

Tonry (2001) 'Punishment Policies and Patterns in Western Countries', in Tonry, M. and Frase, R. (eds) (2001) *Sentencing and Sanctions in Western Countries*. Oxford: Oxford University Press.

Tonry, M. (2002) 'Setting Sentencing Policy through Guidelines', in Rex, S. and Tonry, M., *Reform and Punishment: The Future of Sentencing*. Cullompton: Willan.

Vennard, J., Sugg, D. and Hedderman, C. (1997) *Changing Offenders' Attitudes and Behaviours: What Works?*, Home Office Research Study No. 171. London: TSO.

Von Hirsch, A. (2002) 'Record Enhanced Sentencing in England and Wales: Reflections on the Halliday Report's Proposed Treatment of Prior Convictions', *Punishment and Society*, 4(4): 443–57.

Chapter 7

Sentence management: a new role for the judiciary?

Neil McKittrick and Sue Rex

Introduction

In this chapter we consider the implications of the proposals for a new review function for the courts in the Halliday Report (Home Office 2001), now incorporated in the Criminal Justice Bill 2002, in relation to 'custody-minus' or the new suspended sentence. Before considering the review function, and in order to inform our discussion, we look at the variety of present arrangements by which the sentencer is brought into managing or reviewing sentence. We begin with the power to defer sentence, which will be strengthened under provisions in the Criminal Justice Bill.

Present arrangements

Under the present law, the judge makes an informed sentencing decision in each individual case, influenced by:

- the facts of the allegation, admitted or proved;
- the presence or absence of relevant previous convictions;
- any aggravating features regarding the offence/offender;
- any mitigating features regarding the offence/offender, including remorse;
- any relevant guideline cases or sentencing guidelines;
- any pre-sentence report (PSR), in the adult court prepared by a probation officer, or medical/psychiatric report before the court.

If the decision of the court is that the offender should be sentenced to a custodial sentence, the judge passes sentence and is then *functus officio*. Except in the case of life sentences, where the judge may make a recommendation as to how long the offender serves in prison before his release, the judge has no further role to play in the matter. The sentence is administered by the prison service and in some cases, and later, by the Parole Board. If the decision of the court is that the offence is serious enough for a community penalty, the judge, on making the order, hands over the administration of the sentence to the relevant agency – the probation service, or the curfew order ('tagging') service provider. Implicit in this handover is the full management of the sentence, including the decision whether or not to bring enforcement action.

There are nonetheless a number of circumstances in which the judge may continue to be involved in the case. One is by asking for a progress report as to how the particular form of community penalty is working. Judges are encouraged to make a sparing use of this power. However, it can be of value where a judge has taken a particular interest in the offence or the background or plight of the offender, or, perhaps, where there is a chance that the offender will comply with what might have been a particularly imaginative community disposal.

Deferment of sentence

Another way in which a judge can retain an interest in the case, at least for a limited period, is by deferment of sentence, which gives the judge some scope to manage sentences by setting targets for offenders (though not as part of the sentence).[1] There are strict restrictions on the use of this power. First, sentence can only be deferred for a maximum of six months. Second, there must be clear reasons or 'goals' behind any decision to defer, which should be spelled out to the defendant in plain English. Third, the consent of the defendant is required before the power can be used. It emphatically may not be used because a court 'does not know what to do', in other words to put off what may be a tricky sentencing decision.

There can be no doubt that this power is greatly underused. It is not clear whether that is because of the restrictions on its application or because there is a natural wish on the part of the court and the defendant to deal with the case and get it out of the way. The court may well wish to 'grasp the nettle', even when the sentencing decision is problematical, and the defendant may wish to know his or her fate. It is a commonly held belief that the defendant always wishes to 'put off the evil day', but that is by no means always so. The interests of the victim must also be considered, but at this juncture seldom are. When the power to defer is used at present, the decision to defer is almost always 'defendant related', in the sense that he or she is obliged to refrain from some activity or perform some task to meet the goals laid down by the court. Such an activity or task, if performed, may well prevent offending generally and therefore benefit the wider community. The defendant may be required to attend a probation course on some relevant subject, or drink or drug counselling. Compliance or substantial compliance with such a goal will lead to a court taking a more lenient view of the offence than might otherwise be the case. That the power to defer should usually only be exercised to meet what might be termed the defendant's needs is perhaps hardly surprising. Deferment as an option for sentencers does not usually come from the court itself, but is identified (often with appropriate goals) by a probation officer in a pre-sentence report, and sometimes by defence counsel/solicitor. As will be seen, there is no reason why deferment has to be exclusively (or even mainly) a 'defendant-related power'. It could be used, for example, to develop victim empathy and demonstrate remorse.

The report of the Review of the Sentencing Framework in England and Wales – widely known as the Halliday Report (Home Office 2001) - certainly saw greater potential in the power to defer sentence, recommending:

> A new interim review order should be created, enabling deferral of sentences to be strengthened with proper safeguards.
>
> (Recommendation 32)

This recommendation was accepted (Home Office 2002), and incorporated in the Criminal Justice Bill (albeit without the new terminology). The aim of the strengthened power to defer sentence is to enable sentencers to request additional undertakings and give the probation service a more active role in monitoring compliance and reporting back to the sentencing court. As now, the defendant must consent and sentence can be deferred for a fixed period of no more than six months, during which he or she undertakes to perform specified voluntary commitments, such as:

- reparation;
- voluntary attendance at drug/alcohol treatment programmes;
- participation in restorative justice schemes.

We would argue that any exercise of this extended power must be careful. The goals set may be demanding, but must not be Draconian. They must be capable of fulfilment by the defendant within the appropriate timescale with all the limitations in terms of skills and commitment that he or she may have. He or she must not be given such difficult tasks as to be 'set up to fail', though there is no evidence to suggest this occurs under the current power. Moreover, the goals must be explained to him or her clearly, so that an informed consent to defer must be obtained. Currently, the goals are noted on the court record. In many courts a written copy of the defendant's obligations are given or sent to him or her. The defendant knows precisely where he or she stands and knows the period of commitment. This allows for *finality* in the sentencing process – a time at which sentence is pronounced, and that can be identified as the sentence of the court for the crime committed. Finality is of benefit to the community at large. There must be clarity and finality in the judicial process rather than the risk of vagueness and opacity if proceedings are seen to continue without apparent end.

The suggestion (Home Office 2001) that commitments under the strengthened power might include reparation or participation in restorative justice schemes raises the possibility of one imaginative development of the power. (Here, our view is fortified by the recommendation in Lord Justice Auld's (2001) review of the Criminal Courts in England and Wales for the 'development and implementation of a national strategy to ensure consistent, appropriate and effective use of Restorative Justice techniques across England and Wales'.) That is, to use the order not only to deal with the defendant's 'problems' (the alcoholism, homelessness or drug addiction which has led him or her into crime) but as a vehicle to test his or her remorse.

Defendants who plead guilty promptly to a criminal charge are entitled to a discount off their sentence, often of about one-third. They know this. They are certainly advised of it by counsel. Many defendants are genuinely remorseful, certainly for themselves in that they wish that they had never got involved but also for the victim of their crime. Often counsel will express the defendant's desire to compensate the victim, but invariably no money is available that day. That position must be viewed uncritically because cases are now coming before courts very much more quickly than before and many defendants are of limited means. It is now not uncommon for a defendant to be before the court to answer the charge of assault or criminal damage within a day or two of the offence occurring. Very often the court will dispose of the case then and there, and that disposal will include a compensation order for the damage caused or the pain and suffering inflicted as a result of the crime. Owing to the defendant's limited means, a small weekly payment (perhaps no more than £5) can go towards the payment. Even if payments are regular – and the chances are the enthusiasm will wear off – it may take two years or more for the victim to be compensated. It is often an ineffectual power, 'wooden' in its effect on both the defendant and the victim. From time to time, there has been the interesting debate as to whether the victim should be paid compensation forthwith by the court from fine income, which is then recovered from the defendant.

Could the power to defer be used to test a plea that the defendant is remorseful? Within a certain period, he or she is expected to save up £x towards a likely compensation order or to do a certain number of tasks as reparation for his or her crime. This would have the benefit of being monitored by the probation service straightforwardly, and would come, as in all instances of deferment, with the implicit promise that a more lenient sentence would be passed if the goal or goals were substantially met. It would also expose the important difference between expressions of remorse, however sincere, and proof positive.

Enforcing community orders

One means by which the sentencer can play a role following sentencing is in dealing with breaches of a community order. The expectations upon the probation service in enforcing a requirement of a community order are laid down in National Standards, so that only one warning following an unacceptable failure to comply may be given within any 12-month period. Upon a second unacceptable failure, breach action must be taken within ten working days (Home Office 2000).

When breach action is brought, the court's powers (on admission of proof) are to be found in the Criminal Justice Act 1991 (Schedule 2, para. 3) and the Powers of Criminal Courts (Sentencing) Act 2000 (Schedule 3, para. 5). These include:

(a) imposing a fine on the offender of not more than £1,000;

(b) making a community service order (now a community punishment order);

(c) under certain circumstances, making an attendance centre order;

(d) where the relevant order was made by a magistrates' court, it may revoke the order and deal with the offender for the offence in respect of which the order was made, as if he or she had just been convicted by the court of the offence.

The Criminal Justice and Court Services Act 2000 (section 53) makes important changes to these powers. Where an offender is judged to have failed to comply with a requirement of a community order the court is required to impose a sentence of imprisonment if the offender is aged 18 or over unless it believes that:

(a) the offender is likely to comply with the remaining requirements of the order; or

(b) the exceptional circumstances of the case justify not imposing a sentence of imprisonment (analogous to the power to suspend a custodial term).

These powers will change again under Schedule 7 to the Criminal Justice Bill, which will require the court to do one of the following:

(a) amend the community order to impose a more onerous requirement (though not to increase its overall length);[2]

(b) revoke the order and sentence the offender afresh; or

(c) in the case of wilful and persistent failure to comply on the part of someone aged 18 or older, impose a custodial sentence not exceeding 51 weeks, even if the original offence is not imprisonable.

Even under these new powers, if the (enlarged) community sentence is allowed to continue, the judge (again) has no say in the enforcement process. The only way he or she might informally retain some control of performance is to adjourn the enforcement proceedings and at the same time set specific targets. For example, suppose an offender is in breach of a CPO for 60 hours, and has performed 40 hours satisfactorily but has repeatedly failed to turn up for work subsequently and has no reasonable excuse. As an alternative to proceeding to a determination of the enforcement action, the judge may decide to adjourn the proceedings for, say, a month and tell the offender that he or she is required to complete the balance of the order within that period. If that goal is met, the CS organiser might decide to withdraw the proceedings, but if they proceed the court will dispose of them in a lenient way. The object of the adjournment – the completion of the order – has been met. If the offender fails to comply with the expectation of the court during the adjournment, 'the deal is off' and the court retains all its options for dealing with the breach.

Extending judicial powers: drug treatment and testing

There have been important recent developments or proposals to strengthen sentencers' powers. First, the range of community orders to which offenders can be sentenced has been extended significantly.[3] Second, greater flexibility is emerging in sentencers' ability to combine or mix varying restrictions, for example through extending the range of requirements that can be included in a community rehabilitation order (CRO).

Furthermore, a new role for the court in managing the sentencing was introduced under the Crime and Disorder Act 1998, with the drug treatment and testing order (DTTO). It is helpful to summarise early experience with this new order.

DTTOs can be given for between six months and three years and are not expected to be common. They are intended for serious drug misusers to reduce the amount of crime committed to fund a drug habit. Offenders are required to undergo treatment and submit themselves to drug testing at specified intervals. Crucially for the purposes of the current discussion, there are regular court reviews to monitor progress. The order has now been introduced on a national basis following pilots in Croydon, Gloucestershire and Liverpool between October 1998 and March 2000. So, what was the experience of the pilots?

An evaluation by South Bank University (Turnbull *et al* 2000) found as follows:

- Following a slow start, take-up increased as the pilots established themselves, so that 210 orders were made by the end of the evaluation – nearly three-quarters of offenders recommended to the court for an order.

- There were indications of reduced drug use by offenders subject to orders: the average weekly expenditure reported by 132 interviewed offenders fell from £400 to £25 within the first few weeks of the order; in many cases these reductions were sustained over time and accompanied by reduced criminal activity. Despite such results, the proportion of positive urine tests exceeded 40 per cent for both opiates and crack/cocaine.

- The review process by the court was welcomed by staff and offenders as making a positive contribution to treatment. In Liverpool, the work was shared by two stipendiary magistrates, with the result that four out of five reviews was heard by the original sentencer. For practical reasons, this was achieved only in a third of Croydon cases and a fifth of Gloucestershire cases. It seemed valuable to get the original sentencer to take part in the first and subsequent reviews.

- Frequency of testing, and responses to failed tests, varied between the three sites. Gloucestershire imposed the strictest requirements and experienced the highest revocation rate – offenders were expected to be drug-free within six weeks and the occasional lapse was tolerated (Home Office guidance suggested that a second failed test should lead to formal consideration of breach action). Croydon and Liverpool expected progress towards becoming drug free but not within a specified period of time, and treatment usually continued where tests were positive provided the offender was making progress in addressing his/her drug problem.

It is worth saying more about the experience of court reviews in Liverpool, where over 80 per cent of reviews were held by the original sentencer. Here, the DTTO team negotiated with the magistrates' court that there should be a fortnightly afternoon court session dedicated to reviews. Both the team and the two magistrates who took on this work found that the clear oversight of an individual case and a growing relationship between the drug-using offender and sentencers seemed to be effective both in reinforcing positive progress and in swiftly addressing problems. Problems were experienced when an offender who had mainly appeared before one magistrate perceived the other to be acting differently, and the magistrates sometimes found it difficult to maintain a high level of engagement if they were dealing with a large number of cases in a single afternoon.

Sentence management and review

Under present arrangements, as described above, the judge passes sentence on an offender and then ceases to have any further input into the implementation of the sentence. He or she may be asked to revoke a community punishment order or a community rehabilitation order on the grounds of good progress. He or she may be asked to deal with breach proceedings where an offender is alleged to have failed to comply with some form of community penalty. Is there an argument for developing the role of the court (magistrates as well as judges) to monitor progress of orders, and perhaps use a system of 'carrots and sticks' to reward progress and punish failure? At present, the court is purely *reactive*. Should the court be proactive, an engine for not only dealing with the specific components of sentence but responsible for ensuring they work?

A first, tentative step has been taken with the comparatively new drug treatment and testing orders, as described above. It is too early to say whether regular review hearings, with offenders coming back before (ideally) the same judge sometimes as frequently as once a month, offer any significant improvement over the traditional model under which the order would be made after the court had considered a pre-sentence report, and the court would only see the case again if there was an application to revoke on the basis of the offender's good progress or if he or she was alleged to be in breach of the order. Certainly, it is expensive in terms of the resources of court time. On the other hand, it does give the opportunity for the court, as a representative of the community, to articulate pleasure at an offender's good progress, a not insignificant benefit especially in a section of the community that may often see itself as excluded. Whether this aspect should go as far as the issue of scrolls or certificates to recognise success (in some cases the only success that some offenders have ever achieved) is open to doubt. It would be interesting to see it tried in this country to assess if it is worthwhile.

Perhaps the most radical aspect of *Making Punishments Work* (Home Office 2001) actually lies in its proposals for a new review function for the courts:

> Courts should develop and provide a new 'sentence review' capacity which would deal with breaches of community sentences, hear appeals against recall to prison, authorise pre-release plans for offenders on release from custody and review progress during community sentences and the community part of custodial sentences.
>
> (Recommendation 40)

These are uncharted waters for the courts, which currently have no input into the content of any community-based part of a custodial sentence. The (unspoken) view is presumably that that is a matter best left in the hands of the relevant professionals who have the skills to make that decision. There is a vague corollary with the court's role in approving a care plan in care proceedings. The court does not make the plan, but it may well listen to objections to it and decide whether it is fit for the purpose or whether it is objectionable and should go back to the local authority for reconsideration. In those proceedings, it must be assumed that all parties are represented, and all may have their views to articulate.

No doubt in recognition of the novelty (and possible expense) of introducing a sweeping 'review function', the Home Office (2002) has restricted court review of sentence progress initially to custody minus (the suspended sentence), as well as retaining it for drug treatment and testing under the drug rehabilitation requirement.[4] A related Halliday proposal that the Home Office has accepted is to replace the various community orders with a single generic community sentence containing any of the requirements currently available (according to the Home Office (2002), a 'customised' sentence enabling sentencers to tailor the sentence to the needs of a particular case). So what is the case for giving sentencers a role in the management of a sentence?

The case for change

Contemplation of change to the current arrangements raises the following considerations:

- whether the present division of responsibility between the judiciary and the enforcing agencies should remain unaltered, but perhaps with the expectation that judges will be more willing to stipulate what conditions/work/expectations/treatment they expect to be included in a customised penalty;

- whether the focus of accountability for the success/failure of community penalties should move from the enforcing agencies to the judiciary. If so, what that would mean in practice?

- whether those accountable for the enforcement of orders should have greater discretion to reward progress as well as punish failure;

- whether all sentencing of a custodial nature should, in fact, be 'seamless', i.e. should move through custodial to community phases and be supervised by a judge, presumably the sentencing judge;

- the likelihood that the resources required for imaginative sentencing and effective work in the community will be made available;

- any case for change must be scrutinised against non-discriminatory provision to take account of race, religious, gender and disability issues.

There is also the fundamental question of the proper route by which sentencers should be accountable – and to whom – for their decisions. This raises constitutional considerations relating to the separation of power (judicial and executive), to which we now turn.

Accountabilities and the separation of powers

There is a developing clamour for the judiciary to become accountable, ranging from the proposal that judges should spell out the component parts of a sentence to the suggestion that judges should be made responsible to some other body/agency for the 'success' or 'failure' of their decisions. However, a belief that the judiciary is not accountable now is misconceived. Judges are accountable to the Lord Chancellor, and it is possible for judges to be removed under certain circumstances. For example, a district judge (magistrates' courts) may be removed from office by the Lord Chancellor on the grounds of incapacity or misbehaviour (see section 10A(3), Justice of the Peace Act 1997, as substituted by section 78, Access to Justice Act 1999).

Another route through which judges are accountable, for all individual decisions, is the appellate system. This provides rights of appeal against the grant and refusal of bail, and against conviction and sentence, by both the prosecution and defence. Procedural irregularities can be corrected on appeal under the developing doctrine of judicial review – the more so with arguments under the Human Rights Act 1998 – and accountability for a particular interpretation of the law can be challenged by an application by 'a person aggrieved' for a case stated. In all these cases, accountability is guaranteed under the law, and is underwritten at each level because the proceedings are themselves open to public scrutiny. It is only in small categories of sensitive cases, perhaps most typically those involving young people, that the media are limited in what they may report.

Nor do sentencers have an entirely free hand in sentencing decisions. The Court of Appeal provides starting points through its sentencing guideline judgments, an arrangement that will be strengthened when a Sentencing Guidelines Council, chaired by the Lord Chief Justice, is established under provisions in the Criminal Justice Bill (clauses 160–6). Sentencing guidelines produced by the Council will apply to all criminal courts and provide common starting points in approaching sentence that courts will be obliged to take into account. The Council will be required to consult the Home Secretary on its draft guidelines and submit an annual report for ministers to lay before Parliament.

Without entering into a debate about whether it would be proper or useful to introduce judicial 'performance indicators', a systematic and thorough method of judicial training enables the judiciary to keep up to date with trends in penology, sentence outcomes and the cost of sentencing. This has the added virtue of promoting consistency of approach to common problems, including but not exclusively those of sentencing. The establishment of the Judicial Studies Board and the manner in which it has developed has been a significant factor in keeping the judiciary abreast of new developments in the law, for example the extensive programme of training before the implementation of the Human Rights Act 1998. The Board is an independent body and was originally conceived as being run by 'judges for judges', but its courses are far from limited in scope or insulated from outside influence. The curriculum has been extended to cover almost every aspect of judicial training and a wide range of subjects. These compulsory courses demonstrate that it is possible to influence judicial thinking by the provision of written materials and presentations on current trends, new legislation, sentencing costs and outcomes, aided by discussion groups and residential and non-residential seminars.

The Home Office and ACOP have recently placed considerable priority upon the enforcement of community orders, and improvements in compliance with requirements have been measured (see Hedderman and Hearden 2001). However, the adequacy of the current arrangements for the supervision of offenders in the community remains controversial. The probation service came in for criticism in early 2001, not only for the number of serious offences committed by offenders who were under its supervision, but for 'under-reporting' in which it was found that some probation areas failed to tell the Home Office about offenders charged with serious offences (see *The Times*, 12 February 2001). This led an editorial in the same edition to declare:

> Those who carry such responsibility for public safety have a duty to supply the tools by which their success might objectively be judged. The general reticence and reluctance from the probation service creates profound misgivings. The excuses proferred by chief officers – ignorance of the guidelines or unspecified 'misunderstandings' – are patently unacceptable. At best they suggest a lackadaisical attitude ill-befitting any part of the criminal justice

system. At worst they look like an entirely self-motivated cooking of the books.

In considering whether the probation service should retain responsibility for the supervision and enforcement of community orders and the extent to which the exercise of those responsibilities might be overseen by the courts, it is necessary to bear in mind its existing range of accountabilities – to the Home Office (through Key Performance Indicators (KPIs) and National Standards), to HM Probation Inspectorate with its programme of local and thematic inspections, and locally through probation boards. Another consideration is the extent to which it is desirable to maintain a distinction between the judiciary and the executive (the judge and the enforcing agency), and the impact that implicating a judge in the management and enforcement of a community order would have on his or her capacity for impartial judgment.

The judge as reviewer?

An important practical question is how the review function is intended to operate – whether this will be in such a way as to secure the intended benefits. According to the Criminal Justice Bill, it is open to a court making a suspended sentence order (or a drug rehabilitation requirement) to provide for each review to be undertaken at a court hearing. However, it is not entirely clear in what circumstances a hearing will be considered appropriate (as opposed to a paper-based review), beyond the fact that there must be at least one hearing in the case of a drug treatment and testing requirement exceeding twelve months. Addressing these issues in Chapter 7, the Halliday Report (Home Office 2001) indicated that whether or not there was to be a hearing would depend on the particular function the court was performing in its review capacity. Full hearings, with representation and eligibility for legal aid, were envisaged only when new restrictions on liberty were possible. Examples included resentencing on failure of a community sentence, dealing with appeals against recall to prison and increasing the intensity of the community part of a custodial sentence. Reviews of a pre-release package would be paper-based (with hearings via a TV link), as would progress under a community sentence (or under the community part of a custodial sentence) where the expected outcome was a reduction in the intensity of sentence.

Whether a paper-based review will achieve much in terms of helping to engage and motivate the offender is questionable. The benefits of the drug treatment and testing procedures are surely partly that they bring the offender into face-to-face contact with the judge or magistrate during the course of the sentence. Thus they strengthen the links between the judicial and the administrative elements of the sentence (see Turnbull *et al* 2000). 'Rewarding' the offender who is making good progress in a community order or under a suspended sentence through lifting some of its penal measures (e.g. discounting a certain number of hours of compulsory work) may well motivate him or her. However, there is a danger that it will lose some of its impact – and become a routine expectation – if not accompanied by a court appearance.

Another important question is what the role of the judge is to be. Is the judge to be a contributor to the process, for which role he or she may be singularly ill-equipped, or is the judge there to arbitrate on the arguments and suggestions put forward by others? In our view, the latter is the traditional role of the judge. He or she should be a person who listens carefully to what is said, hears all sides, may make a measured but limited contribution him or herself and then adjudicates. Any proposal that the judge should him or herself 'enter the arena' in a particular case would be potentially compromising to his or her independence in any future dealings he or she may have with the case. This should not imply in any sense that the judge should be uninterested in playing his or her part to ensure that *generally* facilities exist to maximise the chances of success of this important stage of the process, such as by lending support to ensure that there are suitable accredited courses available in the locality and by visiting and supporting them and their providers generally. That same judge may have to deal, fairly and impartially, with some form of breach proceedings or an application for recall or revocation (at any rate some application requiring use of judicial powers). If he or she has already taken a proactive part in the future management of the case, then such impartiality is in danger, perhaps of not being actually compromised, but at the very least of being seen to be compromised.

Conclusion

The heart of the Halliday proposals is a change to the role of the judge in the criminal courts. In an era of managerialism, it is argued that the judge should develop from being an impartial arbiter making decisions on evidence or submissions and on material in reports prepared by professionals in their field to become a proactive 'hands-on' figure, specifying particular conditions here, accredited courses there and review hearings everywhere. In a criminal justice system, often seen as out of tune with the needs and wishes of society generally, the development of a 'manager culture' and accountability may have some superficial attractions. But if the judge is to become sentence manager, who in those cases where management proves unsuccessful will discharge the role of the judge? The judge cannot easily fulfil both roles. Lord Devlin stressed that the role of judges was as 'keepers of the law' and as 'arbiters between the government and the governed'. These proposals blur the judicial and the executive functions and reinvent the judge as a manager. They must have significant implications for the judicial role and quite what sort of 'animal' judges might become in the future. In the light of these larger implications, it is to be welcomed that the Criminal Justice Bill has adopted the relatively cautious stance of applying Halliday's proposals only to the suspended sentence for the time being. This will allow a period of careful testing and reflection before any further enlargement of the judicial role, perhaps along the lines of drug courts and re-entry courts as in the very different US jurisdiction.

Notes

1. See section 1, Powers of Criminal Courts (Sentencing) Act 2000.
2. The Criminal Justice Bill replaces the different community orders with a generic 'community order' comprising one or more of a wide range of requirements, for example: unpaid work; a programme or activity; a curfew or exclusion; residence; mental health, alcohol or drug treatment (clause 170).
3. The Criminal Justice Act 1991 introduced the combination and curfew orders; the Crime and Disorder Act 1998, the drug treatment and testing order and, for young offenders, the reparation order and the action plan order. The Criminal Justice and Court Services Act 2000 added the exclusion order (section 46) and drug abstinence order (section 47), and enabled a community rehabilitation order (previously a probation order) to include additional requirements relating to drug abstinence (section 49), curfew (section 50) and exclusion (section 51).
4. See clause 173 of the Criminal Justice Bill; in addition, clause 161 gives the Home Secretary power to provide for the court review of community orders.

References

Auld, Lord Justice (2001) *Report on the Review of the Criminal Courts of England and Wales* (Auld Report). London: TSO.

Hedderman, C. and Hearden, I. (2001) *Setting New Standards for Enforcement: The Third ACOP Audit*. London: South Bank University and Association of Chief Officers of Probation.

Home Office (2000) *National Standards for the Supervision of Offenders in the Community*. London: Home Office.

Home Office (2001) *Making Punishments Work*. London: TSO.

Home Office (2002) *Justice For All*, CM 5563. London: TSO.

Turnbull, P. J., McSweeney, T., Webster, R., Edmunds, M. and Hough, M. (2000) *Drug Treatment and Testing Orders: Final Evaluation Report*, Home Office Research Study No. 212. London: Home Office.

Chapter 8

Is sentencing in England and Wales institutionally racist?

Amanda Matravers and Michael Tonry

Criminal justice agencies are queuing up to accuse themselves of treating minority suspects and offenders unfairly. Some see progress in the willingness of heads of public institutions to declare their organisations 'institutionally racist'. Notable converts include Chief Constable John Newing, then President of the Association of Chief Police Officers; David Calvert Smith, Director of Public Prosecutions; and Martin Narey, then Director General of the Prison Service. Beyond the criminal justice system, the English theatre sector has labelled itself institutionally racist (Brown *et al* 2001).[1] These declarations follow Sir William Macpherson's controversial redefinition of the term, in his report on the death of black teenager Stephen Lawrence, to include unwitting discrimination on the part of organisations (Macpherson 1999).

The judiciary, by contrast, remains wedded to notions of 'racism' and 'discrimination' that limit the reach of those terms to purposeful, knowing or reckless behaviours (Faulkner 2002). This is the line taken by the Halliday Report on the Sentencing Framework for England and Wales (Home Office 2001), which expresses its disapproval of purposive 'improper discrimination' and urges that 'the general principle applying to levels of punishment should be one of equal treatment, regardless of cultural, religious, or ethnic background' (2001: 16).

We deal in this chapter with hard problems relating to English sentencing and sentencing policy. Neither 'institutional racism' nor the traditional conception of invidious racism that governs discussions of sentencing tackles the core issues of disparate outcomes and differential treatment of members of racial and ethnic minorities. We are mostly concerned with disparities that affect black[2] people because they are particularly acute and different from the problems experienced by other minority ethnic groups. These problems will not be ameliorated through accusations and the use of polemical phrases like institutional racism and positive discrimination, but through a comprehensive refashioning of policies and practices that produce unwarranted disparities.

The chapter is divided into three sections. In the first section we focus on institutional racism and explain why the use of this label is of limited help in efforts to understand and alter policies and practices that disadvantage black people. In the second, we discuss racial disparities in sentencing and, Halliday's subject, sentencing policy.

In the final section we present a set of proposals for reducing unwanted disparities and developing policies that do less damage to members of ethnic minority groups. Some of these call for disparity audits of proposed new policies and of existing practices; the aim is to compel policy-makers to think about the effects of policies on different groups and to force them to make open and deliberate decisions that take predicted or existing disparities into account. Another calls for a substantial reduction in sentence lengths and prison populations. Black people are heavily over-represented in the prison population and a substantial drop would benefit them disproportionately. Finally, we propose a renewed and proactive commitment to the diversity training and positive action programmes that are already in train. Although their benefits are occasionally derided, there is much to be gained from genuine and thoughtfully conceived attempts to promote understanding of diversity issues and to increase the employment and promotion of ethnic minority people within the criminal justice system.

I. Institutional racism

In this section we work through some of the major policy literature on institutional racism in the criminal justice system of England and Wales to suggest that, as the term is commonly used, sentencing and the courts are indeed 'institutionally racist'. We also suggest that this is an unhelpful conclusion that does not take us any closer to a solution to the complex problem of racial disparities in sentencing.

A fundamental difficulty with terms such as 'racism' is that they are polar words, conversation stoppers rather than conversation starters. To say that someone is racist, fascist, bigoted, sexist or homophobic is to accuse them of something hateful. Not surprisingly, people accused of acting hatefully become defensive, and often they respond by taking offence, stalking away or vehemently denying the accusation.

In many cases, of course, the use of polar words is intentional, designed to unmask a racist or a bigot with the aim of curtailing their offensive practices and behaviours. In such cases, defensive behaviour is only to be expected. People associated with organisations decreed to be 'institutionally racist' on the other hand are uncertain of what they are being accused: whether they are being identified as personally racist, or whether the accusation refers to some more complex and ambiguous process wherein they are identified with but not responsible for racism within their organisation. Their responses range accordingly from acceptance through bewilderment, anger and disbelief (see, for example, the submissions of Sir Paul Condon, Commissioner of the Metropolitan Police, to the Lawrence Inquiry – Macpherson 1999: chapter 6).

The phrase 'institutional racism' evokes strong and polarised opinions. That is why we dislike and distrust it. The use of polar words that make people defensive is not a good way to manage a conversation about a difficult subject. A more productive way is to try to reach agreement that a problem exists, to search for evidence of its causes and extent, and then to search for strategies to solve or ameliorate it. This is particularly true with regard to racial disparities in the courts and in prisons. There is little credible evidence that sentencing or imprisonment disparities are solely or largely the product of racial bias or enmity or ill-will toward ethnic minority offenders (Reiner 1993; Smith 1997; Bowling and Phillips 2001). That being so, searching out and removing racist judges and other officials, or eliminating policies that intentionally discriminate, will not do much to reduce disparities. Neither will focusing the debate on the presence or absence of institutional racism.

The way in which criminal justice and other organisations have picked up the term 'institutional racism' and run with it might suggest that it leaves little room for ambiguity. This is not the case. Even Sir William Macpherson, who is regularly (though erroneously) credited with its creation, admitted prior to the publication of his eponymous report that he had struggled to define the concept. The definition on which he settled is becoming one of the most quoted passages in the criminal justice literature:

> The collective failure of an organisation to provide an appropriate and professional service to people because of their colour, culture or ethnic origin. It can be seen or detected in processes, attitudes and behaviour which amount to discrimination through unwitting prejudice, ignorance, thoughtlessness and racist stereotyping which disadvantage minority ethnic people.
>
> (Macpherson 1999: 28, 6.34)

Macpherson's definition is artless, almost incoherent. 'Racist stereotyping' is surely racist per se; the hard problem is stereotyping which, though not ill-motivated, results in differential treatment of ethnic minority offenders. Likewise, prejudice, if 'unwitting', can't be prejudice in a pejorative sense. We take Macpherson's statement to be an effort to refer to disadvantaging practices that are not consciously ill-motivated: a serious problem. However, the use of a polar word in this debate ensures that substantive issue about the source of racial disparities continues to be subsumed by arguments over semantics. The emotive nature of the phrase 'institutional racism' seems to compel people to return to it like the archetypal criminal to the scene of the crime, even though they know that to do so will prove counterproductive at the very least. During a recent speech delivered to black and Asian Home Office employees, the Home Secretary rekindled the debate by departing from his script to criticise the concept of institutional racism for 'missing the point'. This gave rise to a welter of newspaper headlines about 'Blunkett's blunder' as well as several feature articles discoursing upon the derivation and relevance of institutional racism. Ironically – if unsurprisingly – the hacks were not falling over themselves to discuss the real topic of the speech, which was the success of the Home Office in meeting ethnic minority recruitment targets (*The Guardian*, 15 January 2003). In a similar way, the conclusions reached by the 320-page report of the Commission for a Multi-Ethnic Britain (Parekh 2000) were telescoped into a media-fuelled debate about the racially-loaded nature of the term 'British' (see Jasper 2003).

In its original form, the term – as coined by US black power activists Stokely Carmichael and Charles V. Hamilton in 1967 – referred to two forms of racism, overt and covert. While one involved individual acts of racism by whites on blacks, the other involved acts by the white community on the black community. Crucially, however, both forms involve deliberate exclusion on the grounds of race with the purpose of subjugation (Carmichael and Hamilton 1967). Much of the current confusion arises from the assumption (possibly shared and certainly propagated by Macpherson himself) that discrimination within the justice system also takes two forms: namely intentional racism by individuals ('bad apple' racism) and unintended racism by organisations ('institutional' racism). However, Macpherson's much-quoted definition sees institutional racism as a product of 'unwitting prejudice, ignorance, thoughtlessness and racist stereotyping'. There are surely three phenomena to be distinguished here: racism of the overt, intentional, bad apple kind; racism of a less overt but still deliberate kind that results in racist stereotyping; and processes and behaviours that, though not racist in intent, result in differential treatment of members of ethnic minority groups. Whether the third phenomenon may usefully be described as racism of any kind is doubtful.

Unfortunately, most subsequent interpretations follow Macpherson in eliding the latter two phenomena, with counterproductive results. At the individual level, those within institutions may feel personally stigmatised and defensive because it seems that they are themselves being accused of racism. This defensiveness may fuel a 'backlash' like that described by Denman (2001), wherein a group of Crown Prosecution Service Staff anonymously returned a compact disc sent out by the Equal Opportunities Unit on the grounds that it was 'unrequested and unwanted' (p. 97). Another form of 'white backlash' has been associated with recent legislative initiatives focused on racially motivated offending (FitzGerald 2001). Macpherson's criticisms of the police for failing to recognise the impact of less serious crime on minority communities prompted the redefinition of a racist incident as one which is 'perceived to be racist by the victim or any other person'. Recorded racist incidents rose exponentially in the two years following the Macpherson Inquiry (Home Office 2000, 2002a). While there are many ways of interpreting these figures (including better recording by the police), the increase in the proportion of victims of racist incidents recorded as white by the Metropolitan Police supports explanations that identify an element of 'white backlash', in which white crime victims (possibly with the collusion of some police officers) perversely identify a racial motivation for offences perpetrated by black offenders (FitzGerald 1999 2001; HMIC 2000; see also Burney and Rose 2002).

Alternatively, the institutional racism label may encourage the blameless and the 'bad apples' alike to feel exonerated, since the problem is anonymous and impersonal, within the system rather than within them. In addition to fostering racist attitudes and inertia within institutions, the institutionally racist label is bound to dent the confidence of those on the outside, particularly members of ethnic minorities. Insiders and outsiders alike may regard the label as permanent and feel pessimistic about the possibilities of reform.

The terms of reference for Sylvia Denman's report on race discrimination in the Crown Prosecution Service included an investigation of the extent to which institutional racism exists within the Service (Denman 2001). Denman attempts to shed some light on Macpherson's statement by discerning two distinct strands in his definition:

The first … identifies what may be termed 'systemic factors', which, in their result, produce outcomes in terms of service delivery and employment which are less favourable to one ethnic group than another. The second strand, contained in the reference to 'unwitting prejudice, ignorance, thoughtlessness and racist stereotyping', refers to pervasive, unconscious discrimination on grounds of race.

(p. 91)

In other words, Denman distinguishes two forms of 'racism', neither of which is really racism and which are characterised, unsurprisingly, by their invisibility to those who engage in them. Denman further suggests that institutional racism should be understood not in relation to 'traditional racism' but in contrast to it. The difficulty of accurately conceptualising this version of institutional racism is illustrated by the overlap in examples given by staff in the 'race discrimination' chapter and those given in the 'institutional racism' chapter. Manifestations of institutional racism cited include managers who have reacted dis-missively to ethnic minority staff who participate in race equality initiatives, trivialisation of offensive remarks relating to race and undermining of ethnic minority staff both internally and with outside agencies (pp. 94–5). We cannot be the only readers who find it difficult to 'contrast' such behaviours with racism. In spite of her conclusion that the CPS is institutionally racist, the fundamental elusiveness of the phenomenon is revealed by Denman's comment that managers 'must make an emotional and intellectual leap of faith' in order to understand and combat it within the organisation (p. 95). There is an 'Emperor's new clothes' feel to all this that is underlined when denial by white or black staff that racism is a problem in the CPS is characterised as racism in the one case and false consciousness in the other (p. 97).

Our subject, however, is sentencing and Denman's is primarily employment practices within the CPS. Institutional racism in the context of prosecutorial decisions merits only three pages in a report that runs over one hundred pages. Even in this section, the main evidence for the impact of institutional racism on prosecutorial decision-making rests on guilt by association with the employment practices described in previous sections of the report (see p. 99).

Denman acknowledges the central failing of institutional racism as a concept – namely that it provides no guidance to efforts to ameliorate the unfair treatment of minority ethnic groups – at the outset and in the conclusion of her consideration of its existence within the CPS. In the light of her belief that '[t]here is limited value in seeking to determine whether an organisation such as the CPS is or is not "institutionally racist" (p. 92), it is difficult to understand why she apparently expended so much effort doing precisely this. However, even those who share Denman's reservations about the analytical value of the term, argue for its cathartic effects and see it as a call to action or, in the current phrase, a 'wake-up call' for organisational cultures.

It is certainly possible to see Macpherson's 'institutional racism' as a galvanising concept. In the aftermath of the Stephen Lawrence Inquiry, police acceptance of responsibility at the organisational level opened the door to a wide range of initiatives designed to secure a more accountable and representative police service. Looking beyond the police, the Home Secretary's Action Plan (Home Office 1999) sets out the 'post-Lawrence agenda' for a range of criminal justice agencies.

However, similar initiatives were in train prior to Macpherson (see, for example, HMIC 1997, 1999) and the extent of their debt to the term is unclear. The association of institutional reform with racism has arguably hindered as much as it has helped. The example of the CPS has been given above. The Eclipse Report notes that of 125 theatres invited to a working conference on institutional racism in the theatre sector, fewer than a quarter attended, with the vast majority failing to respond to the invitation (Brown *et al* 2001). This lack of interest in itself would be interpreted according to the Denman formula as evidence of institutional racism, but again this is a tautological conclusion that leads nowhere.

The difference between Macpherson/Denman and Halliday is the difference between differential effects, outcomes or impacts and improper or intentional discrimination. However, these competing definitions are conceptual red herrings, neither of which addresses the problem at issue. The core problem in sentencing and punishment is differential outcomes, which are oversimplistically explained in institutional racism analyses and overlooked by improper discrimination analyses.

Black people in England and Wales are, relative to their numbers in the population, six or seven times more likely to be confined in prison than are whites, and, when charged with crimes, are more likely to be imprisoned and to receive longer sentences (Home Office 2002a). Considerable research effort has been devoted to explaining these differences (e.g. Hood 1992; Reiner 1993; Bowling and Phillips 2001). The explanations generated by empirical research focus on five factors, which for clarity of reference we number: (1) offending patterns;

(2) criminal histories; (3) offender characteristics other than race or ethnicity; (4) case processing variables; and (5) 'racist', as Denman would call it, or 'improper', as Halliday would call it, discrimination.

Among convicted persons in prison, the research evidence on the cause of group differences in imprisonment rates is reasonably clear, consistent and uncontroversial. Findings from Roger Hood's (1992) landmark study of black/white differences in Crown Court sentencing in the Midlands are typical. The overrepresentation of black people in prison is explained in the following way: 70 per cent of the differential resulted from black overrepresentation among persons appearing for sentence (factor 1); 10 per cent was attributable to offence seriousness and criminal history (factors 1 and 2); 13 per cent was attributable to case processing differences (factor 4); and 7 per cent was not explained (factors 3 and 5).

Hood's study is eleven years old, but his findings are not idiosyncratic. Other studies by other researchers in other places using other research designs might differ in detail; however, there is no reason to predict the broad patterns of findings would be substantially different. The likeliest source of different results is what researchers call 'sample selection bias'. This simply means that things that happened earlier in the process may have made black and white offenders appearing for sentence systematically different. If, for example, the less serious robbery cases involving white offenders were handled in the magistrates' courts or diverted from prosecution altogether, the remaining white robbery cases would on average be more serious than the black robbery cases. If data showed that white offenders received harsher sentences than black offenders, without more knowledge we could not know to what extent that resulted from anti-white bias, or from the greater average seriousness of white robberies, or from some combination of both. Alternatively, sample selection bias could produce a misleading finding of no racial difference in sentencing if blacks and whites received comparable average sentences. The data would not reveal that the less serious black robberies were being punished as harshly as the more serious white robberies.

Another form of sample selection bias could exist if police officers didn't arrest whites or observed different practices concerning white arrests. Particularly for more minor crimes, such as some drug-related and public order offences, police discretion could fundamentally skew the apparent relation between offending patterns and arrest/prosecution/conviction/sentencing patterns. Or, as some academics have argued, there may be slight racial differences in case outcomes at each case processing stage, all of which are too subtle or too small to be identified by research on disparities but taken cumulatively they may cause major distortions (see, for example, Bowling and Phillips 2001).

We use Roger Hood's findings here to illustrate a series of analytical problems. Hood found that a number of factors influenced racial differentials. Most are not indicators of 'racial' or 'improper' discrimination as defined above, though they would be tarred with the 'institutional racism' brush if it were applied to sentencing. That is to say, most illustrate systemic effects that disadvantage black defendants.

Factor 1: offences committed (70 per cent of difference)

Hood found that 70 per cent of the imprisonment difference resulted from group differences in convictions. Black arrest rates are higher than those of whites for violent crimes, and violent crimes typically receive harsher penalties than property crimes. This means that blacks will on average receive longer prison sentences than whites because of the mix of offences they commit by comparison with whites. The longer sentences are the result of the application of the sentencing tariff deriving from the decisions of the Court of Appeal. Thus more black people are in prison partly because proportionately more are sentenced for the kinds of offences that customarily receive prison sentences and partly because the sentencing tariff prescribes particularly harsh sentences for offences of which proportionately more black people are convicted. Presumably racial patterns in convictions are well-known to the high judiciary. If so, knowledge that harsh penalties for street robbery, for example, will disproportionately affect black offenders can fairly be imputed to the Court of Appeal.

Factor 2: criminal history (less than 10 per cent of difference)

If black defendants on average have more extensive criminal records than whites, a policy of increasing sentences on account of prior convictions will disproportionately affect black offenders. This is not easy to disentangle because Hood attributes 10 per cent of the difference to offence seriousness, which includes both criminal history and extra-statutory offence seriousness factors. It is clear though that criminal history makes some difference. In so far as blacks as a group have more extensive average criminal histories than do whites as a group, they will to that extent be treated more severely.

Factor 3: offender characteristics (less than 7 per cent of difference)

Hood found that offender characteristics explained 7 per cent of the difference. Bail/remand decisions, by analogy, are often influenced by whether defendants have stable employment, a stable home, a family or an education. At sentencing, offenders who have some positive social links are more likely to be sentenced to community penalties than are offenders who do not. These pro-social factors are less likely to characterise black than white defendants. Sometimes these factors are taken into account in sentencing studies and sometimes they are not. Inevitably, some factors are left out.

Factor 4: case processing variables (13 per cent)

Hood attributes 13 per cent of the differential to the effects of case processing practices, of which the largest part resulted from black defendants' lesser likelihood of pleading guilty and if pleading to do so later in the process. Court of Appeal guidance on sentence discounts for guilty pleas awards a one-third discount for early pleas, lesser discounts for later pleas and no discount when a defendant is convicted at trial.

Factor 5: racial bias (less than 7 per cent)

Hood's residual 7 per cent is often cited as the measure of racial bias, but it is not simply that. It refers to *unexplained variation*, which can include what statisticians call 'noise', or random variations. It can also include the influence of unmeasured but unbiased factors. If, for example, being a primary care provider to children were not included as a variable but was a factor that influenced decisions, it would be part of the unexplained variation. So would systematic bias in decision-making. Taken at face value, Hood's findings suggest that the likely impact of racial bias on imprisonment disparities ranges from no impact to 7 per cent.

As an empirical matter, whatever people may suspect or want to believe, most of the imprisonment disparity affecting black offenders results from group differences in offending. Some is attributable to group differences in social and economic characteristics and criminal histories, some is attributable to the unintended side effects of case processing policies, and some, probably, results from 'improper discrimination'. No credible research or other quantitative evidence exists, however, that convincingly demonstrates that racial bias or enmity is a major factor.

The preceding paragraph dealt with empirical evidence and empirical conclusions. Whether Hood's findings (and similar conclusions reached by other researchers) should be interpreted as evidence that there is little discrimination in sentencing depends on the conception of discrimination that is used. Employing Halliday's notion of purposeful 'improper' discrimination, the evidence suggests there is not much. However, most of Hood's explanatory factors – the sentencing tariff, prior convictions, offender characteristics, case processing variables – could be labelled as institutional racism under the Macpherson/ Denman formulation. Disparities associated with those factors result from 'practices, conditions and norms' that through ignorance or thoughtlessness disadvantage black offenders.

Hood's research makes the 'institutional racism' epithet especially difficult to resist because it so clearly shows the adverse disparate effects on black people of the existing guilty plea discount. No judicial figure from the Lord Chancellor and the Lord Chief Justice down can credibly claim not to know that discounts foreseeably exacerbate imprisonment disparities. The guilty plea discount is a practice known to result in harsher punishments for blacks than for whites, but for reasons that have nothing to do with guilt or innocence or with culpability-linked notions of deserved punishment. That should make it fall squarely into Denman's language: ' "institutional racism" is unconscious or systemic in nature' (p. 93).

Defenders of the courts will no doubt immediately and indignantly deny that contemporary English sentencing practices are institutionally racist and insist that bias is deeply objectionable and, except possibly on the part of rogue or insensitive judges, absent from the courts. Similar claims were made by senior Crown Prosecution Service officials in relation to allegations of institutional racism in CPS promotion, retention and grievance procedures (Denman 2001: 32). As noted above, Denman treats such claims as evidence of psychological denial (pp. 96–8). Presumably critics of the courts would adopt the same stance.

Sleight of hand is the only way English sentencing can escape the indictment of institutional racism. The convention so far has been to apply Halliday's 'improper discrimination' analysis to the courts rather than Denman's 'institutional racism' analysis. It is not obvious, however, why the courts should be judged by one standard and prosecutors, the police service and prisons by another.

So, are the English courts institutionally racist? On Macpherson/ Denman's terms, yes. But this is the wrong answer to the wrong question. The unhelpful nature of the term is the problem rather than the belief that the courts somehow pass the institutional racism test that the police, prisons and prosecutors fail. The concept of institutional racism does not bestow analytical clarity. Rather it gets people's backs up and obscures serious social problems. The racial disparities arising from the guilty plea discount policy are 'systemic' in nature but that does not make them institutionally or any other kind of racist. Disparities point up a serious policy problem that cannot be solved by throwing the word 'racist' at it. The problem is that the undesirable foreseeable disparities are counterbalanced in many people's minds by the need to foster guilty pleas and the common belief that plea discounts are an indispensable means to that end.

In the next section we look at the role of race in individual sentencing decisions. First, though, to show that analyses of these problems are no more tortured in England than elsewhere, we describe Ontario's effort to grapple with the subject. Following allegations of police bias in controversial incidents involving black suspects and white police officers in Toronto, the provincial government appointed the Commission on Systemic Racism (1995). 'Systemic racism' was defined as policies and practices that systematically disadvantaged minority offenders whether or not they were meant to do so. The problem, as in England and all Western countries, is that some minority groups are economically and socially disadvantaged compared with the majority population. As a result they are less likely to be granted bail, more likely to be represented by state-funded lawyers, for those reasons more likely to be convicted, and so forth. All these contingencies, like England's guilty plea discounts, resulted in disparate black/white outcomes. There is no question that, as defined, they meet the systemic racism test. As solutions, the commission proposed the common litany of steadfast opposition to bigotry, sensitisation training for officials, efforts to diversify the professional cadres, and more research.

II. Sentencing

So what can be done to reduce disproportionate imprisonment of black offenders and related appearances of injustice and challenges to the legitimacy of the criminal justice system? There are four sets of possible approaches to the disparity issue. Some relate to sentencing, some to sentencing policy, some to processes and practices that exacerbate disparities, and some to the organisation and operation of the judiciary.

Sentencing policy

Promulgation of meaningful, discretion-reducing presumptive guidelines for sentencing is the most promising way to attack unwarranted disparities. Because sentencing standards in guidelines almost inevitably are based primarily on conviction offences and some measure of prior convictions, they reduce the latitude for judges consciously or unconsciously to base sentences on other factors that may be related to or correlated with race. Every evaluation of American systems of presumptive guidelines has shown that racial and gender disparities were reduced after guidelines took effect (Tonry 1996: chapter 2).

Those tasked with the development of guidelines must confront a wide range of issues that impinge on racial disparities.

Sentence severity

The most effective way to reduce minority imprisonment would be to reduce the use of imprisonment overall. No politically saleable reform proposals for tinkering with sentencing criteria will have dramatic effects on the six to seven times over-representation of black offenders in prison. If, however, the prison population were reduced by half, or all prison sentence lengths were reduced by half, black people in absolute terms would benefit. From the perspective of blacks as a group there would be substantially greater benefit if absolute levels of imprisonment were halved, even if the six to seven times disproportion continued, than if the prison population stayed where it is or went up and the rate of disproportion declined somewhat.

Table 8.1 shows the hypothetical numbers. If the ratio were reduced from seven- to six-to-one, but levels of imprisonment continued as they now are, the black imprisonment rate would fall by 80 per 100,000 people. If the ratio remained the same, but the number of prisoners was halved, the black imprisonment rate would fall by 280 per 100,000. Three-and-a-half times more black people would be spared imprisonment if the total prison population were halved than if the ratio of disproportion were reduced by 14 per cent, which is on the high side of what is likely.

Race

It goes without saying that race itself should not be a criterion in sentencing. It may, however, be instructive to look at the way some of

Table 8.1 Hypothetical disparity in incarceration rates by ethnicity

	Black	White	Ratio
Imprisonment rate (assumed)	560	80	7:1
Imprisonment rate if less disparity	480	80	6:1
Reduction in prison per 100,000	80	0	
Imprisonment rate (assumed)	560	80	7:1
Imprisonment halved	280	40	7.1
Reduction in prison per 100,000	280	40	

these dilemmas have played out in relation to gender, where the correct decision is not so obvious. Most empirical analyses (in a number of countries including England) of the role of gender in sentencing have concluded that, controlling for crime and criminal record, women are less likely than men to be sentenced to imprisonment, are likely to receive shorter prison sentences and are more likely to be sentenced to community penalties (Home Office 2002b). The sentencing policy problem is that it is everywhere assumed that gender per se is not a legitimate criterion in sentencing. Policy-makers must decide to sentence men like women, sentence women like men or use the combined male/female averages as the basis for guidelines for everyone. We know of no jurisdiction anywhere that has reduced sentences to female average levels.

The issue of black defendants is different. Since there is evidence that black people are sentenced more severely than whites, setting guidelines on the basis of white or average levels should reduce sentences for black offenders.

Another possibility that we do not propose but raise for the purposes of analysis is the use of race as a mitigating circumstance. Black people could, for example, be given a one-third discount on sentence. This may seem an outlandish suggestion, but something like it is discussed and even openly applied to aboriginal offenders in parts of Australia (Roberts and Doob 1997) and Canada (Broadhurst 1997).

Section 718.2(e) of the Canadian Criminal Code, for example, provides: '[A]ll available sanctions other than imprisonment that are reasonable in the circumstances should be considered for all offenders, with particular attention to the circumstances of aboriginal offenders.' There is an equivalent section in the Youth Criminal Justice Act (which took effect on 1 April 2003).

One rationale for such policies is that aborigines have shorter life expectancies than non-aborigines and thus a specific term of imprisonment represents a greater deprivation of liberty. Another rationale is that aborigines are disproportionately from economically and socially disadvantaged backgrounds that make crime a more difficult option to resist. A discount is conceived as an act of remedial social justice that takes account of disadvantage.

An explicit race discount is not realistic in England for a variety of reasons. The most important is the implication it would carry that minority offenders are less morally autonomous or responsible than whites and therefore are less deserving of punishment. That would be a morally intolerable implication and would be deeply stigmatising. A second objection is social – such a policy would elicit widespread resentment among the majority population and increase the likelihood of a 'white backlash'. A third is utilitarian – if marginal differences in penalties have any deterrent effects it would not be unreasonable to suppose that reduced penalties would result in increased crime. This would have the perverse effect that disadvantaged people whose social or economic circumstances render them more vulnerable to the allure of criminal opportunities will face lesser punishments if they commit an offence.

Social and economic factors

Assuming any explicit use of race in sentencing is outlawed, the related question arises of whether other factors correlated with race should also be forbidden. Social class, educational attainment and employment record are examples. They are correlated with race. Whites score higher on average on all these variables than do blacks. To allow any explicit use in sentencing of race-correlated factors foreseeably disadvantages minority defendants. Use of race-correlated factors as mitigating circumstances means that more whites than black receive mitigated sentences. Use of race-correlated factors as aggravating circumstances, perhaps because they are predictors of higher reconviction rates, means that more blacks than whites receive aggravated sentences. Any systematic reliance on such factors disadvantages minority defendants.

A sentencing system that systematically imposes less severe penalties on middle-class and white defendants than on lower-class and minority defendants is intuitively unfair and unjust. Most US guideline systems banned race-correlated factors as sentencing criteria for just this reason. Unfortunately that seems to have been the wrong decision. The difficulty is that forbidding judges to take regular employment or a stable home life into account to a defendant's benefit in order to avoid favouritism to advantaged offenders also prevents their taking it into account to benefit disadvantaged offenders. And, since there are many more disadvantaged than advantaged defendants in criminal courts charged with serious crimes, the disadvantaged lose out.

The lesson we draw is that judges should be given broad authority to mitigate sentences on the basis of social factors, but on an individualised rather than an across-the-board basis. Some advantaged offenders might benefit but since they are a small minority of offenders the majority would be disadvantaged and disproportionately they would be members of minority ethnic groups.

Another way to deal with race-correlated social factors is to authorise their use in explicit sentence discounts. This carries all the negative implications that race discounts would carry – implications of lesser autonomy and responsibility, stigmatisation, social resentment, perverse incentives – and would be equally impossible to justify.

The best way forward is to tackle issues openly and honestly, identifying factors that cause or worsen disparities, doing whatever research or enquiry is needed to understand how they operate and why, and then systematically considering whether policy objectives whose pursuit causes disparities, like the aim of inducing guilty pleas, are more important than the aim of reducing disparities. Some of these discussions will be heated and some acrimonious but surely it is better to talk them out in public than to allow the issues to fester in silence while minority defendants continue to experience unfair treatment.

Sentencing laws

A wide range of laws and practices exacerbates racial disparities. If, for example, ethnic minority people are over-represented among people prosecuted for drug-related offences, increasing penalties or enacting mandatory minimum sentences for drug crime will disproportionately affect black offenders.

One way to attack this problem would be to require that all proposals for sentencing legislation be accompanied by or subjected to disparate impact analyses that project their distributive effects by gender and for minority and majority nationality and ethnic groups. This doesn't feel like a radical proposal, but no country does it.

The causes of racial and ethnic disparities invariably include policies that in principle apply to everybody but in practice disproportionately affect particular groups. Yet policy-makers continue to shy away from addressing racial issues in the criminal justice system directly. One explanation for this could be a combination of bad motive and hypocrisy. Some people argue that many features of the US federal war on drugs that disproportionately affect black people are best explained this way (Tonry 1995). Other reasons for avoiding disparity impact analyses is that the issues they raise are difficult and sensitive. Because of their stark character, we take two US examples: drug law and capital punishment.

The US Anti-Drug Abuse Act of 1986 establishes mandatory minimum sentences for cocaine offences that prescribe punishment for the sale of 5 grams of crack cocaine that is as harsh as that for the sale of 500 grams of powder cocaine. This is commonly called the 100-to-1 rule because the same penalties attach to crack offences as to powder offences 100 times larger. On paper, the law has nothing to do with race. In practice, however, because blacks typically sell crack and whites typically sell powder, the distinction produces longer sentences for black than for white drug dealers and worsens racial disparities in imprisonment.

These disparate effects were foreseeable in 1986 when the '100-to-1' distinction was enacted. If disparate impact projections and analyses were an obligatory part of the legislative process, policy-makers would have had explicitly to weigh wanted crime prevention effects against presumably unwanted but foreseeable disparate impacts on white and black defendants. This would have had the salutary effect of forcing realistic assessments of what preventive effects were likely and how confidently they could be expected to occur. Perhaps after such deliberations, Congress would still have enacted the 100-to-1 rule, but the decision would explicitly have been made that the likely gains from enacting the law outweighed the undesirable side effect of punishing black people more severely. Possibly the likely drug-abuse reduction gains would have been deemed so speculative as to fail to justify the disparate effects at all or at least such a significant differential. In either case, such analyses would force the making of explicit choices between crime-control policy goals, whether expressive or substantive, and the goal of social/racial inclusion.

Moving to our second example, the difficult issues raised by disparate impact analyses are illustrated by the US Supreme Court's decision in *McCleskey v Georgia*, 481 US 279 (1987). The court accepted the validity of empirical evidence that, all else being equal, capital punishment in Georgia was much more often ordered for blacks who killed whites than for black-on-black, white-on-white or white-on-black killings. The court had then to decide whether to allow McCleskey to be executed in the face of evidence that people like him are more likely to be executed because of their and their victim's race, or to accept the inferences raised by the statistical evidence and effectively end capital punishment in Georgia (and, by implication, the rest of the country). In the face of evidence that race matters, the court nonetheless held that statistical evidence was immaterial and that only proof of racial bias in the individual case was relevant. McCleskey's lawyers could not show this – few biased judges or lawyers openly admit that they are acting discriminatorily – and McCleskey was duly executed.

In explaining the court's decision, an obviously troubled Justice Lewis Powell pointed out that the logic of McCleskey's claim – that statistical evidence of inexplicable racial disparities raises a presumption of bias that the state must refute – might apply throughout the criminal justice system. The court could have avoided that result by asserting that 'death is different', but in principle Justice Powell was right. It could of course be argued that statistical evidence of unaccountable disparities *should* raise presumptions of bias.

The sensitive issue that follows this difficult one is whether race should be taken into account in deciding whether to increase penalties for homicide under English law.

The analysis would apply also to mandatory minimum sentencing laws covering violent and drug crimes. The threshold problem is that black offenders are arrested for homicide and for violent and drug crimes more often relative to population than are whites. For the purposes of argument we take arrest percentages to be a sufficiently accurate indicator of racial patterns of serious violent crime (the best evidence is that for violent crime – arrest proportions are reasonably valid indicators; drug arrests are another matter). A proposed law increasing the minimum prison sentence to be served for homicide to 25 years would, because of the racial offending pattern, disproportionately affect black offenders. Over time, as a result, the racial disproportionality in the English prison population relative to population would worsen. The question is, would this be a good thing or a bad thing?

Preventing crime is a good thing, but so is preventing racial disparities. If we knew that the increased lengths of sentence would through deterrent and incapacitative effects decrease the homicide rate by X per cent or save the lives of Y plus or minus ten people, the trade-off could be considered. Does an estimated crime-reduction effect of a particular amount justify an increase from, say, 11 to 15 per cent of the prison population who are black? What if no crime reduction effect could credibly be estimated? Could any increase in racial disproportions be justified, or any increase in penalties that would disproportionately affect black people? Whatever the crime reduction estimate, does it matter that violent crimes, especially homicide and rape, are heavily intra-racial, and thus that violent black offenders tend to have black victims? Punishing violent offenders more harshly will, if punishment has crime prevention effects, reduce victimisation rates and dis-proportionately benefit potential black victims.

Comparable analyses of the projected effects of alternative public policy choices are commonplace in other settings. Estimates of lost life are weighed against cost in road building and vehicle design. Of course, no action can be made completely safe and cost is inevitably a consideration. If all cars were design-limited to ten miles an hour and built with heavy steel bodies, there would be fewer road traffic injuries and fatalities. Decisions to make cars faster, lighter and cheaper to build necessitate higher actuarial estimates of projected injury and death rates. The trade-offs are explicitly discussed. Similar trade-offs should be discussed, and explicit choices made, in relation to race and sentencing.

Criminal justice practices

As Hood's research shows, English guilty plea discount practices result in longer sentences for black offenders. And, as much other research has shown, the use of social factors as criteria in bail decisions, release decisions and risk prediction instruments has disproportionate adverse effects on ethnic minority offenders.

One way to address this would be to subject all criminal justice system practices to disparity audits to establish whether and to what extent they exacerbate or ameliorate disparities in outcomes affecting members of ethnic minorities. This is a variation on the last point and the argument is much the same.

Decisions about pre-trial release, for example, often give weight to social factors such as the defendant's educational background, vocational skills or family status. These factors are not insignificant. The question is whether the individual will appear for trial, and indicators of social stability or connections are plausible criteria for predicting the defendant will not vanish. Unfortunately, comparatively more black people than white are economically and socially disadvantaged. They are therefore less likely to benefit from the consideration of social factors and more likely to be held in custody pending trial. In addition, a large body of research shows that defendants held in pre-trial custody are, all else being equal, more likely to receive prison sentences and to receive longer prison sentences (even after pre-trial time in custody is factored in) than offenders released before trial. This means that pre-trial detention practices create another disparate impact for ethnic minority defendants. Fortunately, these disparate impacts can easily be reduced once the problem is recognised. Other factors related solely to current or past criminality provide as good predictions of appearance at trial (Blumstein *et al* 1983: chapter 2).

Inducements to plead guilty provide a second, more complex example. In most countries, defendants from some disadvantaged minority groups are less likely than majority group members to plead guilty, and when they do plead guilty to do it later in the process. Most systems provide sentence reductions, openly or otherwise, to defendants who plead guilty. We have already referred to England's progressive-loss-of-mitigation doctrine which explicitly provides a one-third reduction of sentence to defendants who plead guilty at the outset with successively lesser reductions for later pleas (hence 'progressive loss'). Because they plead guilty less often than whites, and typically later, black offenders lose on both counts. This is a particularly ironic and unfortunate outcome, given that such non-co-operation seems likely to result in part from black people's understandable alienation from a criminal justice system in which they believe they are unfairly treated both as suspects and defendants.

Disparate impact audits would force policy-makers explicitly to decide whether the discount's presumed cost-reduction goals outweigh the foreseeable disparities that will result. Judges often assume that the courts will grind to a halt if defendants are not offered substantial incentives to plead guilty, but there is little evidence that this would occur. The limited amount of evidence from plea bargain bans in America suggests that most defendants will plead guilty even when they are not offered sentencing concessions (Blumstein *et al* 1983: chapter 3). At any rate, analyses of discount practices would require officials to weigh estimates of associated cost savings against the amount of increased imprisonment endured by black offenders, and force explicit debates on the question of whether the cost savings justify the increased racial imprisonment disparities the policy entails.

The implementation of the last two proposals is essential if the over-representation of black offenders in English prisons is to be reduced. However, while the necessary research and statistical analyses are not difficult, the policy decisions often are. The illustration of bail-or-jail criteria is comparatively straightforward. Once the problem is recognised, criteria that do not treat groups of offenders differently can be substituted for ones that do. More difficult are instances such as the US 100-to-1 rule, where the goal – try to reduce the direct and indirect effects of drug trafficking – seems desirable but the effect – treat black defendants much more harshly than whites – does not. The obvious options are to accept the unwanted racial disparity, to abandon the drug policy goal or to compromise. Had the choices been this starkly presented, our money would have been on the third option. Black crack defendants would still have been sentenced more harshly than white powder defendants, but the differential, and the resulting racial disparities, would have been less. That would have been a small victory, but a victory nonetheless.

Criminal justice organisation

We raise two key themes here: diversity training and sensitisation, and positive discrimination. The former was a keystone of Lord Scarman's programme for restoring the relationship between the black communities and the police following outbreaks of rioting and public disorder in 1980 (Scarman 1981). A perceived lack of progress in improving such relationships is often laid at the door of diversity training, in train with calls for more radical solutions. We are in sympathy with such calls, but we remain convinced of the value of a well-conceived and properly targeted diversity training programme. As with all programmes, however, what counts is not the original conception so much as its implementation in practice. Done sensitively in a way that does not insult employees or explicitly or implicitly accuse them of racism, such training can reduce stereotypes, enhance familiarity with others' outlooks, customs and beliefs, and encourage a healthy, tolerant atmosphere. Done poorly, it can foster resentment, hostility and backlash, and worsen relations between groups, as in the CPS example given above.

One way of neutralising the divisive potential of diversity initiatives would be to decouple them from racism and link them instead with a broader equal opportunities agenda. This is not to suggest that training about race inequality should be subsumed under the general heading of 'diversity' training, which might encompass other forms of discrimination such as gender, disability and age. However, it is crucial to combine recognition of the insidious effects of race discrimination with a shared commitment to the fairer treatment and maximised potential of all.[3]

This brings us to our second theme, positive discrimination. Although well-meant, the term is culturally loaded in a way that discourages efforts to help enhance the lives and life chances of members of disadvantaged minority groups. The phrase itself is an oxymoron. Though one standard sense of the word 'discrimination' is positive, as in 'discriminating taste', in the context of ethnic relations it is used in a negative sense to describe a bad thing. Positive discrimination is thus a 'good bad thing', which is nonsensical and fails to communicate determination and enthusiasm in the effort to increase diversity. It also, by implication, asks those whose ethnic identity places them beyond the remit of positive discrimination to embrace negative discrimination – a 'bad bad thing'. Hence the cries of 'racism in reverse' that regularly accompany attempts to redress race-based inequalities.

Given the current political climate and in the light of increasing divisions between white and ethnic minority communities (see the Cantle Report 2001), the difficulty of acting decisively for the minority without alienating the majority cannot be overestimated. In order to succeed, it is important to alter the perception that initiatives aimed at the empowerment of one group automatically disempower the other.

Words matter. 'Positive discrimination' is right up there with institutional racism as a mechanism for derailing the substantive issue of unfair treatment. Conceived as positive or affirmative action (a neutral word), though, the connotations are potentially less polarising and divisive. There is a place in the English courts and other criminal bureaucracies for positive action to promote ethnic minority employment and participation in the criminal justice system. There is also, now, a legal imperative in the form of the Race Relations (Amendment) Act 2000. This amendment to the 1976 Act places a general duty on all publicly funded organisations to promote race equality by eliminating unlawful racial discrimination and promoting equality of opportunity and good relations between persons of different racial groups. One way of complying with the law is through positive action, permitted under section 37 of the Race Relations Act 1976 and section 47 of the Sex Discrimination Act 1975. The legislation neatly illustrates the difference between 'action' and 'discrimination', permitting measures which encourage and develop the potential of people from under-represented racial groups ('positive action'), while stopping short of allowing race to be taken into consideration at the point of selection ('positive discrimination').

The evidence is mixed as to whether ethnic minority judges and other criminal justice practitioners act differently to, or make different decisions from, their white counterparts. It seems reasonable to hypothesise though that greater numbers of ethnic minority officials will make the system more sensitive to cultural differences and may enhance its legitimacy in the eyes of ethnic minority offenders and citizens.

III. Conclusions

Sentencing and punishment policies and practices in England and Wales have produced stark differences in imprisonment rates for black and white offenders. While there is little evidence of 'improper discrimination' in the courts, it is clear that a number of existing policies and practices cause or worsen racial disparities in imprisonment.

Our title asks, 'Is sentencing in England and Wales institutionally racist?' It is a provocative question, and for that reason, we think, permissible in a title, but on the substance of the matter it is neither fair nor useful. The answer 'no' implicitly accepts the legitimacy of the concept; the answer 'yes' admits that it characterises the courts. If the term 'institutional racism' accurately describes the Crown Prosecution Service, the police service and the prison service, it is hard to see how the courts and sentencing can escape it. There are disparities in sentencing and some of them, as Roger Hood's research shows, are the foreseeable if unsought consequences of well-established practices and policies.

The use of the term 'institutional racism', however, obscures rather than advances understanding of racial disparities in sentencing and stymies progress towards their reduction. Its incorporation of the polar word, racism, implies that bad motives – either in creating disparities or allowing them to continue – lie at the heart of the problem. But if bad motives are not really at work, the accusation will lead nowhere. If judges and others involved in sentencing believe that they are not racists, they will feel there is no problem to resolve. Even if there are some judges who do have bad motives, drumming them out (and of course they should be drummed out) will not significantly reduce sentencing disparities.

Unwarranted racial disparities in sentencing and racial differences in the handling of cases are real problems and they can be addressed and diminished. But this will require more than polar words, however galvanising. It will require sustained hard work and some hard choices, the most pressing of which have been the subject of this chapter.

To conclude, a serious effort to reduce the disproportionate damage current practices cause would include at least the following elements:

1. Repeal all mandatory minimum sentence laws and in general cut all sentence lengths by half.

2. Establish presumptive sentencing guidelines based solely on conviction offences and criminal histories.

3. Authorise judges to mitigate sentences in all cases on the basis of social and economic factors.

4. Require that disparity analyses and projections be carried out for all proposed penal legislation, estimating the effects of the legislation on offenders disaggregated by gender and ethnicity.

5. Require disparity analyses of all existing penal laws to isolate their respective contributions to current imprisonment disparities.

6. Conduct disparity analyses of all existing policies and practices reasonably believed to cause or exacerbate imprisonment disparities to isolate their respective contributions to correct imprisonment disparities.

7. Establish and maintain throughout the criminal justice system proactive but non-accusatory diversity sensitisation and training programmes.

8. Establish coherent and responsibly implemented programmes of positive action in the employment, retention and promotion of members of ethnic minority groups throughout the judicial system.

Notes

1. See also 'Racism "rife" in English theatre', *The Guardian*, 19 April 2002.
2. Our terminology reflects the four codes (white, black, Asian and other) adopted by the Home Office for the purpose of co-ordinating information on ethnicity in the criminal justice system (see Home Office 2002a).
3. See Home Office (2002c) for the Home Office's current thinking on this issue.

References

Blumstein, A., Cohen, J., Martin, S. and Tonry, M. (1983) *Research on Sentencing: The Search for Reform*, 2 vols. Report of the National Academy of Sciences Panel of Sentence Research, Chapter 3. Washington, DC: National Academic Press.

Bowling, B. and Phillips, C. (2001) 'Prosecution and Sentencing', in *Racism, Crime and Justice*, Longman Criminology Series. London: Longman.

Broadhurst, R. (1997) 'Aborigines and Crime in Australia', in Tonry, M. (ed.), *Ethnicity, Crime and Immigration: Comparative and Cross-National Perspectives*. Chicago: University of Chicago Press.

Brown, S., Hawson, I., Graves, T. and Barot, M. (2001) 'Eclipse Report: Developing Strategies to Combat Racism in Theatre', unpublished report, Arts Council of England, East Midlands Arts Board, Theatrical Management Association and Nottingham Playhouse Initiative.

Burney, E. and Rose, G. (2002) *Racist Offences: How is the Law Working? The Implications of the Legislation on Racially Aggravated Offences in the Crime and Disorder Act 1998*, Home Office Research Study No. 244. London: Home Office.

Cantle, T. (2001) *Community Cohesion: A Report of the Independent Review Team*. London: Home Office.

Carmichael, S. and Hamilton, C.V. (1967) *Black Power: The Politics of Liberation in America*. New York: Vintage.

Commission on Systemic Racism in the Ontario Criminal Justice System (1995) *Report*. Toronto: Queen's Printer for Ontario.

Denman, S. (2001) *Race Discrimination in the Crown Prosecution Service*. Crown Copyright.

Faulkner, D. (2002) 'Taking Account of Race, Ethnicity and Religion', in Rex, S. and Tonry, M. (eds), *Reform and Punishment: The Future of Sentencing*. Cullompton: Willan.

FitzGerald, M. (1999) *Final Report into Stop and Search*. London: Metropolitan Police Service.

FitzGerald, M. (2001) 'Ethnic Minorities and Community Safety', in Pitts, J. and Matthews, R. (eds), *Crime, Disorder and Community Safety*. London: Routledge.

The Guardian (2003) 'Institutional Blunderer' (leader), 15 January 2003.

Her Majesty's Inspectorate of Constabulary (HMIC) (1997) *Winning the Race: Policing Plural Communities. HMIC Thematic Inspection Report on Police Community and Race Relations*. London: Home Office.

Her Majesty's Inspectorate of Constabulary (HMIC) (1999) *Winning the Race: Policing Plural Communities Revisited. HMIC Thematic Inspection Report on Police Community and Race Relations*. London: Home Office.

Her Majesty's Inspectorate of Constabulary (HMIC) (2000) *Winning the Race: Embracing Diversity. Consolidation Inspection of Police Community and Race Relations*. London: Home Office.

Home Office (1999) *Stephen Lawrence Inquiry: Home Secretary's Action Plan*. London: Home Office.

Home Office (2000) *Statistics on Race and the Criminal Justice System: A Publication Under Section 95 of the Criminal Justice Act 1991*. London: Home Office.

Home Office (2001) *Making Punishments Work. Report of a Review of the Sentencing Framework for England and Wales (July 2001)*. London: Home Office Communication Directorate.

Home Office (2002a) *Statistics on Race and the Criminal Justice System: A Publication Under Section 95 of the Criminal Justice Act 1991*. London: Home Office.

Home Office (2002b) *Statistics on Women and the Criminal Justice System: A Publication Under Section 95 of the Criminal Justice Act 1991*. London: Home Office.

Home Office (2002c) *Training in Racism Awareness and Cultural Diversity*, Development and Practice Report No. 3. London: Home Office.

Hood, R. (1992) *Race and Sentencing*. Oxford: Clarendon Press.

Jasper, L. (2003) 'Report Confused on Reality of Racism', *Socialist Campaign Group News*, No. 184, February 2003.

Macpherson, Lord (1999) *The Stephen Lawrence Inquiry*, Cm 4262.1. London: TSO.

Parekh, B. (2000). *The Future of Multi-Ethnic Britain: The Parekh Report*. London: Profile.

Reiner, R. (1993) 'Race, Crime and Justice: Models of Interpretation', in Gelsthorpe, L. (ed.), *Minority Ethnic Groups in the Criminal Justice System*, Cropwood Conference Series No. 21. Cambridge: Institute of Criminology.

Roberts, J. and Doob, A. (1997) 'Race, Ethnicity, and Criminal Justice in Canada', in Tonry, M. (ed.), *Ethnicity, Crime and Immigration: Comparative and Cross-National Perspectives*. Chicago: University of Chicago Press.

Scarman, Lord (1981) *The Brixton Disorders 10–12 April, 1981*, Cmnd 8427. London: TSO.

Smith, D. (1997) 'Ethnic Origins, Crime, and Criminal Justice in England and Wales', in Tonry, M. (ed.), *Ethnicity, Crime and Immigration*. Chicago: University of Chicago Press.

Tonry, M. (1995) *Malign Neglect*. New York: Oxford University Press.

Tonry, M. (1996) *Sentencing Matters*. New York: Oxford University Press, chapter 2.

Chapter 9

Custody plus, custody minus

Jenny Roberts and Michael E. Smith

The Criminal Justice Bill published in November 2002–2003 substitutes a single 'community order' for the various community penalties which are separately authorised in current law, and the Bill would provide courts with several new ways to impose short prison terms – 'custody plus', 'custody minus' and the 'intermittent custody order'. Taken at face value, these reforms at the high-volume, lower end of the sentencing tariff offer imprisonment in new and more attractive wrapping and, as we explain below, passage of the Bill might well tip the balance of disposals further towards custody. But their stated intention is quite the opposite.

These provisions of the Bill spring from John Halliday's *Report of a Review of the Sentencing Framework for England and Wales*, which decried the 'lack of utility' in short prison terms (Home Office 2001: iv) because they 'literally mean half what they say' – after the first half is served in prison, nothing is required of the offender, nor is anything done to change him or his circumstances in ways that might avert new offences, rendering the second half 'meaningless and ineffective' (*ibid.*: 3). This theme was further developed in the White Paper, *Justice for All*, which declared that sentences to prison for less than twelve months are 'usually ineffective' (Home Office 2002: 92) and, more bluntly, that they 'increase the chances of reoffending' (*ibid.*: 102). As the White Paper explained it, short prison sentences do not afford enough time for effective work to be done on offending behaviours before release on licence, and they afford 'no support or supervision after release [for] any meaningful be-havioural or rehabilitation work [with the result that] reoffending rates for short-term prisoners are high' (*ibid*: 92) And high they are. Halliday highlighted the 60 per cent rate of reconviction, within two years of discharge, among offenders sentenced to prison for twelve months or less who were discharged in 1996. He found virtually the same rate of reconviction, after two years at risk, among those who had been sentenced to community penalties (Home Office 2001: 126).

To bring the reoffending rates down for both groups, the White Paper promised widespread implementation of more robust, individually-tailored, non-custodial penal measures. The Bill requires that all offenders sentenced to less than twelve months custody also submit for a specified time to a probation officer's supervision and comply with the 'onerous' demands of programmes now being built upon 'principles of effective practice' which have been drawn from research and grouped under the happy heading 'What Works' (Home Office 2002: 108; Home Office 2001: 6).

The 'What Works' principles emphasise cognitive-behavioural interventions, which the Home Office expects will be (and be perceived to be) more effective than probation supervision and the other community penalties have been to date. Halliday suggested that well-designed and well-run programmes might reduce reoffending by 5–15 per cent (Home Office 2001: 130). The expected effectiveness of the programmes – some to begin in custody, some sited entirely in the community – is essential to the plausibility of the White Paper's proposals, because if the new sentences are not more effective than the old, reoffending rates will remain high, increased public confidence in sentencing will not be warranted and sentencers will be unlikely to reduce their reliance on prison.

There are two paths to solution of the problems caused by ineffective short prison sentences, but the paths lead in opposite directions: make short prison sentences more effective, or effectively discourage their use. The White Paper and the Bill pursue both strategies simultaneously, which risks stimulating greater use of short prison sentences (as they come to be seen as useful at last), while undermining the effectiveness of the new supervision techniques and the 'What Works' programmes on which hopes are pinned for bringing down the rate at which offenders reoffend.

A hope of discouraging courts' use of short prison terms can be seen in the Bill's effective prohibition of sentences that imprison for more than 13 weeks but less than six months. Under the Bill's provisions, an offender sentenced to a year or more in prison will be released on licence, as he must be under current law, after serving half the sentence in custody. Thus the Bill's provisions leave intact courts' authority to keep an offender behind bars for six months or longer by imposing prison sentences of twelve months or more – which power will remain reserved to the Crown Courts. For shorter prison sentences, imposed by magistrates' or by Crown Courts, the Bill requires sentencers to specify a number of weeks between 2 and 13 to be served in custody before release on licence. This narrowing of the range of permissible short prison sentences may prove a more modest reform than it at first appears: in 2001, only 8 per cent of adult offenders received into prison arrived on prison sentences that would be eliminated by these provisions of the Bill (Home Office 2003: 91, table 4.8), and on a given day this segment of short-stay prisoners constituted less than 3 per cent of the adult prison population (Home Office 2003: 85, table 4.4). It is nevertheless worth asking whether offenders who in the past have attracted prison sentences requiring that three to six months be spent in custody will draw longer or shorter prison sentences if the Bill's provisions are enacted. We return to that question below.

A simultaneous attempt to make non-prison sentences more attractive to sentencing courts and to the public can be seen in the Bill's introduction of a new, omnibus community order – described in the White Paper, probably correctly, as 'more effective', 'tougher' and 'more demanding' than community penalties as we know them. The White Paper hints at a hope that the new community order will displace some prison sentences, so that sentencers can 'focus custody on dangerous, serious and seriously persistent offenders and those who consistently breach community sentences' (Home Office 2002: 13). The White Paper aims high – for non-custodial sentences that actually reduce reoffending, for use of those sentences actually to suppress crime and increase public protection, and for the public to notice and, as a result, develop greater confidence in sentencing and in the sentences imposed. It is hoping for a lot.

Prediction of the reforms' likely effects – on reoffending rates, on the prison population, and on public confidence – is complicated by other provisions in the Bill which, in effect, make any prison sentence of less than a year an additional requirement of a community order. The new custody plus sentence is in effect a community order commenced by up to three months' imprisonment. Custody minus, relabelled 'suspended sentence order' in the Bill, is a community order for which the consequence of an offender's failure to comply with its community requirements – a short prison stay – is fixed by the court at the time the order is imposed. It differs from the unadorned community order only in this prior specification of this custodial consequence for violating one of its community requirements.

Introduction of the custody plus sentence – imprisonment followed by a community order – invites sentencers to trade the greater retribution available at the next step up the custody tariff (six months' actual imprisonment on a twelve-month sentence) for what the White Paper suggests should be appreciable gains in public protection from enforcement of community requirements selected by the sentencer from a full menu of incapacitating and therapeutic conditions. Wrapping shorter periods of custody in community orders tailored to the needs and circumstances of individual offenders might render short prison sentences less destructive, but making them (or making them appear to be) more 'effective' does seem likely to frustrate the parallel attempt to discourage their use. More worrisome, unless short sharp shocks of prison are shown in future research to improve outcomes of the new cognitive-behavioural programmes flowing through the Home Office accreditation process, the custodial element of custody plus should be expected to diminish or negate the positive 'programme effects' promised by the 'What Works' initiative. Thus the attempt to make short prison terms less ineffective, by adding licence requirements of participation in otherwise 'effective' programmes, is likely to undermine the prospect that the programmes will achieve the marginal reductions in reoffending that might otherwise be expected from offenders' participation in them.

Custody plus, by making available within a prison sentence the presumed benefits of modernised probation supervision thickened with cognitive-behavioural programmes, curfews, drug or alcohol treatment, compulsory community service and other punishing, incapacitating or therapeutic requirements, is likely to prove a very attractive sentence indeed. Not least of its attractions, in these 'tough on crime' times, is actual and immediate imprisonment (albeit, for only 2 to 13 weeks), augmented by the additional punishment of each requirement of the licence.

The White Paper neatly paired 'custody plus' with 'custody minus' – a sentence assembled from the same menu of community requirements in which the imprisonment is held in reserve, perhaps to avoid some of the upfront damage to an offender's prospects anticipated from the custodial period of custody plus and to make reduced reoffending a more plausible outcome of offenders' participation in accredited cognitive-behavioural programmes and their supervision by probation agents trained in the new techniques.

The starting point for any consideration of custody plus and custody minus prison sentences is, therefore, the wholly non-custodial community order. Using it, courts may impose on an offender any, or several, or perhaps even all of the existing community penalties. But it also occupies a central place in the new scheme of short prison sentences – each is a community order or its operational equivalent, wrapped around a sentence to prison for between 28 and 51 weeks, within which a 'custodial period' of between 2 and 13 weeks is specified by the sentencing court. Operationally, the community order would become the standard sentence in all cases warranting less than a year in prison except those disposed of by fines.

The complexity of the framework obscures the reality that these new prison sentences make the imprisonment a requirement of the community orders in which they must be embedded. This is the most dramatic change – in the great majority of criminal cases sentencing courts will no longer need to choose between a prison sentence and a community penalty, or between one community penalty and another. The White Paper blurs distinctions between sentences provided in current law because 'We need effective sentences in the community which are flexible enough to meet the particular needs of a case, where the courts are not forced to choose between options' (Home Office 2002: 91).

For offenders not thought deserving of more than a year in prison but deserving more punishment than a community order, the sentencing options would be as follows:

1. Custody plus – a prison sentence of 28 to 51 weeks, requiring a custodial period of not less than 2 nor more than 13 weeks in prison to be served up front and be followed by at least 26 weeks on a licence to which the court may attach one, or several, or all of the same requirements available in a community order.

2. Custody minus – a prison sentence in the same 28 to 51 week range, suspended during the term of what is, in substance, a community order of six months' to two years' duration.

3. Intermittent custody – a prison sentence selected from the same range, during which 14 to 90 'custody days' would have to be served behind bars, in periods specified by the sentencing court, and the remainder served on a temporary and then final licence to which the sentencing court may attach some of the same requirements available to it through a community order.

There is much that warrants careful attention in such a complex scheme for combining custodial and non-custodial penalties. But the appearance of custody plus and custody minus in the sentencer's tool kit most sharply brings into focus the conceptual and practical problems that accompany all attempts to fuse custodial and non-custodial penal measures. Those difficulties are the subject of this chapter.

Each of the new sentences poses two pair of questions: First, 'What is the purpose of the imposed, threatened or suspended custody?' and 'What are the prospects of its achieving that purpose?' Second, 'What is the purpose of the rest of the sentence – the community order in which the custody is embedded?' and 'How plausible is the whole sentence as a means for achieving it?'

The White Paper refers throughout to three policy objectives for these additions to the sentencing tariff: to shore up public confidence in sentencing and in sentences, to better protect the public and to more effectively reduce reoffending by those who have been sentenced. In addition, there are hints of hope in the White Paper, as there were in the Halliday Report, that courts' use of the new penal measures will moderate growth in the prison population.

The prison population has risen by more than 50 per cent in the last ten years. This was not an accident; it is the natural consequence of a hardening of public and political attitudes toward offenders everywhere (Garland 2001; Tonry forthcoming). It is not surprising, then, that the White Paper's plea for moderation is expressed in utilitarian, not normative terms:

> High prison numbers mean staff have to spend more time supervising the additional offenders. This reduces the amount of time prisoners can spend outside their cell in education, training or work. Many offenders are in prison for too short a period of time for much rehabilitation to take place but long enough to disrupt their lives and make them even more likely to offend … High prison numbers also lead to constant transfers to prisons all over the country. This means a prisoner may well have to move before he or she completes a rehabilitative programme, and they may well be moved to a prison far from home. 43% of sentenced prisoners say that they have lost contact with their families since entering prison, as do 48% of remand prisoners. Research shows that prisoners are six times less likely to reoffend if contact with their families is maintained.
>
> (Home Office 2002: 106)

The government has set itself no small challenge – simultaneously to reduce or at least constrain the size of the prison population while making community penalties more punitive, demanding and un-forgivingly enforced.

Our principal aim in this chapter is to examine the custody plus and custody minus sentences (and to take a quick look at intermittent custody) and their rationales, and to anticipate, if we can, their likely effects on public confidence, public protection, reoffending rates and prison population growth. We first describe the proposed new penalties and then, by asking and answering a series of questions, try to puzzle out what they are expected to accomplish and why.

I. Custody plus

The rationale for custody plus seemed simple enough when Halliday proposed it. His report plausibly attributed the persistence of high reconviction rates among recently released short-stay prisoners to the utter lack of resettlement assistance to them after discharge from custody, and to their wholly unsupervised condition in places where, when last at liberty, they committed their offences. The 'plus' was to provide that resettlement assistance, to monitor offenders' progress (or lack of it) on licence, to require or prohibit specific activities to reduce the risk manifested individually by each offender in his circumstances, and to require offenders' participation in cognitive-behavioural programmes tailored to deal effectively with their offending behaviour.

True, the 26-week maximum for a custody plus licence seems too short a time for such work really to take hold, but the Halliday Report and the White Paper plainly looked to the 'seamless' construction and the prospect of seamless administration of the sentence to compensate for that limitation. The hope is while offenders are serving their 2 to 13 weeks in prison, they will be enrolled in one of the accredited programmes now under development by the prison and probation services and will finish it up on licence.

Thus was born a prison sentence in which custody – though an undisguised punishment valued for its penal burden – is conceived as well as a necessary component of the resettlement work that imprisonment makes necessary. The first of many questions we have about this rationale is the subject of the following subsection.

What's the custody for in custody plus?

Custody is what makes this sentence a prison sentence, of course, but why make imprisonment the prelude to the new cognitive-behavioural programmes and 'What Works' supervision plans, from which the Home Office so clearly anticipates significant gains to public protection?

It is not because the research base from which the programmes spring shows them to be even more effective if begun in custody. The opposite is more likely true (Liebling 2002). Incapacitation? The custodial period is so short that its purpose cannot plausibly be to protect the public by incapacitating the offenders. Deterrence? Halliday and the White Paper make a convincing case that short prison sentences do not dissuade offenders from reoffending (or at least are no more effective in this regard than community penalties), and that they disrupt the naturally occurring processes which keep most of us on the right side of the criminal law most of the time – those cognitive-behavioural effects of school, family formation and labour market engagement without which deterrence has little force (Bottoms 2001).

Without suggesting there are no better explanations to be found for the custody in Custody Plus, we want to examine three:

- First, the custodial period might be thought necessary as a foundation for subsequent, non-custodial work on the skill deficits (particularly in the cognitive realm) and on the antisocial attitudes (however acquired) which, under currently favoured criminological theory, explain an offender's criminal behaviour and which, if not supplanted by healthy cognition and values, might explain the impotence of short prison sentences.

- Second, the custody might be thought necessary to make more palatable to sentencing courts, and to the public, a sentence otherwise indistinguishable from a community order (which, by promising support for the offender's resettlement and offering programmes to treat his emotional, cognitive, residential and employment deficits, might appear insufficiently punitive, no matter how effectively it suppresses aggregate reoffending rates).

- Third, the custody might well have no purpose other than to punish: a purpose which trumps the public's interest in being more secure from crime, and which reveals the promise of reduced reoffending rates to be thin cover for *schadenfreude* – our pleasure in the misery of others.

We think this third explanation has more to it than Halliday or the White Paper would lead us to believe. They propose to win the public's confidence by supplying 'effective' sentences which the public is presumed to desire out of self-interest. But any plausible strategy to win public confidence without crass appeal to penal populism is likely to require an imaginative campaign to increase the public's knowledge about how security is and is not put at risk by offenders in our midst –

and about how little sentencing and sentences have to do with it (see Roberts *et al* 1998). The White Paper's failure to recognise the need for such a campaign does not bode well.

Is the custody for rehabilitation?

This first, somewhat surprising explanation for the custody in custody plus is advanced in the Halliday Report, but so is the second, and both figure prominently in the White Paper. Rehabilitation seems an implausible rationale, in part because the very idea that imprisonment will improve human beings has been out of favour for so long, and in part because the prison and probation services lack the resources, the administrative and professional skills, the integrated information systems and the genius to use them creatively that seem necessary for 'joined up' delivery of tens of thousands of custody plus sentences per annum.[1] As a practical matter, the early weeks of any offender's imprisonment are so chaotic, and the transitions to prison and back to community so disruptive, that, even if a cognitive-behavioural programme of demonstrated effectiveness is begun before the start of a custody plus licence period, the marginal impact on future offending of adding the custodial phase to the programme is likely to be vanishingly small.

The prison overcrowding of recent times has meant that prisoners are frequently moved around the system, disrupting delivery of even rudimentary treatment, making impossible their more than passing participation in more ambitious programmes, and making very hard the planning and preparation required for the circumstances of a prisoner's release to be other than risky, for him and for his community. The notion emerging from the White Paper – that, before long, short-sentenced prisoners will be moved through in-prison programmes of proven effectiveness in reducing reoffending, and then be marched through neatly joined-up community programmes which pick up where the custodial work left off – is wishful thinking.

The chances of prisoners even being assessed for suitability for interventions during short custodial sentences are remote, and the prospects of such assessments being followed by initiation of interventions appropriately tailored to their offending behaviour are currently non-existent. Indeed, with a few exceptions, prisoners serving much longer periods in custody are not offered such opportunities.

Good liaison arrangements between prisons and the probation service are prerequisite to effective linking of custodial and supervisory elements of a sentence and a smooth transition from the one correctional setting to the other. But for short-stay prisoners today, it is difficult to ensure that simple practical issues are satisfactorily dealt with. There would need to be considerably enhanced resources, especially in prison probation teams, just to bring the administration of release arrangements for the large population of short-stay prisoners into line with the arrangements for those approaching release from long sentences. In practical terms, a person sentenced to two weeks in custody and six months on licence would probably have to be issued with instructions for reporting following release at the court, at point of sentence, to ensure that he or she received them.

Notwithstanding all those reasons for scepticism, a prospect of continuities in treatment between prison and probation is likely to be very attractive to sentencing courts and to the public whose confidence is being sought through the reforms – so long as it retains its surface plausibility.

Is the custody somehow for parsimony?
The second answer to the question 'what's the custody for?' can be more fully stated this way: sentencers might be induced to impose less (scarce and presumably ineffective) prison time, and more of the (presumably more effective) community requirements available in community orders if they could attach those same community requirements to prison sentences of strictly limited durations. Even the most robust non-custodial penal measures tend not to excite as much public support as do often less effective but undeniably harsher prison sentences – as the Halliday Report's survey of public and sentencers' attitudes shows (Home Office 2001: 108–25; see also Roberts 2002) – not because the public judges prison to be more effective for its long-term protection from crime, but because the public is (or is thought to be) so willing to trade the prospect of that security for the immediate gratification of its punitive appetites.[2] The custody in custody plus can be understood, then, as an obvious attempt to make the essentially non-custodial penal measure more palatable.

This is a dangerous calculus. Even if some sentencers, inclined to impose a prison sentence of a year or more in a category of cases, sometimes will be drawn to use custody plus by the opportunity it gives them to impose community requirements in the licence period, other courts will surely find custody plus more attractive than the community order they would otherwise have imposed because the new prison sentence permits use of the clearly punitive prison cell without sacrificing the presumed benefits of community requirements available in community orders. At present, when a case perceived by a court to be right on the 'in/out line' forces a choice between plain custody and a community sentence involving supervision, sentencers sometimes comment informally that it is the absence of supervision attaching to the custodial sentence which leads them to impose the community sentence. The introduction of custody plus would be likely, in such cases, to tip the balance the other way.

Two weeks of prison and six or more months of correctional supervision and participation in accredited non-custodial programmes is, indeed, likely to draw many courts to use the new prison sentence when, under current law, they would have serious reservations about imprisoning. The upbeat 'plus' label coupled with the tough connotations of 'custody' encourages this in the current policy climate, which conditions sentencers and those who assist them to avoid being labelled 'soft'. Demand for imprisonment would be likely to increase, both as a result of offenders currently not sent to custody at all being sentenced to custody plus, and as a result of the failures of many to comply with licence requirements imposed in the hope of reducing their risk of reimprisonment, or promoting their resettlement, or both.

There is irony here. The cognitive-behavioural deficits that purportedly lie behind persistent offending stand in the way of offenders' compliance with community requirements, including the cognitive-behavioural programmes designed to help them stop offending. It is obvious that returning offenders to custody for their failures to comply, if made a general policy, would reduce the chances of their completing the programmes of intervention on which we are asked to rely for longer-term public protection and reduced reoffending. Further, if offenders sentenced to custody plus often fail to comply with requirements imposed to help them avoid reimprisonment, as we expect they will (particularly if the requirements prove to be as 'tough' and 'demanding' as the White Paper describes them), breach proceedings are likely to pour a significant portion of this group back into prison. That would reverse any relief from prison population growth that might be achieved by making the shorter prison sentences more attractive than longer ones. It will be hard to think of parsimony in the use of custody as an important objective of custody plus should this come to pass.

But it is also be hard to imagine a near-term Home Office policy effectively discouraging the enforcement of licence requirements which are made part of custody plus orders, in light of policy initiatives in recent years which have tightened enforcement of the ordinary community penalties. If vigorous enforcement is to remain a priority for the correctional services, relief would come only from courts making the community requirements of custody plus sentences *less* demanding. Yet, if the community requirements imposed by custody plus orders turn out to be as 'robust' as the White Paper suggests they should be (Home Office 2002: 108), and if they are in fact well designed to reduce reoffending, then diluting them to make compliance more likely would diminish the public protection they are expected to secure. That ought to *decrease* public confidence in sentencing and sentences – and the ultimate rationale for introducing the new sentence would evaporate. Conversely, if the community requirements of custody plus licences turn out not to be well designed to increase public protection, if they are not likely to reduce reoffending, why ever should an offender's failure to comply with them cause us to throw him back into custody in the name of enforcement? The only answer we can imagine is the *schadenfreude* that haunts the orderly precincts of the White Paper and the Bill.

We can imagine many sentencing courts finding nearly irresistible the prospect of two weeks in prison coupled with 26 to 50 weeks of community supervision and compelled participation in programmes pre-certified by the Home Office as effective for suppressing re-offending. Mothers with small children? Surely someone will care for the kids for two weeks so that the important cognitive-behavioural programme can get underway. The productively employed? Surely employers will treat a couple weeks' absence as unpaid holiday. Surely two weeks away, at prison, will not put accommodation at risk. Surely relief care could be arranged for invalid relatives – after all, that is what Social Services are for! If notions such as these tip the balance at sentencing from community orders to custody plus, large numbers of offenders will be exposed to imprisonment who would otherwise not be, and who have not been so exposed in the past.

What is the 'plus' for in custody plus?

Considered together, the Halliday Report and the White Paper offer half a dozen explanations for the 'plus'. The most plausible is that it attempts to give meaning to the whole sentence – Halliday's response to his observation that 'sentences of less than 12 months literally mean half what they say [because] release is automatic at the half-way point' and nothing is done to or with the offender thereafter (Home Office 2001: 3). In his view, if community requirements were added,

> these prison sentences would mean what they said, instead of half of what they say. Prisoners under supervision would be liable to recall to prison administratively, on breach of conditions, with a right of appeal. In the event of recall, re-release would be possible only for those with 4 months or more left to serve at the recall point,

and on the authority of a review hearing. Liability to recall to prison on breach of conditions would make this potentially a sentence almost as severe as one of 12 months under the new framework.

(Home Office 2001: 24)

Halliday was surely right to find fault with existing law. First, for nothing at all to be done to or for offenders during the second half of the sentences imposed on more than half of those sentenced to prison,[3] and for that fact to be widely known, drains legitimacy from the sentencing system – an unhappy result for a system of laws whose aim is to secure compliance from those who might be disposed to break them.

Second, public confidence very likely suffers today from it not being generally known what is required of offenders serving community sentences; it would be reasonable to expect at least some gain in public confidence from the imposition of community requirements in custody plus sentences when, by operation of other provisions of the Bill, courts would be obliged to refer to the full content of the sentence when pronouncing it – *if* the pronouncements were to reach the public and the public were to understand them. The persistence of public ignorance of what sentences are pronounced and how they are carried out is cause for scepticism about the 'meaning' of the plus reaching the public audience (Roberts 2002).

Is the 'plus' for additional punishment?

Halliday did not justify any of his proposals by direct reference to the national pleasure taken in the imprisonment of others, but he was clear (as are we) that the community requirements of the 'plus' element of this sentence will be imposed for the punishment of offenders, whether or not they are in fact 'effective' in reducing their subsequent offences. Community requirements restrict autonomy and liberty, as does prison, and the demands they make on offenders for cognitive and behavioural transformation represent burdens as great or greater than the burdens of 'doing time'. In acknowledging this, Halliday also acknowledged that, if courts are permitted to pick and choose licence requirements from the community order menu to fit them to the needs and risks presented by individual offenders up for sentencing, the resulting penal burdens imposed will vary without regard to differences in offenders' deserts. To Halliday, this variability in resulting penal burdens was ultimately desirable, because those found unsuitable for demanding community requirements – for reparation, for punishment through unpaid work, for restraint by electronic monitoring or for any of the other permissible licence conditions – and those for whom such requirements are unavailable locally could justly be sentenced to serve correspondingly greater portions of their sentences in custody. Having asserted the acceptability of sentence differences of this kind, under the principle of 'limiting retributivism', Halliday was able to argue the converse – that the unmistakably punitive quality of community requirements imposed in custody plus sentences would justify shortening the custodial periods with which they would be combined. Running through the White Paper and Halliday narratives is the hope that just such an exchange, occurring daily in sentencing courts across the land, would help bring prison population growth under control at last.

It strikes us as implausible that sentencing practice is, or can be, so finely calibrated. Courts are no better equipped than the rest of us to assess the relative punitive weight of the requirements which might be imposed in the 'plus' element of this sentence and they would be hard pressed to determine the imprisonment equivalent of a programme obligation avoided by offenders unsuited to it or unable to participate because of limited programme availability. Nor is there any real constraint in the equation. An individual offender's desert cannot be expressed with any precision, and the punitive weight of a given penal measure cannot readily be found – a problem if it is necessary to measure the weights of community requirements in a custody plus order, which becomes insurmountable when those requirements are fused, in a single sentence, with imprisonment and the possibility of recall. Because durations of confinement can be given numerical expression, there seems to be general agreement that sentencers can vary the durations of custody to make prison sentences proportionate in the sense that longer ones are allocated to the more serious offences and more blameworthy offenders. Perhaps. But even if sentencers have a mental scale by which the magnitude of one offender's desert may reliably be compared to another's, there seems not to exist a mental scale by which to measure the penal burdens of what Halliday called the 'variable constituent parts' of a custody plus sentence.

Not only do offenders (like the rest of us) differ in their capacity to comply with such requirements, they differ in whether or not they experience a particular 'requirement' as punitive. For example, although an unpaid work requirement is objectively punitive (restricting, as it does, an offender's liberty and autonomy), anyone who has administered this form of punishment has heard some offenders express gratitude for the 'opportunity' to serve others, or even (from a memorable, marginalised offender serving out his community service sentence at a Senior Center in the South Bronx) thanks for 'the best job

I've ever had'. Given the distinct possibility of offenders finding some community punishments pleasurable, and the research evidence that a community service order is more effective in reducing reoffending when the offenders value it as a 'worthwhile' experience (McIvor 1992), just desert principles would warrant an *increase* in the custodial period when a custody plus community requirement is valued by the offender (or by most offenders) subjected to it.

In reality, it is extraordinarily difficult to array community punishments by their punitive effect on offenders so that the greater punishments can be visited upon those more deserving of them, or so that those spared the punitive burden of a community requirement can be required to serve a longer time in prison. The persistent belief, in academic and policy circles, that we are capable of such penal calibration is, in our view, cognitive error (Fitzmaurice and Pease 1996).

Is the 'plus' for neutralising custody's criminogenic effects?

If not for additional punishment, perhaps the community requirements in custody plus orders are to contain the damage short prison sentences cause. Custodial periods as short as 2 weeks and no longer than 13 weeks are too short for proper assessment and delivery of cognitive-behavioural treatments in the prison, but are too long for an offender's ties to remain intact. The net effect on reoffending rates, even if 'What Works' programmes are successfully mounted in the prisons through which short-stay prisoners flow, is not likely to be positive – unless when a prison phase is grafted onto longer-term cognitive-behavioural and substance abuse treatment programmes, the work undertaken during the licence period is significantly advanced. Halliday reported that evaluations are expected of 'pathfinder' programmes designed to do just that (Home Office 2002: 131), but at present there is no evidence to support a claim that the effects of these interventions are *improved* if begun in custody. It is curious that, despite the drumbeat of claims for 'evidence-led' policy and for programmes that 'research has proven effective', neither Halliday nor the White Paper offer empirical support for the notion that it is 'effective practice' to spread cognitive-behavioural programmes over custodial and community phases.

Yet the 'plus' in custody plus clearly is intended to compensate in some way for custody's injuries to the social infrastructure that is likely to be necessary to the maintenance of a crime-free life by those whose offending led to their imprisonment the last time they were at liberty in our midst. In this sense, the 'plus' is for public protection, short and long term. And the White Paper makes a convincing case that imprisoning offenders without at least neutralising the effects of custody on their subsequent behaviour puts them and the communities to which they are discharged at greater risk than do community sentences. Custody plus is presented in part as a solution to the problem, under existing law, that neither the sentencing court nor the prison service has legal authority to condition in any way the licence period of a prison sentence of less than a year. As roughly two-thirds of prison sentences have been of this kind,[4] most prisoners have been released directly from custody into communities where their activities are wholly unsupervised and where their needs for employment, for housing and for the other essentials of resettlement are rarely addressed by the probation service. As their circumstances after release aggravate the risk of their reoffending, it is hardly surprising that well over half are reconvicted within two years (Home Office 2001: 126).

The solution may not be so simple as to extend to short prison sentences the licence supervision available following longer prison stays, though the idea has obvious merit. At present, however, the standard form of licence supervision following release from prison is regular one-to-one contacts between offender and probation officer, and it focuses on solving practical problems and encouraging the offender's efforts to find employment and to settle down. This form of supervision grew out of the traditional approach to voluntary after-care and, when it is used, it still attracts a relatively good response from offenders. Rates of compliance are good – better than those for supervision on community sentences, as gauged by compliance with the requirements of supervision and by the rate of completing supervision without breach or reconviction. Licence requirements are standard, and issued by the prison governor (or the Parole Board). Additional requirements may be added, usually when proposed by the supervising probation officer, and generally with the aim of supporting resettlement. But intrusive and demanding requirements of the type likely to dominate custody plus orders are found at present only in the cases of those considered to present risk of serious harm, who are released from terms of imprisonment of four years or more – and their licence conditions are most likely to have been imposed by the Parole Board.

Custody plus invites courts to impose such requirements following very much shorter terms of imprisonment. We think it obviously desirable that this be made possible in appropriate cases – an extended period of electronic monitoring and curfew, or a requirement to stay away from specified areas or persons could do much to extend the incapacitative effects of short prison sentences in cases where that degree of incapacitation would significantly contribute to public protection in the short term, help keep offenders from reoffending and facilitate resettlement work. It needs to be noted, however, that under present arrangements it has not been possible for licence requirements to be imposed which represent serious follow-on to work undertaken in prison, unless the offender has been sentenced to four years or more in custody. A few other recently released prisoners are persuaded to undertake programmes voluntarily, usually ones they had agreed to as part of a community sentence they did not receive. But *courts* have no substantial experience of imposing community requirements on those released from custodial sentences, and there is no evidence to be had about the likely levels of compliance with intrusive requirements of the kind contemplated for custody plus licences.

High rates of failure to comply with custody plus licence requirements should be expected, given what has been reported about failures to comply with programme requirements in some of the 'pathfinder' programmes wending their way through the accreditation process. Interim findings from a prospective evaluation of one such programme, 'Think First', revealed that 42 per cent of those whose participation was required by community rehabilitation orders or punishment and rehabilitation orders failed even to show up. Another 28 per cent failed to complete the programme (half of them before they had attended even four sessions). It might be worth risking such rates of non-compliance – it might be worth the resources necessary to compel compliance, perhaps even to punish non-compliance – if compliance were likely to very substantially diminish offenders' further offences. The plausibility of that occurring is called into question by the awkward fact that, although offenders who completed the 'Think First' programme under study were *less* likely to be reconvicted than offenders who failed to complete it, the improvement in reconviction rate for completers was *smaller* than for the custodial comparison group, even taking into account risk differences between the groups. Of course, programme effects cannot be reliably determined from comparison of completers with non-completers, but it cannot seriously be suggested that compelling participation in the 'Think First' programme 'worked' for the offenders in this study (Ong *et al* 2003).

Is the 'plus' for resettlement of offenders?

Halliday's idea for the 'plus' was that the 'package' of requirements 'be geared to public protection, rehabilitation and resettlement' (Home Office 2001: v). Was his use of the term 'resettlement' muddle or spin? To probation officers, and to the voluntary organisations from which the task of resettling prisoners was inherited in 1966, the term had no connotations of deliberate punishment. Resettlement was the rationale for voluntary contact between released prisoners and those offering them such assistance. Over the following decades, various forms of compulsory supervision following prison release were introduced – both to support effective resettlement and to protect the public. More recently, as national standards have shifted the focus of all forms of supervision in a more punitive direction, emphasising regularity and frequency of reporting, voluntary after-care has all but disappeared from the workload of the probation service.[5] Prisoners released to a custody plus licence would probably be bemused to learn that the requirements that expose them to reimprisonment originated in the belief that a society that incarcerates has a corresponding duty to resettle.

There is no good argument against providing a period of resettlement to follow any time in custody. Human decency requires it, and it holds the possibility of rebuilding the ties to family, community and labour market which are disrupted by imprisonment, thus encouraging desistance from further offending and thereby enlarging public protection. But attaching demanding and intrusive requirements to the licence period is not what has been meant by resettlement and conflicts with its original premise. Of course, there are likely to be gains for the offenders and for the rest of us when licence requirements are suited to the offender's needs – and the offender complies. But the benefit is likely to be confounded by hasty and inaccurate targeting of the programmes, by indiscriminate use of other licence requirements, and by excessively punitive responses to failures to comply. Indeed, unless the interventions are carefully targeted and the offenders are skilfully supported by their supervisors, we will see a great many offenders who, having completed the custodial part of their sentences, are returned to prison for being unwilling or unable to comply with the part of their sentence that is designed to help them not reoffend.

If it is discovered that courts can design packages of community requirements which in fact reduce reoffending among large numbers of offenders recently released from short stays in prison on custody plus sentences, and if it proves possible for courts to accomplish that without it appearing to the public that offenders are 'walking free' after only 2 to 13 weeks behind bars, nothing would justify continuing use of custody plus for those cases rather than community orders carrying the same community requirements. That happy prospect is not in sight – in part because evidence of the 'effectiveness' of the new programmes is not nearly as strong as Halliday and the White Paper suggested, but more because the sensibility of these times is to debate questions of effectiveness while indulging punitive appetites.

II. Custody minus (the suspended sentence order)

The proposal for a custody minus order[6] in the White Paper involved much more than bringing suspended sentences back onto the tariff. The suspended sentence it would replace was, after all, too easily characterised as 'walking free' to get much use. And, for reasons rehearsed in the preceding section, the sensibility of the current period places high value on tough and 'demanding' sentences. Not surprisingly, the White Paper resurrected suspended prison sentences as toughened up community sentences:

> Custody Minus ... will give judges and magistrates the power to put an offender into custody and suspend the sentence for up to two years on condition that the offender undertakes a demanding programme of activity in the community. Any breach will lead to immediate imprisonment.
>
> (Home Office 2002: 93)

It is risky to threaten immediate imprisonment for any breach of a community order whose requirements will range from an exclusion requirement, whose contribution to public protection might be great, to the details of participation in a particular accredited programme. It is a risky toughness both because an offender's failure to comply might more usefully be used as an occasion to revisit the question what should be required of him and why, and because most human beings, offenders included, become *less* compliant when threatened than when they are required to do what they have come to understand as useful to themselves. It would seem no more likely that offenders would comply with the 'demanding' community requirements of custody minus sentences, backed by the White Paper's promise of mandatory imprisonment for failure to comply, than that they would comply with the same requirements imposed through custody plus. Perhaps because of this, the Bill abandons the requirement of immediate imprisonment for an offender's failure to comply with a suspended sentence order. The Bill gives the court power to vary the terms of the order, or to substitute a more onerous requirement, or to remove altogether a requirement that an offender seems unable to meet. This is a welcome 'climbdown' from the uncompromising enforcement policy introduced by the Criminal Justice and Courts Sentences Act 2000.

As it stands, after the March 2003 amendments to the Bill, a court imposing a suspended sentence order would specify a definite period of imprisonment to be served in the event the offender is later found to have 'failed without reasonable excuse to comply with any of the community requirements', but the court handling violation of the order may:

(a) order that the suspended sentence take effect with its original term and custodial period unaltered,

(b) order that the sentence take effect but with the substitution of a lesser prison term or a lesser custodial period, or

(c) impose more onerous community requirements, or extend the supervision period or the operational period of the original order, up to the durational limits available to the original sentencing court.

Schedule 9 also provides that when a court orders the imposed and suspended prison sentence to take effect (with or without variation of the original term and custodial period), the court 'must also make a custody plus order'. In short, if the prison sentence is given effect upon breach of a suspended sentence order, it is to be executed as a custody plus sentence within which the offender, when released on licence, is put at risk of return to custody for breach of conditions very like the conditions whose breach triggered his imprisonment.

Custody minus seems to have evolved into a provision for sentencing *de novo*, when it appears to a reviewing court that an initially imposed 'package' of community requirements was not well-designed to keep the particular offender out of trouble or was imposed in expectation of events that have not materialised.[7] It is impossible to predict how courts will respond to the grant of such open-ended power to revisit original sentences. From our informal conversations with judges and magistrates it appears that many prefer to think of their past decisions as having been, for the most part, remarkably prescient – a psychological trait distributed generally in the population, probably because of its contribution to our mental health. This makes it harder than reason suggests it should be for a decision-maker to come to a different view of a matter already decided, even when a good reason for a change of mind is presented. Nevertheless, when violation of a community requirement is not itself a crime and causes no substantial harm to the person or property of others, the possibility of adjusting a custody minus order to make achievement of its original purpose more plausible seems more likely to enhance public protection than certainty that prison will follow violations.

Halliday envisioned an active role for courts in reviewing the progress and the difficulties offenders encounter in the course of non-custodial sentences, and in making mid-course adjustments where adjustment rather than enforcement would be likely to advance the purposes of the sentence (see Home Office 2001: 49). It is a pleasant surprise to find in the Bill the core of Halliday's proposal that courts be given a 'sentence review capacity'. At the time, the proposals provoked more doubt about their practicability than enthusiasm for the contribution they might make to the fairness and effectiveness of sentences[8] (McKittrick and Rex, this volume).

Periodic sentence review is important if sentencing purposes are important, because the effect of a particular sentence on a particular offender is highly contingent on changing facts and circumstances. The effects eventually realised through the execution of any sentence – particularly a community sentence or the non-custodial element of one of the new short prison sentences – must be shaped by facts not knowable to the court at sentencing: the offender's values and habits of mind should be expected to change during execution of the sentence (including changes of the kind sought by cognitive-behavioural programmes), his circumstances are likely to change too (including changes sought or fought by the supervising probation officer) and, particularly during this period of innovation and retooling in the correctional services, there are likely to be modifications to the programmes and supervision techniques available to a court and changes in what the research suggests are their effects. The complexity of community orders (imposed as such, or as the medium in which a short prison sentence is embedded) makes sentence review – even sentencing *de novo* – preferable to breach and imprisonment when a community requirement of the sentence fails to achieve the offender's compliance.

Fortunately, the Bill permits this review and amendment of community requirements for each of the new short prison sentences and the community order, not only when a failure to comply is brought to a court's attention but also when an offender or responsible officer requests it during the course of the sentence.

There nevertheless remain problems with the purpose and meaning of the custodial element of a suspended sentence: if imprisonment is part of and deserved as the offender's punishment, why does he not serve it except upon his failure to comply with a separate community requirement? If the threat of custody is designed to encourage compliance, how can courts deal justly with offenders who turn out to be unable to comply without undermining this deterrent effect? And if the purpose of the custodial element is only to deter non-compliance with community requirements – if the sentencer's intent was that the offender *not* be imprisoned – execution of the custodial part when deterrence fails is exceedingly hard to explain. These matters were not really addressed by Halliday or the White Paper, nor was the case for custody minus convincingly made. There is a suggestion in the White Paper that the suspended sentence, by holding a position up-tariff from the community order, allows non-custodial sentencing in a wider band of cases. But that possibility has vanished with the Bill's clear specification of review rather than imprisonment as the first response (after a statutorily required warning) to an offender's failure to comply with the order. The strongest rationale for this sentence may be the opportunity that comes with it for review of the whole sentence, arising from its breach.

III. Enforcement generally: relating purpose to consequences

Whether one of these new sentences is commenced in prison or in the community, it surely matters why a particular community requirement was included in the order to begin with. It most obviously matters when questions of enforcement arise. If a requirement was included because the sentencing court found it a plausible means of near-term public protection from an articulable risk of harm to the persons or property of others, then non-compliance with that requirement ought to trigger a search for a requirement more likely to advance that protective purpose. Prison might be required, but to reach for custody automatically, or before canvassing the less damaging and (usually) less costly non-custodial possibilities, would be irrational – unless the kind and degree of risk presented by the offender in his present circumstances has been re-examined and revealed to be greater than was believed at the time the sentence was imposed.

Irrational, but understandable. Understandable not because 'public confidence in a reformed sentencing structure will only be established if the new sentences are effectively enforced', as the White Paper would have it (Home Office 2002: 97), but because there is in all of us a tendency, when others ignore our demands or treat them with contempt, to lash out at the source of the irritation we feel. It is not for their capacity to lash out in irritation, however, that courts are given the job of sentencing offenders – sentencing is entrusted to courts because of their capacity for deliberation, for dispassionate fact-finding, and for reasoning to plausible and fair dispositions by application of law to relevant facts. It is this latter view of courts' competence that led Halliday to propose the 'sentence review function' for them; it animates the Bill's provisions for periodic court review of suspended sentence orders and for the courts' exercise of discretion as to consequence when an offender is shown to have failed to comply with a community requirement of any of these orders.

'Enforcement' has in recent years become nearly synonymous with effectiveness – in part because it is easier simply to be tough than to be effective in complex undertakings such as increasing public protection or reducing reoffending, but perhaps more in the hope that talk of 'tough enforcement' will defeat the 'soft option' tag that probation in particular, and community sentences in general, tend to attract. The White Paper continues in this vein, although there appears to be no evidence that talking tough actually reassures the public or protects against accusations of being soft.

It is not obvious what public interest is advanced by imprisoning offenders who were at the time of their sentencing not thought to deserve prison for their offences. Nevertheless, enforcement has become a dominant concern of probation service supervision, to the point where the organisational focus on it may thwart the probation service's capacity to deliver interventions that might actually reduce reoffending. The first national standards for community sentences were prescribed in 1989, and they have been ratcheted up ever since. Here are some results from South Bank University's three audits of the service's enforcement of community sentences, the third involving a sample under supervision six months after a more stringent set of enforcement standards had come into effect (Hedderman and Hearnden 2001):

- 53 per cent of offenders attended all their appointments or had acceptable reasons for absences;

- after National Standards allowed offenders to accumulate two unacceptable absences before being breached, the compliance rate rose to 78 per cent in the second audit and 84 per cent in the third audit;

- 73 per cent of offenders in the third audit who failed to comply more than once were breached or recalled to prison; and

- only 7 per cent of offenders in the third audit got as far as a third failure to comply with requirements – half of these were breached and 14 per cent were formally warned. The comparable figure for the second audit was 21 per cent, of whom 84 per cent were breached or warned.

Taking into account the social context from which the community sentence population is drawn, these audit results suggest that weaknesses in enforcement practice may be close to the irreducible minimum. It is obvious, however, that the White Paper's hope to 'ensure tough community sentences are a credible alternative to custody' could not be achieved simply by skilful presentation of these findings to the public.

IV. Effectiveness: 'What Works' and the risks of evidence-led penal policy

Running through the Halliday Report and the White Paper is an enthusiasm for cognitive-behavioural approaches to work with offenders on reducing their reoffending, and for the principles of effective programme design which have been drawn from meta-analyses of evaluation studies. In one sense it is easy to understand the excitement. After decades of labouring under the negative cloud of 'Nothing Works' – the unforgettable but regrettable title of Robert Martinson's 1974 article – the statistical techniques of meta-analysis have shown his implication to have been wrong. In short, and not surprisingly, programmes of sound theoretical design, targeted on offenders whose reoffending is (according to the theory) likely to be suppressed by them if executed well, are likely to yield measurable improvements in the participants' reoffending rates. There is much more to the 'What Works' initiative than this, and some of the work done under that banner has gone far to marginalise fanciful programme ideas and expose incompetent programme delivery. But the 'measurable' improvements expected from thorough-going embrace of the 'What Works' principles are only that – measurable.

Measurable improvements – gains of 'statistical significance' – are what have excited the research community. And the excitement of researchers, so often sceptics about the plausibility of Home Office initiatives in the past, has somehow excited the policy world to an extraordinary degree. The Halliday team's enthusiasm for 'What Works' is evident throughout his Review, but his (optimistic) projection of the improvement that can be expected if 'What Works' principles are built into the sentencing framework, if the national prison and probation services adopt those principles in their supervision of offenders and if they retool and train staff to deliver, at scale, accredited programmes incorporating those principles, is only 10 to 15 per cent. With rates of

reconviction within two years of sentence hovering around 60 per cent –
successful execution of these ambitious reforms should not be expected to
yield reconviction rates lower than the 51–57 per cent range.

We find it hard to understand how public confidence is likely to be
restored by sentences which more than half the time are followed by
reconviction within two years.

There is much of value in the 'What Works' literature, valuable work
has been stimulated by the 'What Works' initiative and offenders will
likely benefit from the spread of accredited programmes – even from the
process of accrediting programmes. But the benefits are not likely to
include a durable rise of public confidence and there is a real danger that
probation practice, divorced from its traditional approach to working
with offenders and the situations in which they are found, will atrophy.
And *that*, we think, could prove costly to public protection and,
ultimately, to what remains of public confidence in sentencing.

Cognitive-behavioural approaches have captured the imagination of
the national probation service, although experience suggests that there is
not likely to be one effective approach to the complexity of criminal
behaviour. Indeed, examination of the evidence cited to justify the choice
(meta-analytical studies in Canada and the United States) reveals that
more powerful effects on reconviction rates can be secured by effective
attention to improving offenders' labour market position (Lipsey 1995).
Employment, while likely to advance public protection and reduce
reoffending, could not be presented as a demanding penal measure
almost as tough as imprisonment. It is not obvious, however, that an
informed public would choose prison (even prison embedded in
community orders) over the potentially transformative effect of getting
offenders into paid employment and keeping them there if the choice
were plausibly presented to it.

Right now, the probation service is preoccupied in an effort to push a
mass of offenders through 'pathfinder' programmes. The object is to
find out if the programmes are as effective as theory suggests and to
demonstrate that they are. The policy commitment to delivering
reductions in crime levels through this strategy is so strong that
generous funding has driven out good sense about careful selection of
offenders for the programmes. Lack of time to prepare and underpin the
work involved has plagued the effort, as has the simultaneous
restructuring of the service. It appears that the initiative has been
compromised by the same muddle about enforcement, toughness and
effectiveness that burdens the White Paper: because enthusiasm for
'What Works' coexists with a commitment to tough enforcement, the
White Paper discusses effective interventions as if they were necessarily

'tough and demanding'. But effectiveness and toughness do not necessarily coincide, and there is some evidence in the research literature showing that intensive supervision designed purely with toughness in mind is relatively ineffective (Petersilia and Turner 1993). Toughness ought to be particularly carefully balanced with justice when dealing with damaged and disadvantaged people who have no stake in society. The White Paper fails to recognise that offenders are usually found among the deprived and victimised and it fails to deal with the problem that offenders with most to gain from high quality, theoretically rigorous, well executed interventions are the least likely to do so because of the very deficits the interventions are designed to remedy.

V. Public confidence

We have already explained why we think the White Paper's and the Bill's preoccupation with public confidence is misplaced. A 5 to 15 per cent reduction in reoffending rates from the current 60 per cent is unlikely to galvanise enhanced public confidence. Nor, conversely, is it obvious, from what is known of public opinion about these matters, that the public would prefer incarceration rather than employment or assignment to better targeted treatment programmes and behavioural controls for offenders who violate conditions or commit new minor offences. Public confidence in the criminal justice system is important, but these are not likely to be the best ways to achieve it (Roberts *et al* 2002). There is no evidence to justify pursuit of public confidence by introduction of tough new penal measures, or effective new penal measures for that matter. There is, instead, abundant evidence that public confidence is not likely to be affected in any way by such tinkering (Roberts 2002).

Research commissioned by the team that produced *Making Punishments Work* (Home Office 2001) explored the attitudes of the general public to sentencing (Chapman *et al* 2002). It was demonstrated that ignorance about sentencing could be reduced by the provision of information, and support for disposals other than imprisonment could be increased. Attitudes about and lack of confidence in sentencing were similarly modified by the provision of information.

More generally, this research identified reducing offending as the most important purpose of sentencing in the public's view (Home Office 2001: 109). This could prove an obstacle to achieving the increased public confidence sought by Halliday and the White Paper, because it may be harder to generate 'measurable' improvements at scale than the 'What

Works' literature suggests it will be, but also because the public has demonstrated repeatedly that the reality does not necessarily affect its view – a 10 per cent improvement in the reoffending rates is likely to leave intact the public demand that sentences reduce reoffending.

Conclusion

The reconfiguring of community penalties initiated in the Halliday Report, with and without embedded terms of imprisonment, is a work in progress. Halliday's initial proposals – a single community order, custody plus, elimination of 3–6 month real-time prison terms, community controls in the second half of longer prison terms – were ambitious. Augmented by the proposals in the White Paper and provisions in the Bill for intermittent custody and custody minus, the scale of change is daunting. If laws effecting these changes are enacted, the job of implementing them will be enormous. There will be difficulties in obtaining and deploying the resources required for such an effort, and difficulties in developing the capacity for coordination, for matching offenders to programmes and for operating programmes effectively to produce the promised effects.

There are mysteries here concerning how the new penalties are to be enforced, whether official confidence in the 'What Works' principles and programmes is warranted, and whether and how their implementation can be expected to raise public confidence in the justice system. The aims are to increase public confidence, enhance public protection, reduce reoffending rates and reduce or constrain prison population growth. We are sceptical whether these are realisable goals for so complex a set of proposals.

Notes

1. How many custody plus sentences should be anticipated? In the text we explain why custody plus is likely to be a popular sentencing choice, why it is likely to be preferred over the unadorned community order and over the suspended sentence order and intermittent custody. Thus the potential pool is very large. Any of the more than 60,000 individuals received into prison in 2001 on sentences of less than a year might draw a custody plus sentence when courts are authorised to use it (Home Office 2003: 91, table 4.8), as might any of the more than 100,000 who began community sentences in 2002 (Home Office 2002: 18, 20).

2. The public's assessments may be much more complex than that (see Roberts 2002). Halliday, for example, found from sampling public opinion for his Review that the public consider the combination of custody and community supervision the most effective way to reduce future offending. Halliday particularly noted that '72% thought that a 3-month + 3-month sentence would be more constructive than a 6-month prison sentence', and he emphasised that *'The informed public were even more enthusiastic, with 84% believing custody plus supervision was more constructive than custody only'* (Home Office 2001: 112, emphasis in the original).

3. Of the 90,523 receptions of prisoners on immediate custodial sentences in 2001, 67 per cent (60,840) had been sentenced to less than 12 months (Home Office 2003: 28, table 1.12 – Receptions into prison under sentence: by type of prisoner and length of sentence).

4. In 2001, for example, nearly 50,000 of the 69,554 adults received into prison under sentence of immediate imprisonment arrived on prison sentences of 12 months or less – sentences for which the Bill would substitute custody plus, custody minus and intermittent custody – and 40,615 (58 per cent) were prison sentences of six months or less (Home Office 2003: 91, table 4.8).

5. At the end of December 2001, only 924 persons were receiving voluntary supervision following release from custody – a precipitous drop from the years preceding the Criminal Justice Act 1991 (Home Office 2002: 38, table 5.3).

6. The suspended sentence order is a marketing nightmare. 'Custody plus' sounds somehow better than, more than, custody itself, but 'custody minus' suggests something less than custody, perhaps not really custody at all. 'Suspended sentence' does not solve the problem, but borrows the label of a product not highly valued in the past. In the rhetorical frame of the White Paper, 'custody unless' would have been a better choice: Criminal Justice Bill (March 2003), Schedule 10, Clause (7)(2).

7. This resentencing power is subject to some sensible limitations. For example, a reviewing court cannot impose requirements it could not have imposed at the original sentencing, it cannot impose treatment requirements to which the offender objects and, when substituting a new requirement for one originally imposed, it must substitute a requirement of the same kind. See, for example, Criminal Justice Bill (March 2003), Schedule 9, Clauses (14) and (15).

8. Although the Bill's language appears to grant courts considerable leeway when handling violations of custody minus orders, the White Paper had a much more limited purpose in mind:

> Special hearings, or 'review courts', will enable sentencers to order the offender to appear before them at any stage of the sentence and allow them to amend any sentencing requirements they have made. This might result in a toughening up of the conditions if the offender was showing signs of failure, immediate imprisonment in the event of failure, or a less onerous sentence if there was good progress.
>
> (Home Office 2002: 94)

References

Bottoms, Anthony (2001) 'Compliance and Community Penalties', in Bottoms, A., Gelsthorpe, L. and Rex, S. (eds), *Community Penalties: Change and Challenges*. Cullompton: Willan.

Chapman, B. Mirrlees-Black, C. and Brawn, C. (2002) *Improving Public Attitudes to the Criminal Justice System: the Impact of Information*, Home Office Research Study 245. London: Home Office.

Garland, D. (2001) *The Culture of Control*. Oxford: Oxford University Press.

Hedderman, C. and Hearndon, I. (2001) 'To Discipline or Punish? Enforcement under National Standards 2000', *Vista*, 6(3), 215–24.

Home Office (2001) *Making Punishments Work: Report of a Review of the Sentencing Framework for England and Wales*. London: Home Office Communications Directorate.

Home Office (2002) *Justice for All*, CM 5563. London: HMSO.

Home Office (2003) *Prison Statistics England and Wales 2001*, CM 5743. London: TSO.

Fitzmaurice, C. and Pease, K. (1996) *The Psychology of Judicial Sentencing*. Manchester: Manchester University Press.

Liebling, A. (2002) 'The Uses of Imprisonment', in Rex, S. and Tonry, M. (eds) *Reform and Punishment: The Future of Sentencing*. Cullompton: Willan.

Lipsey, M. (1995) 'What Do We Learn from 400 Research Studies on the Effectiveness of Treatment with Juvenile Delinquents?', in McGuire, J. (ed.), *What Works: Reducing Reoffending – Guidelines from Research and Practice*. Chichester: Wiley.

McIvor, G. (1995) 'CSOs Succeed in Scotland', in Tonry, M. and Hamilton, K. (eds), *Intermediate Sanctions in Overcrowded Times*. Boston: North Eastern University Press.

Martinson, R. (1974) 'What Works? – Questions and Answers about Prison Reform', *Public Interest*, 35(2), 22–54.

Ong, G., Roberts, C., Al-Attar, Z. and Harsent, L. (2003) *Think First: An Accredited Community-based Cognitive-Behaviour Programme in England and Wales. Findings from the Propective Evaluation in Three Probation Areas*. Probation Studies Unit, Centre for Criminological Research, University of Oxford.

Petersilia, J. and Turner, S. (1993) 'Intensive Supervision Probation and Parole', in Tonry, M. (ed.), *Crime and Justice: A Review of Research*, Vol. 17. Chicago: University of Chicago Press.

Roberts, J. (2002) 'Public Opinion and Sentencing Policy', in Rex, S. and Tonry, M. (eds), *Reform and Punishment: The Future of Sentencing*. Cullompton: Willan.

Roberts, J., Hough, M., Smith, M.E. and Dickey, W.J. (1998) 'What If Corrections Were Serious about Public Safety?', *Corrections Management Quarterly*, 2(3), 12–30.

Tonry, M. (forthcoming) *Thinking about Crime*. New York: Oxford University Press.

Chapter 10

Reducing the prison population

Michael Tonry

For a period of some months early in 2002, though in retrospect it seems like minutes, rumours circulated that the then newly-appointed Home Secretary David Blunkett thought too many people were in prison and the imprisonment rate too high. The Home Office created a not-very-secret working group on getting the prison population down and Blunkett, speaking at the Prison Service Annual Conference in Nottingham, gave a speech consistent with that agenda. Director General Martin Narey (2002) called it 'the most important speech that has been made at a Prison Service Conference for many years ... It signals an alternative to the inexorable rise in the size of the prison population.'

The winds quickly changed direction. Neither Blunkett personally nor the government generally any longer tries to talk down the imprisonment rate. The 2002 White Paper (Home Office 2002) proposed changes calling for longer sentences for violent and sexual offenders and greater use of imprisonment in enforcement of breaches of community penalties. The Criminal Justice Bill submitted late in 2002 followed suit. Numerous other policies under consideration – for remand and punishment of young offenders, for control of antisocial behaviour, for sentencing of rape and other sexual offences – call for or imply increased use of imprisonment. In April 2003, when the prison population reached another record high, *The Guardian* reported that the government, anxious about unwanted media focus on the subject, announced that daily figures will no longer be released.

Blunkett was not alone in calling inconsistently for tougher punishment policies and measures to reduce or control the prison population. A

Cabinet-level committee of ministers met weekly in 2002 to oversee policy concerning the rapid increase that year in street robberies, especially in London and especially of mobile telephones. Lord Woolf, though reiterating assertions that too many people are sent to prison for too long and issuing an opinion late in 2002 calling for reduced use of prison sentences for first-time burglars, earlier in 2002 issued a notorious opinion directing that 18 months was an appropriate sentence for taking of mobile phones. The Lord Chancellor's department early in March 2002 announced the establishment of fast-track courts for violent crimes. All of this, by promoting a sense of crisis and fanning public anxieties, fosters a climate of business as usual and more of the same.

There is no reason why England's prison population cannot be reduced substantially should government leaders wish it so, even though the subject inevitably is politically difficult and contentious. A sizeable number of jurisdictions have made the decision to do so and succeeded. Finnish policy-makers decided in the late 1960s that the incarceration rate of 160 per 100,000 could not be justified, in comparison with the rates in other Scandinavian countries of 50–70 per 100,000, and over 30 years held to that goal. By the mid-1990s, the Finnish rate of 60–65 per 100,000 was in the middle of Scandinavian rates (Lappi-Seppälä 2001). The Germans in the late 1960s and early 1970s decided that prison sentences under six months did more harm than good and decided through use of fines and prosecutorial diversions to reduce their use. In one year, the number of prison sentences of six months or less fell from 130,000 per year to under 30,000, and has fluctuated around the latter number ever since (Weigend 2001). North Carolina policy-makers decided in the early 1990s, primarily for cost reasons, that prison population growth should be restrained. The prison population stabilised, in contrast to an average doubling in American states during the 1990s, and North Carolina's imprisonment rate, 7th among the 50 states in 1985, was 35th in 2000 (Wright 2002). The North Carolina example is especially striking since North Carolina is a conservative Southern state in which law-and-order politics are strong and racial tensions are high, and in which voters typically elect conservative Republicans to the US Congress and Senate (including Republican Senator Jesse Helms, the most conservative of them all). The French on a regular basis decide the prison population is too high and in the single strokes of broad-based amnesties and pardons reduce it by as much as a third (Kensey and Tournier 2001).

It is possible the December-2001-to-February-2002 Blunkett will re-emerge and again want to reduce the use of imprisonment in England

and Wales. This essay surveys the range of options that is available should that happen. There are basically only two options for reducing prison populations: front-door options – sending fewer people there or sending them there for shorter periods; and back-door options – letting them out sooner. Sections I and II examine the options available. In examining them, I adopt an agnostic stance concerning the purposes of punishment, on the rationale that it is better first to consider the possibilities and then to consider whether in principle there is good reason to reject them. Some options are more politically viable or realistic than others and section III, a brief conclusion, offers what seems to me a practicable programme for prison population reduction.

I. Front-door strategies

Front-door strategies range from changes in sentencing laws through changes in policies for dealing with breaches in conditions of community penalties and parole. I list as many as I can think of.

Repeal mandatory minimum sentencing laws

Jack Straw put all three of Michael Howard's mandatory minimum laws into effect. Centuries of research show that mandatory penalty laws often cause imposition of penalties that everyone directly involved believes to be too harsh, which is unjust (Tonry 1996: chapter 4). Sometimes they lead practitioners wilfully and disingenuously to circumvent their application, which is unprincipled. Repeal of all such laws, including the mandatory life sentence for murder, would avoid both undesirable effects. Severe penalties will no doubt continue to be the norm for cases involving serious crimes, but extenuating circumstances will often justify less severe penalties and the need for prison beds will fall.

Rationalise all sentencing laws

Current law concerning penalties for driving under suspension, for example, limit judges' sentencing options to fines and prison sentences, thereby forbidding use of community penalties. This forced choice makes no policy sense. Elimination of all such anomalies would have demonstrable, even if modest, effects on the number of prison sentences.

Establish presumptive sentencing guidelines premised on the policy that lengths of all prison sentences should be reduced by some percentage (10 per cent? 50 per cent?) from current levels

There is nothing magic about the current sentencing tariff or current practices. Countries vary widely in their sentencing norms and individual countries vary substantially over time. Data provided in the Halliday Report (Home Office 2001) demonstrate that average lengths of prison sentences and the percentages of cases receiving prison sentences both increased substantially during the 1990s. There is no substantive reason why effort could not be made to return to, say, 1992 levels or to reduce sentences across the board by some specified amount. The evidence from the US (Reitz 2001) and Holland (Tak 2001) is that judges' behaviour can be changed by guideline systems in which they must either impose an authorised sentence or give reasons for doing otherwise, subject to the defendant's right of appeal to a higher court.

Reduce guideline judgement starting points for all crimes by some percentage (10 per cent? 50 per cent?)

If the Court of Appeal in its judgements ambitiously pursued Lord Woolf's sometime public agenda to reduce prison use, it could do so. All the points made under the previous heading apply here. The only difficulty is in knowing whether sentencing judges and magistrates would take notice. Martin Wasik, chair of the Sentencing Advisory Panel, is but one of many who have noted that no convincing empirical evidence exists that issuance of guideline judgments affects sentencing patterns (Wasik 2001).

Talk down sentence lengths and use of imprisonment

Chris Nuttall, former head of the Home Office Research and Statistics Directorate, developed statistical reports that dramatically showed that judges were remarkably responsive in their sentencing decisions to both perceived changes in public opinion (sentence lengths and prison committals increased immediately after the Bulger murder, well before legislation was enacted to increase penalties) and to Home Secretaries' calls for harsher penalties. Presumably what goes up can come down. A unified call by government officials from the Prime Minister and the Cabinet down for reduced reliance on imprisonment would influence judicial behaviour. Getting the Cabinet and the Prime Minister to make this call may be an unlikely goal, but strong, unambiguous and repeated calls from the Home Secretary and the Lord Chief Justice are likely, on the basis of Nuttall's work, to do some good. For that to work, however, the message would have to be clear and sustained and not undermined by the Prime Minister. The reactions of both David Blunkett and Tony Blair to Lord Woolf's and the Lord Chancellor's efforts in the winter 2002–2003 to send such messages (both repudiated them) are not encouraging.

Create new credible community penalties backed up by ministers' calls for their use and by sentencing guidelines directing their use

Day fines, DTTOs, Halliday's generic community punishment order, suspended prison sentences and imaginative development of existing penalties all offer opportunities. Day fines in particular have been successfully used in a number of countries to reduce the use of short prison sentences (Germany, Austria, Sweden). So have suspended prison sentences (most of continental Europe). The big problem here is that judges tend to use community penalties for less serious cases than programme developers intend. This can partly be controlled by guidelines.

Strongly discourage the imposition of prison sentences of six months or less

I mentioned the successful German attempt to do this above (Weigend 2001). Here is why the Germans concluded that short prison sentences did more harm than good. There is little reason to believe that short prison sentences have any significant incapacitative effects or that they have any greater deterrent effects than do credibly implemented and enforced community penalties. There is no reason to believe that short prison sentences are useful for rehabilitative purposes. Any time on remand must be netted out. Initial interview and classification processes take at least weeks and usually months. The short period left is generally insufficient for meaningful rehabilitative dosages to be delivered, even assuming that appropriate treatment facilities are available. On the other side, three to six months is long enough to do serious damage to an offender's employment continuity and prospects, to damage his or her chances for a later law-abiding life, and to do considerable damage to partners and dependent children. The social stigma associated with any prison sentence is qualitatively different from that associated with a community penalty. For younger offenders, a short prison sentence provides opportunity for association with older and career offenders and for socialisation into deviant values. The case is compelling. Halliday took a small step in this direction by proposing the elimination of prison sentences between three and six months (Home Office 2001).

Early experience with community service in England (Pease 1985), New York City (McDonald 1986) and Holland (Tak 2001) shows that community penalties can successfully be used in lieu of short prison sentences.

Create a new sentence of intermittent confinement

Persons sentenced to short terms (say under three months) could be given various options that would enable them to keep jobs and support families while serving a sentence on weekends, on week-day nights or during vacation periods. Switzerland has been doing this successfully since the 1970s and simultaneously reduced needs for prison space and reduced collateral damage to prisoners and their families. All of the arguments against use of short prison sentences in the preceding paragraph apply here also.

Create and promote new diversion programmes

One possibility is vastly increased pre-adjudication diversion into drug treatment programmes. Another is rapid development of restorative justice programmes outside the formal criminal justice system. A third, also successfully used elsewhere to reduce use of prison sentences, is to adopt systems of conditional dismissal in which prosecutors negotiate penalties with defendants on condition that the charges will be dismissed (Germany, the Netherlands, Belgium, France, Austria). All of these things in other countries are successfully diverting large numbers of cases from the courts and the prisons.

Prohibit prison admissions at any time when the population exceeds 95 per cent of capacity

The Dutch (Tak 2001), Danes (Kyvsgaard 2001) and Norwegians (Larsson 2001) long forbade admissions into prisons operating over capacity. At times of overcrowding, convicted offenders were placed on waiting lists for later admission. In Holland (Tak 2001), an elaborate classification scheme was developed that determined who was admitted and when and occasionally required the exceptional release of lower-risk prisoners to permit the admission of high-risk prisoners. For human rights reasons, some low-risk prisoners on the waiting lists were eventually discharged. Ninety-five per cent capacity is proposed as a limit because some space is always under repair and some excess capacity is required for unexpected population fluctuations.

Divert all offenders in whose offending drug dependence plays a significant role into drug treatment programmes

Diverting drug-dependent offenders into treatment programmes is a more effective crime-reduction strategy than sending drug-dependent offenders to prison. Results from the NEW-ADAM project of urinalyses of charged offenders showing that large majorities are drug dependent demonstrate the influence of drug use on crime (Bennett, Holloway and Williams 2001). Research in England and the United States shows that well-run drug treatment programmes can reduce drug use and dependence – and criminality – of drug-dependent offenders (Gebelein 2000). A substantial body of research shows that the best predictor of successful drug treatment is the length of time in treatment, no matter whether participants are volunteers or coerced; diversion into treatment with the threat of prosecution of those who fail makes good sense. Since a year in a community drug treatment programme, or even in a residential drug treatment programme, costs less than the £25–30,000 cost of a year's imprisonment, it makes both economic and crime-reduction sense to divert the maximum number of people possible from the criminal justice system into drug treatment programmes.

Adopt more nuanced policies for dealing with breaches of conditions of community penalties and parole

Experienced probation officers know that a breach of programme conditions may or may not signal that an offender is bound to fail. Drug dependence, for example, is now understood to be a chronic relapsing condition, and lapses back into drug use are to be expected. Revoking people for doing something that is to be expected is bad practice. Breaching people and sending them to prison as a consequence is only sometimes a good idea, yet in both the US and England policy-makers have mistakenly adopted zero-tolerance policies. In the US from the mid-1980s to the mid-1990s, the combination of no-drug-use conditions and inexpensive on-site urinalysis contributed to extraordinarily high revocation rates. In many American states, half of all people admitted to prison in the 1990s were probation and parole violators, many of whom had failed drug tests (Blumstein and Beck 1999). In England, Jack Straw famously insisted that violators of Home Detention Curfew be automatically returned to prison. The better approach is to create a presumption that breaches of conditions should not ordinarily lead to revocation into imprisonment but instead should be dealt with on a case-by-case basis. Policies should be developed for use of graduated responses to successive breaches on the model of drug courts.

II. Back-door strategies

Back-door strategies range from broad-based amnesties through changes in release mechanisms. I list as many as I can think of.

Carry out a large-scale amnesty

The French have done this regularly, with the effect that periods of increased sentencing severity such as England experienced in the 1990s and in 2002–2003 can be offset in a stroke (Kensey and Tournier 2001). There are any number of ways it could be done. Save for a defined set of prisoners sentenced for serious violent offences, all sentences could be reduced by a fixed percentage (10 per cent? 30 per cent?), or all offenders eligible for release within a fixed period (three months? six months?) could be released early. There is no reason to worry that this will undermine the law's deterrent effects since the amnesty would be a one-time or unpredictable occasional event that intending offenders could not predict or count on.

Re-establish a broad-based parole release system

Though this would fly in the face of recent truth-in-sentencing and determinate sentencing trends, it would bring important benefits. It would enable parole and prison officials to control prison populations by using release policies as a population-control safety valve. A well-developed system of release guidelines would allow parole authorities to reduce disparities in sentences imposed by judges; although there is little reason to suppose that either guideline judgements or magistrates' guidelines are an effective control on sentencing disparities, a substantial literature on parole guidelines shows that they can achieve consistency in time served (Gottfredson, Hoffman and Wilkin 1978). In addition, in so far as humanitarian considerations or particularly successful participation in treatment programmes argue for early release, a parole agency could make these case-by-case decisions.

Set an absolute prison capacity limit and, once it is reached, forbid admissions except when matched by one-for-one early releases

This is another way to describe the Dutch and Scandinavian prison waiting list systems but focuses on releases rather than admissions. Such systems operated in several American states (e.g. North Carolina (Wright 2002)) in the 1980s and early 1990s under the terms of consent decrees that followed federal district court findings that overcrowded prisons violated minimum constitutional conditions. In each case they focused legislators' attention on prison capacity issues. In North Carolina the policy resulted in the guidelines system previously described that stabilised the prison population. In Texas and Florida they led to massive programmes of prison construction.

Authorise the prison service to petition the courts for resentencing of individual cases

This is a provision of the Model Penal Code. The first proposed draft made every prison sentence 'tentative' for the first year and authorised prison officials to petition for resentencing. The supporting commentary explained that judges have limited opportunity to study the offender and that prison officials may decide that the judge 'proceeded on the basis of misapprehension as to the history, character or physical or mental condition of the defendant' (American Law Institute 1954: 57). There are, of course, other reasons in an individual case, such as changed circumstances or particularly successful programme participation, why prison officials might urge reconsideration of sentence. This would be a considerably less efficient way to deal with such cases than would the reconstitution of a programme of case-by-case parole release review.

Authorise the prison service, while retaining legal control and notional custody of offenders, to release them into community programmes on a case-by-case basis

In an important sense, prisoners are in effect sentenced 'to the custody of the prison service' rather than to prison. Prison officials have nearly unlimited discretion over classification and housing of prisoners. Prisoners may for reasons of administrative convenience or policy be reassigned from one landing of a prison to another, be transferred from one prison to another or be reclassified from one security status to another. Co-operative prisoners are often successively reclassified to lower- and lower-security institutions, including near the end of sentence to open institutions or halfway houses. Except under exceptional circumstances, none of these reclassifications, reassignments or relocations gives rise to justiciable issues coming within the purview of the courts. Under the logic of a sentence being to the custody of the prison service rather than to a prison, there is no reason why the prison service could not transfer prisoners to community locations where they would retain the legal status of a prisoner. A transfer to ad hoc home confinement, for example, would constitute in effect imprisonment within the prisoner's home. During the 1980s in the United States, after the growth in prison population came to seem inexorable but before states were prepared to pay massive sums on prison construction, entrepreneurial prison directors created new back-end community penalties on this rationale (Morris and Tonry 1990). Offenders remained 'in prison' in the 'in the custody of ...' sense, but in their own homes or in work-release hostels. For low-risk and non-violent offenders, this was a win/win/win situation. The prisoner won for obvious reasons. The prisons director won – one less mouth to feed and one less body to bed. The state won because money was saved and pressure to build new prisons was reduced. And legal propriety was not offended because the prisoner remained 'in prison'. Unless legal constraints on the authority of the Director General of the Prison Service prevent such initiatives, this proposal could move a sizeable number of prisoners out of prisons and into 'prisons'.

Extend the example of Home Detention Curfew and create a large and diverse programme of community penalties into which prisoners can be transferred

The great advantage of creating new community penalties under the control of the prison service is that it avoids the problem of judicial 'net-widening'. Evaluations in many countries of new community penalties meant to be used as alternatives to incarceration consistently show that judges prefer to use them for people who would otherwise have received less rather than more severe penalties (Pease 1985 (England); Tonry 1996: chapter 5 (US); McIvor 1997 (Scotland); Tak 2001 (Holland)). This is commonly called net-widening. The foolproof solution to net-widening is to have someone other than judges decide who is assigned to community penalties. If, for example, prison officials were given authority to release prisoners into newly created community penalties, there could be no doubt that the new less-expensive-than-prison programme was used entirely for people being released from prisons. The Dutch created a new programme of 'Penitentiary Sanctions' on this logic, and with it managed to reverse a 25-year increase in prison populations that began in the mid-1970s (Tak and van Kalmthout 2001). Statutes gave prison officials discretion to release prisoners into penitentiary sanctions after they had served one-half of their sentences; previously mandatory release occurred after two-thirds of the sentence. Home Detention Curfew is an early release programme of this type, but there is a great deal of room for many other such programmes.

Re-establish a broad and generous remission programme

Remission rules could easily be made more generous, allowing one-half or larger reductions in the lengths of prison sentences. This is an unusually low-cost, low-visibility way to reduce prison populations quickly.

Eliminate prison service authority to extend lengths of prison sentences as sanctions for breach of prison rules

Current law allows the prison service to lengthen prison terms as penalty for violation of prison rules. That authority should be repealed. Some of the extra time results from behaviour that is not punished in the free community (marijuana use, possession of pornography) and it is hard to see why that should ever be necessary. In any case, prison administrators already possess adequate discretionary powers to punish minor violations (denial of privileges, custody reclassification, use of punitive detention) and serious violations that constitute crimes can and should be referred to the Crown Prosecution Service.

III. What?

There is no free lunch. Except for modest changes that involve small numbers of prison beds, such as ending disciplinary sentence extensions and sentencing anomalies, most changes require political leadership, legislation or both.

A number of significant changes could be made without legislation but not without leadership. The Home Secretary and the Lord Chief Justice could launch a visible and sustained campaign to talk down the prison population. The Lord Chief Justice could lead the Court of Appeal in a systematic programme of reduction in starting points in guideline judgments. With support from the Home Secretary, the probation service could adopt policies calling for more nuanced approaches for dealing with breaches of conditions, the Crown Prosecution Service could establish programmes to divert drug-dependent offenders into treatment programmes and other offenders into restorative justice programmes, and the prison service could exercise its considerable discretion to create something like the Dutch 'Penitentiary Sanctions' programme. Without leadership, none of that is likely to happen.

With leadership and legislation, the sky's the limit. Presumptive sentencing guidelines, new programmes, amnesties, prison waiting lists, revitalised parole, conditional dismissals – they are all possible.

Whether any of this is likely depends on how the penal climate develops. If politicians' belief in Sir Anthony Bottoms's (1995) populist punitiveness remains strong, little that is constructive is likely to happen. Progress is possible if the real David Blunkett is the one who appeared to want to talk the prison population down. If the real one is the fellow who wants to lock up more children, England's overcrowded times are likely long to last.

References

American Law Institute (1954) *Model Penal Code*. Tentative draft no. 2. Philadelphia: American Law Institute.

Bennett, T., Holloway, K. and Williams, T. (2001) *Drug Use and Offending: Summary Results from the First Year of the NEW-ADAM Research Programme*. Home Office Research Findings No. 148. London: Home Office.

Blumstein, A. and Beck, A. (1999) 'Population Growth in U.S. Prisons, 1980–1996', in Tonry, M. and Petersilia, J. (eds), *Prisons, Crime and Justice: A Review of Research*, vol. 26. Chicago: University of Chicago Press.

Bottoms, A. (1995) 'The Philosophy and Politics of Punishment and Sentencing', in Clarkson, C. and Morgan, R. (eds), *The Politics of Sentencing Reform*. Oxford: Oxford University Press.

Gebelein, R. (2000) 'The Rebirth of Rehabilitation: Promise and Perils of Drug Courts', in *Sentencing and Corrections: Issues for the 21st Century*, No. 6. US Department of Justice.

Gottfredson, D., Hoffman, P. and Wilkins L. (1978) *Guidelines for Parole and Sentencing*. Lexington, MA: Lexington Books.

Home Office (2001) *Making Punishments Work*. Report of a Review of the Sentencing Framework for England and Wales (July 2001). London: Home Office.

Home Office (2002) *Justice for All*, CM 5563. London: TSO.

Kensey, A. and Tournier, P. (2001) 'French Prison Numbers Stable since 1988, but Populations Changing', in Tonry, M. (ed.), *Penal Reform in Overcrowded Times*. New York: Oxford University Press.

Kyvsgaard, B. (2001) 'Penal Sanctions and the Use of Imprisonment in Denmark', in Tonry, M. (ed.), *Penal Reform in Overcrowded Times*. New York: Oxford University Press.

Lappi-Seppälä, T. (2001) 'Sentencing and Punishment in Finland: The Decline of the Repressive Ideal', in Tonry, M. and Frase, R.S. (eds), *Sentencing and Sanctions in Western Countries*. New York: Oxford University Press.

Larsson, P. (2001) 'Norway Prison Use Up Slightly, Community Penalty Lots', in Tonry, M. (ed.), *Penal Reform in Overcrowded Times*. New York: Oxford University Press.

McDonald, D. (1986) *Punishment Without Walls*, New Brunswick, NJ: Rutgers University Press.

McIvor, G. (1995) 'CSOs Succeed in Scotland', in Tonry, M. and Hamilton, K. (eds), *Intermediate Sanctions in Overcrowded Times*. Boston: North Eastern University Press.

Morris, N. and Tonry, M. (1990) *Between Prison and Probation: Intermediate Punishments in a Rational Sentencing System.* New York: Oxford University Press.

Narey, M. (2002) 'Opening Speech, Prison Service Conference, 2002', <http://www/hmprisons.gov.uk/news/newstext.asp?246>.

Pease, K. (1985) 'Community Service Orders', in Tonry, M. and Morris, N. (eds), *Crime and Justice: An Annual Review of Research*, Vol. 6. Chicago: University of Chicago Press.

Reitz, K. (2001) 'The Disassembly and Reassembly of U.S. Sentencing Practices', in Tonry, M. and Frase, R.S. (eds), *Sentencing and Sanctions in Western Countries*. New York: Oxford University Press.

Tak, P. (2001) 'Sentencing and Punishment in the Netherlands', in Tonry, M. and Frase, R.S. (eds), *Sentencing and Sanctions in Western Countries*. New York: Oxford University Press.

Tak, P. and Van Kalmthout, A. (2001) 'Prison Population Growing Faster in the Netherlands than in the United States', in Tonry, M. (ed.), *Penal Reform in Overcrowded Times*. New York: Oxford University Press.

Tonry, M. (1996) *Sentencing Matters*. New York: Oxford University Press.

Tonry, M. (ed.) (1997) *Ethnicity, Crime and Immigration*. Chicago: University of Chicago Press.

Wasik, M. (2001) *How Should Guidelines be Produced? How Should They Be Monitored?* Paper prepared for QMW Public Policy Seminar on Policy and Practice for Sentencing. 23 October.

Weigend, T. (2001) 'Sentencing and Punishment in Germany', in Tonry, M. and Frase, R.S. (eds), *Sentencing and Sanctions in Western Countries*. New York: Oxford University Press.

Wright, Ronald (2002) 'Counting the Cost of Sentencing in North Carolina, 1980–2000', in Tonry, M. (ed.), *Crime and Justice: A Review of Research*, Vol. 29. Chicago: University of Chicago Press.

Chapter 11

'Justice for All': A summary of Cambridge conference discussions

David A. Green

The following pages are meant to provide brief summaries of the group discussions immediately following the presentation of each of the conference papers. The summaries comprise the key issues raised by participants over the two-day period and are not meant to be a complete record of all features of the conversations. However, a complete record does exist in the form of transcripts from the original audio recordings of the entire conference proceedings. These transcripts were used to recreate and to reiterate here some of the more significant discussion points that might not be addressed sufficiently in the essays themselves. It is hoped that these summaries will serve to provide for the reader a fuller account of the range of implications and wider concerns generated by the policy proposals in the White Paper, *Justice For All*.

Unprincipled sentencing? The Policy approach to 'dangerous sex offenders' by Amanda Matravers and Gareth V. Hughes

Several participants expressed little confidence that the new provisions in the White Paper would help practitioners better manage sex offenders in the community. Some expressed a preference for a real government commitment of resources rather than the creation of a new sentence, as the procedures and tools already in use were not resourced adequately. In addition, there was suspicion that too optimistic an appraisal of the effectiveness of risk assessment tools might lead to inaccurate reporting during evaluations. Performance targets might be met on paper, but might also misrepresent the reality. One discussant asked if the creation of the new sentence might not provide the pretext for the government to appropriate funds for community supervision programmes for sex offenders, but others disagreed insisting that in the past the government had passed new legislation without a true financial commitment to make it workable.

The point was made that previous convictions were a poor predictor of a sex offender's risk to reoffend, as many offenders convicted of sex offences did not specialise in one kind of offence. Furthermore, satisfactory or even exemplary performance in prison-based re-habilitation programmes was also a poor predictor of future offending behaviour. In fact, a Canadian study was cited which suggested that individuals who were high in features of psychopathy tended to be more adept at convincing the Parole Board they were ready for release. Likewise, in another study similarly diagnosed individuals who tended to take part most rigorously in rehabilitative programmes were the ones most likely to reoffend.

If operated well, it was argued, multi-agency public protection panels (MAPPPs) could effectively differentiate sex offenders and could apply resources differentially to minimise the risk of reoffending. Because they were much better equipped to prevent a sex offender from, for instance, 'grooming' a victim over a long period of time, MAPPPs stood a better chance than did the courts of actually preventing reoffending. The difference was that MAPPPs could effectively set up checks and balances specifically designed for a particular offender.

A commitment to invest appropriately in MAPPPs was advocated, but it was recognised that considerable courage on the part of public officials was needed if community-based programmes for managing sex offenders were to succeed. It was difficult to engage with the public and the media about any positive gains made in community-based pro-grammes for sex offenders because doing so raised awareness of their very presence in communities. Moreover, until more consistent evidence of programme effectiveness was demonstrated, campaigns to gain the support of the public for such initiatives were unlikely to have a great deal of effect.

Many indicated that current resources were insufficient to facilitate suitable supervision and monitoring of sex offenders upon release. In those cases in which parole conditions were not in place after release, law enforcement officers were frustrated because they lacked the power to utilise an imminent sanction on a released offender actively engaging in behaviours linked with his or her past offending. Some welcomed the extension of the post-release supervision period on these grounds, citing its ability to fill the gaps in the current system.

On the other hand, there was a concern that rigorous post-release conditions would only represent the 'high road to more confinement'. Experience in the United States was called upon to illustrate that breaches of such conditions often led ultimately to substantial increases in the prison population.

Further concerns were raised about the fundamental aims of sentencing based on risk assessment. Such sentences could be viewed as instrumental, in so far as they reflected a genuine interest in and proven ability to target particular offenders deemed to be dangerous, or as non-instrumental, whereby the real concern was to reassure an anxious public that such assessment procedures were being utilised and more offenders were to be subsequently taken off the streets. In the latter case, the question of whether or not risk assessment procedures were effective was not particularly important, as the motivation driving the use of such procedures was reassurance, not results. Minimising net-widening effects then was also not necessarily a priority if indeed the goal of risk assessment policies was to target more offenders in an attempt to mollify certain strands of public opinion or the press. Ironically, it was argued, aggressive press coverage of sex crimes has sometimes actually jeopardised efforts to prosecute the accused in such cases by impinging on the rights to fair trial.

One discussant expressed anxieties about the practice of including members of the public in MAPPPs. Ethically, it might be unfair to submit unpaid members of the public to the rigours required in making difficult and potentially perilous decisions about the management of sex offenders in the community. Public service personnel were paid to take such risks and the public were not. Secondly, it was believed that a member of the public might be tempted to go to the press if, for instance, he or she believed that a panel's decision to house an offender in a particular village was unacceptably risky. If this occurred, it could undermine much of the effective work accomplished by the panels.

However, one discussant stressed that public involvement was a step toward counteracting the apparent distrust the public had of the experts charged with managing offenders in the community. Another suggested that the decision to involve members of the public in MAPPPs was a placatory compromise struck after the government decided against the sex offender registry policy of community notification. More imaginative and complex measures might instead include some level of public education about the reality of the risks posed by most sex offenders upon release.

Attention was drawn to several issues overlooked or ignored in the White Paper's proposals for the management of dangerous sex offenders. First, the heavy reliance upon the use of custody drew attention away from strategies that could potentially divert more offenders from custody. Second, the actual mechanics involved in the proposal to expand the remit of the Parole Board was not adequately explained, specifically the question of how the Parole Board's expanded risk assessment role would fit with the prison service's various classification tools and the release plans of the probation service. Third, ethical questions remained unresolved because the indeterminate sentences proposed did not specify satisfactorily enough for some how and when a particular sentence would end.

'Custody plus, custody minus' by Jenny Roberts and Michael E. Smith

Much concern was expressed about the impacts the new custody plus and custody minus sentences were likely to have on the prison population. Custody remained central to the proposals, both as part of the actual sentence served under the custody plus provision, and as a looming threat if conditions were breached under the custody minus proposal. This heavy reliance upon custody could be counterproductive if the intent of the proposals was actually to reduce the number of custodial sentences.

One discussant thought the combination of custody and community supervision was anomalous. Though on one hand the sentences seemed to reflect the sort of rationale found in Germany and Sweden, for instance, where short terms of custody were the norm, these short custodial periods were also coupled with substantial periods of community supervision. As breaches of community conditions occurred, sentencers would be likely to increase their use of custody overall. The more intensive the community supervision was, the more likely and prevalent breaches were to be. Therefore, concerning custody plus sentences, the particular criteria sufficient to recall to prison an offender serving the community supervision component of a sentence needed to be much more clearly articulated to assess its probable effects. Similarly for custody minus sentences, in which failure to comply with the sentence conditions could trigger a prison sentence, the measures to be utilised by judges and magistrates in making this decision were unclear.

Picking up on a similar theme, one participant asked if the point of the new proposals was to make use of more or less custody. Much about the proposals was inconsistent. For instance, regarding the breach of sentence conditions, judges were likely to be split about the purposes of sanctioning a breach. Some might punish a serious breach by choosing a particular treatment-centred disposal which they might expect would effect a change in an offender's behaviour. Others might feel compelled to act upon the 'how dare you theory' and to sanction any breach harshly on principle, regardless of what any evidence base might suggest to be the most effective disposal available. One discussant raised the concern that probation officers might be influenced to change the way they wrote reports for judges and magistrates if such reports could be used to justify custody. Additionally, it was unclear if anyone, including sentencers and representatives of government agencies, intended to take any account of what the costs and consequences of these new sentences might be for the prison population.

Though building public confidence was one of the central intentions of the sentencing reform proposals, little confidence was expressed among discussants that the proposals would significantly accomplish that goal. Even if the probation and prison services relied very heavily upon evidence of 'What Works', there was little to suggest it would have any real impact on public confidence. Some suggested it would be very difficult for successful evidence-based programmes to counter the effects sensational newspaper coverage and politicians' law and order rhetoric had upon public opinion and public confidence. The focus on public confidence created an additional risk, as sentencers might be tempted to give a 'taste of custody' to an offender instead of a community penalty in order to avoid hostile media criticism.

Also, the government had so far failed actively to promote existing effective and promising community sentences. It was said that there did not appear to be any true willingness on the part of the government to examine thoroughly and genuinely whether or not the proposals they advocated were indeed effective. Therefore there was a suspicion that the government's commitment to evidence-based policies was disingenuous, and that information which failed to jibe with the government's views could be suppressed.

As evidence suggested fines were at least no worse in terms of preventing reoffending than many other disposals, the absence in the White Paper of any mention of the use of fines was conspicuous to some. Despite the evidence, there had been a massive drop in the use of fines and most of the pressure to manage offenders had been shifted to the prison and probation services. One discussant argued that the problem with the utilisation of fines was the inability of magistrates to agree upon a formula to calculate them. The result had been a loss of faith among magistrates in their usefulness.

Another discussant referred to the White Paper's stated intention to reserve custody for the serious, the violent and the persistent. This represented a potential 'trap', as there was no clear definition of the term 'persistent'. Many offenders, it was pointed out, were persistent in so far as they tended to have previous convictions, and it was not clear how these previous convictions were to impact their sentences. Some evidence pointed toward a probable consequential increase in the use of custodial disposals for this population. Specifically, the Persistent Offender Initiative to be launched in the spring of 2003 was meant to target for severe sentences all offenders with six recorded offences, not convictions, in the past twelve months. It was very likely then that the 37,000 offenders targeted by this initiative nationwide, many of whom would be individuals with addiction problems and a collection of repetitive nuisance offences, would have a dramatic effect on the prison population. It was unclear how this initiative squared with the White Paper's proposals.

The tendency of the judiciary and the magistracy to circumvent any guidelines they perceived to be unjust represented another difficulty. One cited example was taken from prior experience with suspended sentences in England and Wales. Judges had chosen to impose a seven-month prison sentence in order to avoid the mandatory six-month suspension. Some expressed doubts that the Home Office had adequately studied previous experience with similar sentences.

Some argued that despite the potentially unfortunate consequences the community supervision component of custody plus might have on the overall use of custody and on the prison population, the sentence focused attention on the importance of resettlement efforts following release from custody. Post-release supervision was viewed to be a very encouraging development because, in many cases, offenders were released without any resettlement support. Especially for those released offenders with particularly disorganised and chaotic lives, the opportunity to aid with resettlement for a period of time could significantly decrease their chances of reoffending. However, others pointed out that it was precisely this category of individuals who were most likely to breach their conditions. Furthermore, one discussant thought usage of the term 'resettlement' in the White Paper had a punitive connotation and that it seemed to refer merely to the attachment of additional conditions to an offender upon release. The commitment appeared not to be to successful or meaningful resettlement of offenders in the community, but instead to their intensive disciplinary supervision.

'Sentencing guidelines' by Neil Hutton

Discussion first centred on the importance of getting judges to support and to comply with any guidelines system. Past experience with inconsistent fine enforcement was drawn upon to illustrate what could happen if judges and magistrates were not convinced that a particular disposal was appropriate. In that instance, sentencers stopped imposing fines. Similarly, if the guidelines forbade the use of very short prison sentences, for instance, it was possible judges and magistrates might then impose the shortest prison sentence available under the guidelines, even if it happened to be longer than the one preferred might have been.

As evidenced by the relative lack of judiciary and magistracy participation in the present conference, both as attendees and as co-authors of papers, judges and magistrates had appeared reluctant in some cases to discuss publicly a topic as controversial as sentencing policy, and in other cases to adjust their demanding schedules to make participation possible. They were characterised by one participant as being 'so central and so seemingly disengaged from the process of trying to figure out how to do it better'. However, another discussant pointed out that some progress must have been made behind the scenes for the judiciary even to contemplate the institution of guidelines.

It seemed peculiar to some then that the group charged with drafting the actual guidelines, the new Sentencing Guidelines Council, was to comprise exclusively members of the judiciary and magistracy. However effective the Council eventually proved to be, it was unlikely to produce very much in the near future, it was thought, as such an ambitious venture promised to be highly time-consuming. Some wondered where the judiciary would find the time to take on such a task when some members had indicated that participation in the conference, even for half a day, was too demanding on their time.

Parliament's role in the Council's draft guidelines was of concern to some, though it was still too soon to know how the legislation would define the relationship. It seemed to some to be little more than a 'gesture towards the democratic principle' and that the parliamentary approval criterion would probably not be allowed to subvert the entire guidelines mechanism. A distinction was drawn between two very different ways in which parliament could be involved in reviewing the guidelines. The first was via a 'legislative veto' device, which was used in Oregon. Under this scheme the legislature or parliament were given a fixed period of time to review the guidelines, and if no action was taken by a particular date, the guidelines would become law. This mechanism allowed MPs to avoid voting on the merits and shortcomings of particular guidelines for particular offences. This device was said to be more workable when the submitted guidelines were comprehensive and systematic.

The second mechanism was the 'legislative requirement for approval'. It involved a more critical review of the guidelines and was therefore more susceptible to political pressure and the volatility that often accompanied crime policy debates. If Parliament was charged with reviewing specific offence guidelines in this more 'piecemeal' fashion, the process strongly invited MPs to adopt a tough posture to play to their constituents. This second mechanism of Parliamentary approval was likely to be highly contentious and could consequently lead to sentencing ranges considerably more severe than those specified in the guidelines originally submitted.

Regardless of the manner in which Parliament decided it would give its approval to guidelines, some welcomed the practice. They believed it would lend the guidelines a degree of legitimacy that they might have otherwise lacked without Parliamentary review, while at the some time better insulating judges from public scrutiny in the wake of controversial decisions.

The White Paper's lack of a clear sentencing rationale was a problem for some. It seemed the White Paper reflected a 'cafeteria approach' to sentencing by attempting to mobilise multiple purposes simultaneously. Judges and magistrates needed to negotiate several messages at once. At one time it appeared that desert was the rationale, at others sentencers were meant to assess the risk of reoffending, and at other times the purpose of sentencing was to reduce crime and protect the public. In fact, discussants themselves were clearly undecided about what it was the public wanted sentencing to achieve. Each one of these rationales had a champion in the discussion, as each was argued to be the one most important to the public.

The expectation that sentencing policy would ever on its own significantly impact on crime rates was misguided, according to some, as the number of offenders actually sentenced was but a very small percentage of the total number of offenders committing crimes. If crime rates did drop following a change of sentencing policy, it was very difficult to attribute it to the policy changes. Still, the government was caught in a bind when faced with this issue. Although it must be cautious about setting crime reduction targets it could not achieve through sentencing, it must also appear to be trying to use sentencing policy to reduce crime.

Another problem brought about by a piecemeal approach to drafting guidelines was that of successfully coordinating sentences in a sensible framework. The Sentencing Guidelines Council would need to reconcile differences between Crown Court and magistrates' court sentencing practice with that of the Youth Courts, and still be able to incorporate the work accomplished by the Sentencing Advisory Panel. For instance, when the Sentencing Advisory Panel considered the offence of burglary, it needed to work within the parameters of the existing minimum sentence for a third burglary offence. How all these separate concerns and organisations would be integrated was still very unclear.

It was also unclear how a sentencing guidelines framework could possibly incorporate the other considerations facing judges. For instance, offender characteristics were not the same as offence characteristics. Guidelines were most often offence-centred, but judges were concerned not only with the offence, but with the characteristics of the particular offender. A 'What Works' approach to sentencing would demand it. Incorporating evidence of sentence effectiveness into the framework was further complicated by what one discussant thought was a relative paucity of such evidence, and by a lack of Probation Service funding to make community sentences available. Moreover, the resulting guidelines might be muddled by the simultaneous and multiple sentencing rationales.

Others pointed out that the guidelines would not, however, be entirely custody-centred. They instead would be comprehensive and include community punishments within their remit. If this was to be, the current problem of getting judges to accept the validity of pre-sentence reports – probation service reports intended to match offenders' needs with appropriate and effective programmes – needed to be resolved. Further problems might arise because the authority to specify appropriate sentences would be split among the probation service, the judiciary and, as some suggested, the Crown Prosecution Service.

Some concern was voiced about the disparity between the sentences imposed by the Crown Courts and the magistrates' courts. The great bulk of cases brought before the courts were triable either way, but Home Office research showed wide discrepancies in the use of imprisonment between the two courts for equivalent cases. Crown Court cases were three times as likely to attract prison sentences, which were on average two and a half times as long. These differences reflected a 7 to 1 difference in the use of imprisonment in the Crown Court when comparing matched cases in magistrates' courts. Reconciling this difference would be problematic because either judges would need to take a softer approach, which seemed unlikely to happen, or magistrates would need to get tougher to bring practice in the two courts into line. The latter contingency would further drive up the prison population.

Ultimately, as some pointed out, it was unknown the extent to which judges would comply with any new guidelines system. There was no known statistical evidence indicating the degree to which the Court of Appeal guidelines or those of the Sentencing Advisory Panel had actually influenced judicial practice. However resentful judges appeared to be of outsiders' attempts to limit their decision-making, judicial practice did appear occasionally to be subject to influence by powerful speeches by elected officials and particularly controversial high-profile cases. It remained to be seen what effects a more systematic and broad-based approach would have on judicial behaviour.

'Nuisance offenders: scoring the public policy problems' by Rod Hansen, Larry Bill and Ken Pease

According to one discussant, the description of low-level offending as 'nuisance offending' ran the risk of undervaluing the impact antisocial behaviour had upon the lives of victims, particularly in the poorest neighbourhoods. Several discussants thought it helpful to consider both the consequences low-level offending had on victims and communities and on what communities could do in response to it, rather than to focus on the problem of such offending from the perspective of the perpetrator.

Some thought definitions of 'nuisance', 'prolific' and 'serious' offending were important and potentially dangerous. It would be difficult consistently to apply comparable definitions for these terms without encountering problems of fairness and equity when behaviours were compared across communities. The definition of a nuisance offence in Bath might be entirely different in Cumbria. A sanctioning system of 'escalating responses' would then have differential consequences in different communities.

Apprehension was expressed about the use of anti-social behaviour orders (ASBOs). The two-year period a young person was under the control of an ASBO appeared to some to be excessive. More importantly perhaps, the use of an ASBO appeared to be a clever but dangerous way to skirt the right to a fair trial as guaranteed under Article 6 of the European Convention of Human Rights. As one discussant asserted, according to the Labour Party's paper called *A Quiet Life*, Labour was looking for a method to avoid normal procedural safeguards when dealing with problem young people. Breaching the conditions of an ASBO was criminal and grounds for custody, but ASBOs were being used for a range of non-criminal (what one called 'proto-criminal') behaviours, not all of which were particularly serious. For behaviour deemed to be more serious, an ASBO was an inappropriate sanction as it tended to combine a range of offences and offenders.

Expanding on these themes, a number of ethical and legal questions were raised which focused on police methods of gathering intelligence and on the statutory obligation to share information to which all agencies represented in Youth Offending Teams (YOTs) were subject. Some young offenders intimidated witnesses, a practice adults appeared to be less likely to engage in, perhaps because adults were more often deterred by the probable consequences of doing so. Police were faced with the problem of deciding how to act upon information received from witnesses who were too intimidated to testify. ASBOs were dangerous, some argued, because they loosened the evidentiary rules sufficient to bring a supervision order. Additional fears were raised about how information gathered from the information-sharing arrangements called for in the White Paper would be used. Some feared this represented a dangerous 'back-door' means of subjecting young people to super-vision. It made use of potentially inaccurate and uncorroborated information that, because of the civil nature of the sanction, did not need to withstand scrutiny in court.

The available disposals already in existence were encouraging for some who believed that minor warnings and referrals were doing much to allow young people to avoid court appearances for antisocial behaviour. Other measures were also helpful. For instance, the Intensive Supervision and Surveillance Programme (ISSP) was a successful means of supervising and supporting the most prolific young offenders upon their release from Young Offender Institutions (YOIs), although one discussant believed the period of time for which young offenders were subject to the ISSP was in some cases too short. Others pointed out that the various orders provided some structure and certainty in the often otherwise chaotic lives of the young people subject to them, and that this could have a positive effect on their behaviour.

However, some argued that the focus on the White Paper's proposals to target young offenders overlooked the need for proper investment in early prevention efforts that targeted the risk factors associated with crime. First, the Youth Justice Board had a statutory obligation to reduce crime, but it suffered from being inadequately resourced. The abilities of the agencies charged with preventing offending tended to be con-strained within the time limits imposed by a particular offender's court order. Second, some argued that a wiser tactic was to employ a social welfare approach to children and young people. The risk factors associated with crime were also associated with teenage pregnancy, drug misuse and poor educational attainment. The criminal justice system could only deal with the 'problem person' and not the problems. Therefore it was misguided and myopic to expect the criminal justice system adequately to address underlying issues.

Drawing upon Larry Sherman's research on crime crackdowns, a discussant also stressed the importance of taking advantage of the quiet periods that followed the removal of particular prolific or persistent offenders from the community, those who accounted for large numbers of offences. 'Weed and seed' was not the same as 'weed and wipe your brow', which was the approach traditionally taken by police forces. The seeding was a critical component of a preventative approach, and should include various community defences, like street lighting or witness protection schemes. It was a 'lost opportunity' if the police merely celebrated the removal of particular offenders without attempting to equip the community to deal better with later offending. Others pointed out that the Crime and Disorder Reductions Partnerships were receiving heavy investment and their mission was to focus upon prevention strategies.

'Procedural and evidential protections in the English courts' by Nicky Padfield and Richard Crowley

Regardless of the criticisms levelled at the White Paper's proposals, it was argued that on the issues of hearsay evidence and previous misconduct, the government had undertaken an 'extremely intense and wide-ranging exercise of consultation' with the Law Commission, the Bar Association, the Law Society, the Association of Chief Police Officers, the Crown Prosecution Service and several academic experts. For judges, it appeared that the kind of direct input at the pre-legislative stage such consultation solicited had set a precedent in the way judges were expected to influence policy. It was asserted that the government's decisions were generally consistent with the Law Commission's basic proposals.

One question raised was whether or not there was a current perception that an imbalance between the prosecution and the defence and between the victim and offender needed to be redressed. Some said that if an imbalance did exist between the prosecution and defence, one could make a case that it was the prosecution that was unfairly advantaged. For one thing the availability of resources was much more extensive on the prosecution side, and procedures that tended to lengthen the trial processes were abused by both sides.

The notion of an imbalance was dismissed by several participants who argued that the proposals were meant to simplify and to clarify a convoluted system, and to bring the concerns of victims and witnesses into focus. The admissibility of previous convictions during trial was used to illustrate. Despite existing rules allowing it, there was a 'cultural reluctance' on the part of prosecutors and judges to admit into trial any evidence of previous misconduct on the basis that the practice jeopardised the case. Even when invited to do so, prosecutors were 'scared stiff' of making an application to admit previous misconduct, fearful as they were of having a conviction overturned on appeal. Most preferred to 'soldier on' to get a conviction without it. It was Crown Prosecution Service policy that any case that could not stand up without the evidence of previous misconduct should not be prosecuted.

The case of Roy Whiting, the killer of Sarah Payne, was used to illustrate. Despite the existence of compelling evidence from a similar previous conviction, the judge turned down the prosecution's application to have the evidence admitted so as to ensure the fairest trial possible and to minimise the chances of a successful appeal. Instituting a presumption of inclusion rule for such evidence, which may or may not be included in the legislation, would redress any imbalance and send the message to judges and prosecutors that all evidence was admissible unless a case could be made for exclusion.

Others argued that the notion of summary justice had disappeared, and attrition rates were far too high. Victims, as well as offenders, tended to perceive the trial process as a 'playground for lawyers' where unnecessarily long delays were commonplace. They felt as if the defence was merely dragging out the proceedings to wear down the will and patience of the witnesses and to undermine the prosecution's case on procedural grounds rather than on the more substantive issues. It was believed by some that the White Paper's focus on victims was an attempt by the Labour government to address public opinion for political reasons.

There was nothing in the White Paper, some argued, that allowed prosecutors to move more quickly on a case. Some argued that defence reports at trial were often inadequate, and disclosure of unused material was a problem on both sides. If anything, it was claimed, the White Paper's proposals would make things worse. For example, prosecutors should not have to make an application to use a video link to obtain testimony from a vulnerable witness if the video link and the witness were in place. There should be a presumption to move forward, not to 'produce more paper to justify what you're doing'.

Some concerns were voiced about police powers to set bail conditions.

More research was needed to indicate how many people had appealed against bail conditions set by the police and the reasons more people had not done so. Little was known about how the conditions imposed on bail had affected the remand prison population.

When studying the issues presented to them, the Law Commission's agenda was both to remove anomalies and to render the whole trial process more 'understandable' and more 'sympathetic' to those involved in it. Its reports were commissioned by the Home Office and therefore reflective of a government agenda to speak to the public's perception of the trial process, but there were also technocratic grounds for their reviews. It was argued that the Commission had successfully resisted a populist approach and made its judgments on the basis of fairness.

'Drug-dependent offenders' by Mike Hough and Darian Mitchell

There was apparent consensus concerning the value of drug treatment and testing orders (DTTOs). DTTOs allowed the probation service to utilise a 'holistic' approach, targeting not only the drug misuse, but also the range of additional problems that drug misusers typically faced. The intensive nature of the DTTO facilitated contact with a variety of appropriate agencies, and this focused but multilateral technique was paying dividends.

Though there may have been problems demonstrating the consistent and marked progress of drug treatment programmes of any kind – generating the sort of evidence the tabloid press would find convincing – it was nonetheless heartening for some to observe sentencers using the DTTO with a full awareness of and tolerance for the numerous breaches that tended to characterise participation in any drug treatment programme. It appeared that sentencers had got the message that condemning breaches of a DTTO outright was not necessarily productive, and that some patience was required. This was encouraging news to many discussants.

It was claimed this indicated a shift had occurred whereby the definitions of success and failure had changed. Progress in drug treatment had become an indicator of success, when in early periods what appeared now to be progress – a drop in the frequency of offending or drug misuse rather than a halt to offending or drug misuse – had been defined as failure. This was indicative of the subtle ways in which research knowledge influenced policy. In this case, for years policy-makers used the results of drug treatment evaluations from the 1970s as evidence that treatment methods were ineffective. In time, however, in light of criminal career research literature suggesting that changes in offending needed to be viewed longitudinally to perceive changes in the frequency of occurrence of particular behaviours over time, the same research was reconsidered and found to be promising. The earlier paradigm had been replaced, and relapse no longer necessarily equated with failure.

Sentencers, it was argued, liked the DTTO because it allowed them the rare opportunity to re-engage with an offender after imposing a sentence and to see evidence first-hand of an offender's progress. This perceived success of the sentence review function of the court led a discussant to ask if this evidence supported the use of review courts at the end of a sentence for a wider range of offences and offenders, as the Halliday sentencing review had suggested. Several respondents indicated that the DTTO review should be viewed as a special case. Wider use of review courts would severely 'magnetise resources', both in the courts and in the probation service. Report preparation for the review was highly costly in terms of resources, but worth it in the case of drug-dependent offenders who benefited from the motivating encouragement they received from the review.

Some discussants drew attention to the importance of the motivational work accomplished by the probation service. Probation officers were experienced with motivating offenders to comply with a range of orders, not just DTTOs. Drawing upon a point from the paper given, the probation service was skilled at working with an offender's ambivalence about offending behaviour. The motivational work they accomplished had 'huge importance for the success of community sentences'.

However, some believed that this important work was threatened by the bureaucratic and managerial problems that the enforcement of national standards created. Some agreed that national standards were a good thing in principle, but in practice, the time-consuming nature of the work required to meet them consumed valuable time that could be better spent accomplishing motivational work with offenders. A more streamlined procedure with a less intensive effect on resources was recommended. Others insisted the problems associated with enforcement of national standards extended well beyond the DTTO to all agencies of the criminal justice system. Furthermore, the monolithic and uniform nature of the standards failed to recognise the range of different needs required by the variety of offenders.

One county involved the police in the enforcement of a DTTO, a practice that was viewed to have been successful. Combined with the possible deterrent effects of unannounced police visits to an offender's home, it also allowed offenders to justify abstaining from drug misuse if pressed by their friends to do so.

There was some disagreement among discussants about whether or not prisons were the best places to deliver drug treatment. One asserted that prisons merely served to introduce offenders to drugs and it was therefore unwise to believe that prisons were an ideal venue for treatment. Another was not so sure, citing anecdotal evidence that the mundane prison routine motivated offenders to seek treatment, providing an interesting pursuit while in prison. At the very least, it was argued, failing to attempt to treat drug-dependent offenders while in prison was a missed opportunity. There was agreement that follow-up after the completion of a drug treatment programme was crucial, regardless of the venue in which the programme was provided.

Further research was recommended in order to discern who was being targeted by the use of DTTOs and to determine the degree to which the estimated 150,000 drug-dependent, persistent offenders were being successfully targeted. Research was also needed to determine the degree to which DTTO 'accessibility and eligibility' indicated gender or ethnic bias.

There was some general criticism that the White Paper did not adequately speak to other issues arising from gender and ethnicity. For instance, anecdotal evidence suggested that part of the explanation for the growth in the number of women sent to prison could be found in the relationship between women's offending and drugs. Sentencers were responding to a belief that persistent property offending was tied to drug misuse, as women were engaging in crime to fund the drug habits of their children or partners. As a result, more women were being sent to prison for these sorts of offences than they had previously. If this was the case, drug misuse had clear links to the rise in the women's prison population.

The additional disposals outlined in the White Paper represented meant to augment the DTTO an 'arduous trail', as enormous resources and effort would be required to facilitate the new measures. Experience with getting the DTTO up and running and working properly suggested there would be a great deal of difficult work ahead. Moreover, the task of targeting appropriate schemes for particular offenders would in itself be very difficult to achieve.

Index

Access to Justice Act (1999) 150
Acourt gang 103
acquisitive crime 32, 34
acquittals, wrongful 20
acquitted defendants, reinvestigations
    103–4
actuarial methods, risk assessment 72
addiction model, drugs and crime 31,
    36
Afro-Caribbeans 4
amnesties 218
amphetamines 28, 32
Anti-Drug Abuse Act (1986) (US) 171–2
anti-social behaviour
    blurred line between criminal
        behaviour and 106
    political usefulness of term 80
anti-social behavioural orders 5, 85–92
    Cambridge conference discussion
        233–4
    natural history of an ASBO case 85–7
    reporting 87–92
appellate system 150
appropriate punishment 64
approval (Parliamentary), sentencing
    guidelines 231
arrest rates, black people 164
arrest referral schemes 34, 45
ASBOs *see* anti-social behavioural
    orders
Ashworth, A. 96
Auld Report 1

Bail Act (1976) 100
bail conditions
    Justice for All 100–1
    police powers 236–7
bail legislation, drug dependent
    offenders 38–9
Bath Boy 83–4
Benn, Hilary 13–14
Best Value Performance Indicators 91
bifurcation, sentencing 117, 118
Bingham, Lord 5
black people
    likelihood of confinement 162–3
    racial differentials in sentencing
        163–6
    sentence discounts 169
Blair, Tony 215
Blunkett, David 211, 215
Bottoms, Sir Anthony 4, 118
breaches
    community orders 10, 144–5
    drug dependent offenders 10–11, 44
    probation 10
    revising policies for dealing with
        217–18
British Crime Survey, illicit drug use 29
burglary *see* domestic burglary;
    first-time burglars

Cambridge conference discussions
    224–39